US POLICY AND REGIONAL SECURITY IN CENTRAL AMERICA

US Policy and Regional Security in Central America

Edward Best

St. Martin's Press   New York

First published in the United States of America in 1987
Printed in Great Britain
ISBN 0-312-00212-2

Library of Congress Cataloging-in-Publication Data

Best, Edward
    U.S. policy and regional security in Central America.

    Bibliography: p.
    Includes index.
    1. Central America — Foreign relations — United
States   2. United States — Foreign relations —
Central America   3. Geopolitics — Central America.
4. United States — National security   5. Central
America — National security.   I. Title.
F1436.8.U6B49   1987   327.730728   86-20389

ISBN 0-312-00212-2

Contents

Introduction   1

1 The Origins of Current US Policy   5
The Legacy of the Past   5
The Changing Caribbean Basin   10
Changes in US Foreign Policy   13
Carter and Central America: 1977-79   15
The US Domestic Opposition: 1977-79   17
Carter and the Sandinistas   20
Carter and El Salvador   22
The End of Carter's Policy   28

2 The Development of Current Policy   32
The Reagan Administration and Central America   32
Reagan and El Salvador   38
Reagan and Nicaragua   51

3 Current Perspectives for US Policy   93
Guatemala   95
El Salvador   100
Nicaragua   109
The Improbability of Intentional Military Action   112
Risks of Limited Action, Escalation and Unplanned
    Intervention   117

US Policy and the Contadora Process 120
Rebel Prospects 135
International Pressures and Costs of Current Policy 149

Conclusions 159
Alternative Assumptions about the Sandinistas 160
Recommendations 172

Index 177

Introduction

In the late 1970s, sharpening social and political tensions compounded by deep economic troubles began to produce a crisis in Central America. By the end of 1979, the dynastic dictator of Nicaragua had been replaced by a revolutionary government, the brutal military president of El Salvador ousted three months later by a coup that brought political turmoil and guerrilla war, while a revolutionary movement was given new life by repressive violence under the military regime of Guatemala.

The United States thus faced the challenge of revolution and chronic instability in nearby countries whose internal stability and international alignment it had historically taken for granted. Political concern and the fear of Cuban and Soviet exploitation precluded indifference to the crisis. The inevitable question was what precisely the US could, in the circumstances, do to restore regional stability and safeguard US interests.

Debate about the appropriate US response was given a special intensity by the special characteristics of the crisis. Central America was an area with particularly critical internal problems, and the threatened regimes were notably unstable and undemocratic. This situation could make the roots of revolution understandable in internal terms and internal change seem inevitable and necessary. But it could also seem to make revolutionaries more likely to be radical, instability more likely to spread and be spread, and the area especially vulnerable to external exploitation. A history of US interventionism in the region could make distrust of the US seem understandable in local terms and a change in US attitudes desirable. But a particularly strong anti-Yankeeism in social revolutionaries could also increase suspicions of their sympathy and ties with the US' global adversaries. It was an area in which the US had for decades held, and could expect to maintain, a position of predominant influence and power, which could seem to permit a flexible response to points of internal crisis within the region. But it was an area in which assured US security could be seen as a prerequisite of US global capabilities, and which thereby seemed a predictable target of opportunity for the US' global adversaries. Moreover, reactions to this revolutionary challenge in the US' historical sphere of influence were strongly coloured by broader considerations. The crisis came shortly after other developments had led to a questioning of the nature and strength of US influence in the Caribbean region, and coincided with a period of perceived US setbacks elsewhere in the world, renewed global tensions, and strong domestic debate about the overall direction of US foreign policy.

In this situation, policy formulation and implementation was to be particularly difficult for the US. There was general consensus as to the US' strategic ideal in Central America: a stable isthmus ruled by centrist and democratic regimes and free of Cuban and Soviet influence. There was less agreement, however, as to what constituted an actual or potential threat to US security interests and what were the necessary and appropriate US actions required to avoid such threats. It was also disputed whether the strategic ideal could be fully attained; by what means it might be approached; and what effort and expense should be devoted to doing so, so long as the alternative did not threaten US security.

In those countries in which revolutionaries had not taken power, the policy mix which emerged was to create considerable controversy and face formidable problems. But its stated goals were at least to become relatively clear. In El Salvador, the US would provide economic and military assistance to the government in order to keep the rebels from power without direct US involvement, while at the same time attempting to reconstitute the political centre, support limited reforms and establish a stable and legitimate government. In Guatemala, the US would encourage the military regime, deprived of US military assistance because of its brutality, both to put down a guerrilla insurgency and prepare to leave power. Meanwhile, the US would prop up democracy with economic assistance in Costa Rica, and foster its development in Honduras. In Nicaragua, where despite US efforts a revolutionary movement had achieved outright military triumph and political power, it was to prove even harder to agree what should and could be done, and with what precise objectives. President Carter had hoped to accommodate and moderate the movement which had overthrown a US-backed dictator. President Reagan did not want to accept a regime which challenged the US' historical position in the area, represented a radical change in the regional status quo, and was perceived as threatening a 'second Cuba'. As Nicaragua strengthened its relations with Cuba and the Soviet Bloc, began to build up its armed forces and was seen to be a source of support for revolutionaries elsewhere in the region, there was a growing consensus that something needed to be done. There was still debate, however, as to what was necessary and effective, and what might only prove dangerous or counter-productive.

In 1986 the US Administration can plausibly claim to have had some, if by no means unqualified or irreversible, success in the other Central American countries, with a reduction of domestic and international opposition to its policies there. In Nicaragua, however, the Left-wing government holds out against US pressures and fights US-backed counter-revolutionaries with Soviet arms and Cuban advice, amid continued controversy about US policy instruments, confusion about policy goals, and concern about its possible consequences. American neighbours, supported by European allies, still endeavour to reduce tensions by proposing a comprehensive, negotiated regional settlement which might allow the US to satisfy its fundamental concerns at acceptable costs. Such a settlement, however, remains elusive.

The US Administration remains reluctant to intervene directly against the Sandinista regime. Invasion of Nicaragua would not only be costly, but have serious negative consequences for domestic politics, inter-American and transatlantic relations. It would certainly undo much of the progress that had been made in the rest of Central America, afford a propaganda victory to the Soviet Union, and clearly fail to fulfil the fundamental strategic demand of ensuring that the region need not distract US military attention and resources.

The Administration is also unwilling to accept any settlement guaranteeing the immediate survival of the Sandinista regime 'in its present structure'. That, it feels, would weaken the inter-American system, create a potential threat to the vital interests of the US and the security of its allies, and be seen internationally as a failure of US resolve. It believes that this would impede further progress toward stable democracy in the rest of Central America, be taken as a political success for the Soviet Union, and even constitute the consolidation of a Soviet beachhead on the American mainland.

US policy, centring on support for the Nicaraguan 'Contra' rebels, is presented as necessary in order to avoid an 'agonizing choice' between intervention, arousing fears of 'another Vietnam', or settlement, arousing fears of 'another Cuba'. However, although the strong commitment of the Reagan Administration to the Nicaraguan rebels makes it likely that they would be able to continue fighting for a considerable period, the rebels seem unlikely to be able to bring down the Sandinista regime or to force it into political negotiations. Indeed, it seems likely that the US will sooner or later have to adopt an alternative policy towards Nicaragua.

US policy in Central America since 1981 has had more success in some respects than was expected by its critics, but it continues to face enormous problems. Not only do many of the fundamental dilemmas remain unresolved. In certain respects, they have become yet more difficult and dangerous, and the prospects for their successful resolution, however that may come to be defined, are far from clear.

The first two chapters of this book discuss why and how US policy has developed as it has. The third chapter considers the present situation of US policy, its prospects in the immediate future, and the costs, benefits and wider implications of the broad options left open to the United States in Central America. In particular, it seeks to answer certain fundamental questions concerning the future of US policy in the region.

To what extent can a continuation of policy within current limits be expected to bring regional stability and achieve the US objectives? Can US policy stay within its current limits? What circumstances could lead to direct military action by the US in Central America, and with what consequences? Could a negotiated settlement – necessarily involving the immediate survival in some form of the Sandinista government with which it would be negotiated – be the basis for regional stabilisation and satisfy the fundamental interests of US security? What minimum costs and concessions would this necessarily entail for the US and under what circumstances might the US move toward such an outcome? Are there still openings to make it any less of a 'best worst case' for the US should current policy fail?

1 The Origins of Current US Policy

The Legacy of the Past

Central America has been of accepted importance in US policy for a long time. The exclusory implications of the Monroe Doctrine, the expansion of US power following the Spanish War of 1898, the extension of direct security concerns with the construction of the Panama Canal, and the consolidation of US dominance through the decades of intervention and dollar diplomacy, had by the early 1930s created an enduring set of assumptions about Central America's relation to the US.

Like all the Caribbean Basin, Central America came to have an undisputed strategic significance, not only for the protection of the US mainland, but also for the projection of US power. Since the beginning of the century, then, militarily, politically and, to a lesser extent, economically, the stability and security of the Basin *for* the US was to be seen as a condition of US global capabilities. This had three principal strategic implications. No other global power should be allowed a significant presence; there should be no local threat to the basis of US power projection, whether to shipping and naval power or to the inter-American system; and there should be no local instabilities which might either attract other global powers or distract the US from the exercise of global power. It was, thus, an area of latent global importance to which the US generally wanted to give a very low priority.

With this long-standing strategic premise came a 'hegemonic presumption' that Central America was part of the US' 'historical',

5

even 'natural', sphere of influence, often strengthened by a belief in the US' historic duty, be it to 'manifest destiny' or 'continental democracy', to exert that influence. The US was also assumed to have the unquestioned capacity to exert decisive influence when it believed necessary.

There emerged a 'traditional' pattern of US behaviour toward the region, and perception of its events. Highly sensitive to the international implications of regional events, the US might take direct action where it saw a threat which could not be handled by local allies, except when to do so would directly conflict with global demands.[1] When and where national US interests seemed secure, the region could generally be entrusted to private US interests and reliable local governments. This combination of a special sensitivity to international implications with a confident neglect born of unchallenged hegemony came all the more naturally in Central America in particular. Its significance for US national interests derived almost exclusively from its relation to broader concerns. Having no strategic US installations,[2] strategic resources or massive US investment, it mattered mainly because it was there, between Mexico and the Canal, bordering the Caribbean sea, and inside the US sphere and inter-American system. Except by their own instability, moreover, these small and weak nations could not by themselves seriously threaten US national interests. When Washington's attention was drawn to Central America, therefore, it tended to be given primarily in terms of possible threats to those broader concerns, necessarily by unfriendly outside powers, and with the objective of being able to take stability and security for granted again as soon as possible. International reliability, which included the capacity to maintain internal stability, tended to be the ultimate criterion in perceptions of local actors. The Cold War and the Cuban Revolution only strengthened this tendency to react to internal threats to stability in terms of external threats to security.

There was, thus, a 'traditional' assumption that the US could count upon the international support and internal stability of Central America, and needed to be able to do so for the security of her direct regional interests and for the maintenance of her global capabilities. At least as important, it was confidently assumed that the US had both the right and the capacity to control the course of events in Central America in order to ensure that support and stability when threatened.

By the early 1970s, Central America had not lost its latent strategic significance. Defending US military assistance to the area in 1970, the Commander of US Southern Command, General Mather, argued that it had a 'special importance, since it dominates the land, sea, aerial electronic lines of communication between North and South America and permits access by relatively defensible routes to the raw materials of South America. Not only would lines of communication and area solidarity be threatened; but, a Communist government in Central America would foster the growth of Communism in adjacent countries with obvious threats to the Canal and its operations.'[3] But by then, Central America seemed to have been stabilised and secured and, with the immediate Cuban threat apparently receded, and the US preoccupied elsewhere in the world, the area could again receive the type of low political priority appropriate to the nature of its international importance.

There was an enduring strategic basis to this 'traditional' attitude, but there were also 'traditional' assumptions and sensitivities which were predictably to shape the strategic perceptions of many, when later in that decade this historically assured, and reassuringly secure, area of US influence began to collapse from within.

The reasons for that collapse cannot be attributed exclusively to past US policy. However, that policy of intervention and neglect did substantially help to shape the background to the current crisis both in practice and perception. The emphasis on international reliability, and the practical tendency for maintenance of stability to imply defence of a status quo, led the US visibly to approve or support the continuation of dictatorial and repressive regimes, and outmoded and inequitable socio-economic structures. The US did not implant in Central America either oligarchy or dictatorship, and Washington did not in fact play a simple role in the spread of dictatorships in the 1930s which began those direct traditions of repression leading to the current crisis. In El Salvador, the US had nothing to do with the 1931 coup by General Maximiliano Hernandez Martinez, whose name was taken by one of the modern 'death squads', nor his 1932 massacre of rebelling peasants and execution of the communist leader Farabundo Marti, whose name was taken by the guerrilla armies of today. In Nicaragua, the US had indeed intervened militarily in 1909, 1912–1925 and 1926–1933, directly combating the nationalist leader Augusto Sandino whose name was taken by the Nicaraguan revolutionary movement, and establishing the National Guard against which it would fight. However, the US did not, in fact, directly impose the founder of the dynasty, the Head of the National Guard, Anastasio Somoza, who took power in 1936. Once he was there, however, like his fellow dictators in El Salvador, Guatemala and Honduras, he came not only to be accepted, in this new era of US non-intervention, but also, as an expedient pro-American, to be approved. In the famous phrase of Franklin Roosevelt's which has come popularly to epitomise past US policy in Central America: 'Somoza is a son-of-a-bitch, but he's our son-of-a-bitch.'

The basis for a 'traditional' identification of US interests with undemocratic regimes was laid, but was still reversible. Those who in 1944 overthrew the old-style dictatorships of Guatemala and El Salvador, and tried to remove the old Somoza, were not only not anti-American, but had been positively inspired by the New Deal policies of the US President and by the Democratic Alliance of the Second World War.

The Cold War, however, only helped ensure that there would not be new democracies but new-style dictatorships, for which the US did bear responsibility. Only in Guatemala had a new regime been consolidated after 1944. The perceptions of anti-Communism soon outweighed any interest in fostering non-Communist reform. Guatemala being in the 'backyard', Washington was to be especially sensitive to the influence of the Guatemalan Communist Party, and receptive to the complaints of private US interests affected by reforms. Anxious to prevent consolidation of such an unreliable government in Central America, and not unhappy to show that it could roll back Communism somewhere, the US helped bring about its overthrow in June 1954. This intervention and subsequent neglect of social reform and democratic institutionalisation helped to produce a series of undemocratic regimes in Guatemala and insurgents in whose brutal countering the US would find itself actively involved in the 1960s.

The Alliance for Progress was intended to prevent revolution and Cuban expansion by creating a secure environment for development and evolutionary change in co-operation with the US. Although the Cuban Revolution increased Washington's sensitivity to the region's internal problems, it also increased the immediacy of the external threat. Concern to achieve long-term stability through promoting social reform and development was therefore more than matched by concern to avert immediate external destabilisation by strengthening the internal security of reliable regimes. The emphasis on security, a recognition of the existing role of the army, and the desire to achieve long-term stability without immediate instability encouraged two rather hopeful beliefs: first, 'that the military are not only the sole force of stabilization but . . . also promote democratic institutions and progressive changes of a socio-economic nature';[4] and, second, that local elites would voluntarily accept certain reforms and relinquish some power in order to pre-empt demands for radical change. The broad consequence was to strengthen military establishments which did not prove to be especially interested in democratic institutions, and elites which, while modernising and diversifying, were mostly to show only limited tolerance of demands for social reform and structural change. This process was neither simple nor immediate. There was rapid economic growth in the 1960s, but the regional model had inbuilt imbalances, limitations and vulnerabilities. It also, especially in the absence of significant fiscal and land reforms, tended to increase the concentration of wealth while at the same time creating new and more complex social forces. There was some political liberalisation and democratic opening, notably in El Salvador. The military Government there permitted the formation and activism of new political parties representing this more complex society, including the Christian Democrats, Social Democrats and a party fronting for the still outlawed Communists. However, when a coalition of these three parties won the 1972 elections, it was defrauded of its victory, and its presidential candidate, the Christian Democrat José Napoleón Duarte, exiled after an abortive attempt at a counter-coup by reformist officers. The US Embassy may have saved his life, but did nothing more. The immediate priority was to restore stability. This frustration of the electoral process did not mark the beginning of revolutionary activity in El Salvador. The first group was formed in 1970 by some who had already committed themselves to armed struggle, and organisation of the new repression had begun even before that. But after 1972, revolutionary ranks began to grow, the political centre to be weakened, and the most rigid sectors of the economic elite and the military to reassert themselves amid mounting political violence. Once the immediate violence of the coup was over, however, El Salvador seemed to be sufficiently stable and secure for it, like the rest of Central America, again to receive a low priority in US foreign policy.

The Central America that was taken for granted in the early 1970s was, however, now very different. The pressures arising from fundamental inequities and political exclusion were greater, and the economic model was not only incapable of meeting basic internal demands but especially vulnerable to the international economic shocks of the 1970s. There was a new level and type of political violence. And inflexible responses to the demands of more complex societies, and the radicalising effect on both sides of new influences – such as the Cuban Revolution and liberation theology – brought an increasing element of socially-based ideological polarisation which would make crisis both more likely and more intractable.

This process also had consequences for the US position. For many in opposition, it undermined the credibility of its interest in reform, and fostered the belief that revolution, even wide-reaching reform, implied challenging the US' traditional position in the area. For many with power, it strengthened the belief that America's fundamental interest in stability and fear of Communism would always lead the US to support them against internal challenges, almost whatever they did. This assumption, and their entrenchment in the face of growing internal threats, served not to strengthen but to weaken Washington's capacity to influence those powerful groups. Moreover, as radical opposition groups became stronger and more determined, the more likely it became that they would both be seen as undesirable by Washington and be resistant to its influence. As the US looked away from Central America, it had in fact become more directly involved and implicated in its affairs, while at the same time also losing much of its capacity for direct political influence.

The Changing Caribbean Basin

The Caribbean Basin as a whole had also changed dramatically. The Cuban Revolution in the early 1960s had given a tremendous shock to US assumptions about the Basin. Its global adversary had established a political foothold in the region and even attempted to pose a direct military threat to the US from this area of previously presumed security. Cuban support for revolutionary movements in the region meant that the immediate source of 'external' threat to security and stability was now placed within the region itself. Even when the revolutionary threat receded in the late 1960s, and the question of a direct Soviet military presence was again downplayed after the 1970 'Cienfuegos incident' (when the USSR tried to establish a submarine base in Cuba), these problems remained latent in US strategic views of the region. At least as important, the Cuban experience left a number of bitter memories in US minds, kept fresh by the large number of Cuban exiles in the US. It seemed an unforgettable lesson of how not to handle revolution in the Caribbean Basin, or indeed anywhere else. At one extreme, the consolidation of such a regime was to be seen as the consequence of a mistakenly confrontational policy toward a radical but nationalist movement which had overthrown a dictator linked to the US, forcing it to turn to the Soviet camp to survive.

At the other extreme, the mistake seemed more to have been that the US had been insufficiently tough. This inevitably troublesome and pro-Soviet regime should not have been permitted to survive at all. The attempt at its indirect overthrow through the Bay of Pigs invasion was to be remembered as bringing only international embarrassment for the US. The subsequent missile crisis was to remain an illustration of the potential strategic dangers posed by such a regime. The Kennedy–Khrushchev understanding, by which the Soviet Union removed the offending weapons in return for the expectation that the US would not invade Cuba, was certainly not to be remembered as the kind of diplomatic deal which the US would want to repeat. A Soviet-backed, if nominally non-aligned, regime apparently devoted to spreading revolution was left in place. The determination to allow 'no more Cubas', and to avoid facing the same kind of situation posed by Castro, was thus to be deeply embedded in US perceptions of regional developments.

In the early 1970s, however, the immediate Cuban threat seemed to have receded, while serious problems in other regions were further to distract US attention from the Basin. With the Nixon Administration seeking a reduction in the US military profile throughout Latin America, one trend in the 1970s was to be a gradual withdrawal of some aspects of the US' direct military presence in the region. The number of US military personnel stationed in the Basin fell from a 1968 peak of 25121 to 15688 in 1981, with various military installations and facilities being downgraded or closed, most importantly in Puerto Rico, the Panama Canal Zone and Guantànamo. International Military Education and Training (IMET) programmes declined from more than $13 million in 1968 to less than $2 million in 1980 and the Military Assistance Programme (MAP) from over $37 million to $665000 over the same period. Foreign Military Sales (FMS) deliveries increased relative to MAP, but still accounted for less than 10 per cent of total arms deliveries to the Caribbean Basin area in 1980, as compared to 30 per cent in 1968.[5]

While Central America was being confidently neglected and the US was reducing its military presence, other developments were altering the strategic and political profile of the Basin in ways which laid the basis for both greater US sensitivities and diminished US influence.

There were certain changes in the nature of US objective interests. The Panama Canal was still important, but rather less so both economically and strategically. It retained considerable logistic importance for most conventional war contingencies, as illustrated by the quadrupling of transit by US public vessels during the Vietnam War, but it could not handle aircraft carriers and would thus be of reduced significance in the case of global nuclear war. Its direct economic importance to the US had been falling since at least the 1940s and it could not handle the supertankers which were beginning to carry much of the world's oil, whereas the security of other trade routes and sea lines of communication had the same or increased importance as before. Access to most of the various strategic minerals imported from Caribbean countries, although still not critical except in the event of major global conflict, continued to offer 'the cumulative "conveniences" of ready availability and long-standing commercial relations'.[6] However, in the case of oil, the region's significance was increasing. The Basin had become a major refining centre in the 1950s. By the end of the 1970s, refineries located in the Caribbean were supplying 50 per cent of US petroleum products derived from Middle Eastern and African crude. The region's own known oil reserves were dramatically

11

increased by the discovery of massive new fields in Mexico, and their potential importance to the US was to rise with new concern about the security of supply from the Middle East.

There were also changes in the Soviet military profile in the region. The Soviet Union acquired a new and significant naval presence, made possible by its expanding global capabilities and by the existence of the Castro regime. Nineteen naval and naval air deployments to Cuba took place between 1969 and 1978, of which eleven also entered the Gulf of Mexico,[7] with the quality of the ships being upgraded on each occasion. The Soviet naval presence grew from nothing to an annual average in the 1970s of well over 1000 ship-days in the region. While this represented no more than an average of 3 ships on station, of especial sensitivity to the US, given her experience of submarine warfare in the Second World War, was the Soviet submarine presence. Between 1958 and 1963, Soviet hydrographic research and acoustic survey ships had sailed extensively in the Caribbean. Two diesel submarines and a submarine tender were included in the first naval squadron to visit Cuba in 1969. The US did react strongly in 1970 to Soviet attempts to construct a permanent base for nuclear submarines in Cienfuegos Bay. It secured its dismantling and an understanding that the Soviet Union would not use Cuban ports as a base for strategic operations, but the Soviets did not back down completely. Submarine tenders and ballistic missile submarines continued to be deployed in Cuban waters until 1974, when a brief attempt at *rapprochement* began between Washington and Havana. In 1978, the year of the longest Soviet naval deployment to date and the first patrols flown by Soviet pilots from Cuba, the Castro Government received its first submarine from the USSR. Cuba's overall forces were substantially strengthened by the Soviet Union in the early and late 1970s to include, by 1979, 3 fighter-bomber and 8 interceptor squadrons (including 20 MiG-23s), 2 submarines, 18 large patrol craft, and 62 fast attack craft.[8] Neither the Soviet presence nor the Cuban inventory posed any immediate threat to the US, but the time when the US could militarily take the Caribbean for granted was gone.

At the same time developments of a different nature tended to question both the US' regional position and the international status quo. Economic nationalism, diversification and regional co-operation, and demands for a new international economic order, reflected resentment at US economic policies, the global upsurge in 'North–South' demands, and increasing external economic problems. All aimed at changing the level or nature of US economic influence. Politically, Panama's demands for sovereignty over the Canal were only the clearest example of a rising Latin American nationalism, while there was mounting frustration with the US-dominated Organization of American States (OAS). Diplomatic contacts expanded, and the relative importance of economic relations with Western Europe and Japan grew. There was increased interest in extra-hemispheric political and institutional contacts, notably with Western European political parties and international political movements, which largely reflected a desire on both sides to strengthen democratic alternatives and counter ideological polarisation. Particularly significant was the role of the newly active regional powers, Mexico and Venezuela. They now had much greater economic potential and some economic interest, a variety of political and diplomatic motivations, and – apparently – an international opportunity to take a lead in regional initiatives of an economic and political nature, and to assert their own influence, even at the expense of the US.

The relation between the different dimensions of developments in the Caribbean was to be one of the key factors in the subsequent crisis. Pressures were building in Central America for deep internal changes. There were *de facto* changes – and demands for further changes – in intra-regional relations, regional relations with the US and relations with the rest of the world. There were also changes in the geo-strategic profile of the region. A serious problem would predictably result from any direct association of domestic and regional changes with geostrategic shifts, whether that association arose more from positive encroachment, or from destabilisation promoted by the US' global adversary, or from US perceptions of the negative implications of such developments for its own global position.

In the mid-1970s, however, there was global *détente* and little apparent prospect of further Cubas or unmanageable instability in the region. Talks with Havana failed more because of Cuban activities in Africa than in Latin America. A growing number of regional governments were then restoring relations with Cuba, and many were also expanding diplomatic and commercial contacts with the Soviet Bloc. US concern about these moves was significant only in the case of the few Caribbean countries which had Left-wing governments. Most countries indeed were taking these steps in the context of efforts to reduce ideological tensions in the region, and to prevent the East–West conflict from impeding new forms of international co-operation which would help remove the fundamental causes of regional instability. And the US itself then seemed to be moving away from its 'traditional' attitude.

Changes in US Foreign Policy

Developments in the Caribbean in the early 1960s had left the US with a determination to have 'no more Cubas'. But US public support for the use of military force to prevent further 'losses' had been greatly weakened in the early 1970s by the long war which was then being lost in South-East Asia. Thus not only were there to be 'no more Cubas' but there were to be 'no more Vietnams' either. There was also a new level of concern in the US about the political consequences and moral basis of support for undemocratic allies. A 1974 report from the House Committee on Foreign Affairs concluded that support for repressive dictatorships damaged both the prestige and, because of their inherent instability, the long-term interests of the US. Legislation in 1975 and 1976 empowered Congress to limit economic and military assistance on human rights grounds. Moreover, the feeling grew that the US had both to recognise the limits of its power in a more complex and interdependent world, and to respond to internal and international changes in a positive manner, or risk the antagonism of the emergent forces. The Carter Administration responded to many of these currents with a new foreign policy designed 'to make the U.S. constructively relevant to a world of turbulent change.'[9] It would maintain US strength and be prepared to defend key interests abroad, but with a more flexible diplomacy based on new forms and areas of co-operation, and with an active commitment to human rights to give a new moral content, and restored moral consensus, to US policy. However, there was not only to be a growing domestic opposition to this new policy, which seemed to many only to deepen the US' perceived global weakening and lack of resolve, but considerable inherent dilemmas and internal differences.

The basic problems behind regional instability were agreed to be 'the growing demand of individuals around the world for the fulfillment of their political, social and economic rights.' It was agreed that the US should 'act forcefully when the vital interests of our nation, our allies and our friends are threatened' and 'assist nations threatened by external force to defend themselves.'[10] But how exactly should the US prevent moves by 'our ideological opponents to exploit turbulence for their own selfish ends', without seeming 'to stop the unstoppable – to try to block inexorable political, economic and social changes'?[11] What were the acceptable limits of 'an increasingly pluralistic world' and of flexibly 'capitaliz[ing] on the West's inherent strengths . . . [to] improve our ties to developing countries in a context which does not force them to make an explicit choice between East and West'?[12] Could regional problems be thus isolated from the global conflict by greater US accommodation of new forces? Could that alone prevent them seeking ties with ideological opponents, and could the Soviet Union and its allies be relied upon to play by the same rules? Could the US be more confident in its flexibility in areas of long-standing US influence, or was it not rather dangerous to undermine repressive but allied regimes in areas of vital importance? The Central American crisis was quickly to highlight tensions within the Carter Administration over such questions and reactions to the perceived results of Carter's efforts to explore the path of accommodation were to colour the approach of his successor.

Carter and Central America: 1977–79

Central America at first continued to receive a relatively low priority, given the apparent weakness of existing revolutionary movements and the continued absence of any immediate external threat. Yet there existed a feeling that 'American longer range interests would be harmed by continuing indifference to the mounting desire in Central America for greater social justice and national dignity, as our indifference will only make it easier for Castro's Cuba to exploit that desire.'[13] Moreover, most local governments typified the repressive Right-wing regime, unquestioning alliance with which discredited the US, while the apparent absence of a direct security threat and the strength of presumed US influence seemed to make them a safe and suitable area for a demonstration of human rights concern.

However hopes were soon dashed of easily moving these regimes toward 'viable democracies' through scheduled elections. Those in El Salvador in February 1977 saw another fraud perpetrated against a broad coalition and a new wave of repressive violence. Guatemalan elections in 1978 brought a still more brutal military government, revealing the political strength of the far Right, while many of the most important moderate political leaders were assassinated or forced to leave the country. In Honduras, a coup in 1978 replaced a relatively moderate military government with a harsher regime.

The limited and unclear pressures brought to bear by the US tended only further to weaken US influence in Central America generally. Reports on the appalling state of human rights in these countries led in early 1977 to an ending of military assistance to Guatemala and El Salvador, and to a reduction of military and economic aid to Nicaragua. However, the Guatemalan regime showed more nationalist resentment than political responsiveness, and increased its reliance on alternative sources of military equipment such as Israel. In El Salvador, the effect of that move and the US veto of an Inter-American Development Bank loan was soon undercut as the US responded positively to the promises of reform made in July by the new military President. Approval for that and other loans was restored, despite objections from the Human Rights Bureau, and the next month the US Ambassador defended a draconian new public order law as a justified means 'to combat terrorism.'[14] In the eyes of all parties the credibility of the new US commitment was reduced.

In Nicaragua, the US took an even more confusing position. The reduction of US aid boosted the moderate opposition by creating the belief that, for the first time, Somoza did not have the guaranteed power of the US behind him. Aid restrictions were accompanied by calls for dialogue with the opposition after Somoza's brutal response to the rioting and general strike following the assassination in January 1978 of the prestigious moderate opposition leader Pedro Joaquin Chamorro. While the radical Sandinista National Liberation Front (FSLN) had come back with a series of attacks in October 1977, the moderate opposition, which then held the political initiative, waited for the US to help to remove Somoza. Yet the Administration was uncertain and divided as to whether Somoza should now be propped up to avoid greater instability and any prospect of the FSLN gaining power, or further pressured in the direction of political compromise. In the end, the Administration did almost nothing for months, and the little it did do only made things worse. Its response was complicated by the large pro-Somoza bloc in Congress which succeeded in forcing the President in May to release a suspended package of economic aid. Carter then compounded this lack of clarity with a groundless message congratulating Somoza on an improved human rights situation. Predictably, all sides took this as a mark of US support for the regime. The moderate opposition now formed a Broad Opposition Front (FAO), while the FSLN's active mobilisation during the year, its seizure of the National Palace in August and its September offensive gave it a greater role within the opposition. Deciding at last that Somoza himself should go, the US organised an OAS mediation effort, proposing an interim government of Somoza's party and the FAO, excluding the FSLN but retaining intact the hated National Guard. This unrealistic move only divided and discredited the FAO. Somoza, having survived the autumn offensive, rejected the final proposal for an internationally supervised plebiscite in January 1979. The US continued with rather inconsistent attempts to ensure the succession of a moderate government.

After the FSLN's final offensive began in June, the US unsuccessfully sought Latin American support for another effort at multilateral mediation. At the OAS, the US then made its first public statement in favour of Somoza's resignation, yet it also proposed, at the insistence of Carter's National Security Adviser Zbigniew Brzezinski, that an OAS 'peace-keeping force' be sent to install a 'broadly based government of national reconciliation', along practically the same lines as those proposed in the autumn mediation, even though a provisional Nicaraguan government taking refuge in neighbouring Costa Rica was by then supported by most of the Nicaraguan opposition, and by much of Latin America. The US' proposal for intervention was bluntly rejected. Only when the FSLN was on the verge of military victory in July 1979 did the US stop trying to exclude it from power, and even then it angered it with pressures to broaden the new junta and with its attempts to ensure the continued existence of the National Guard.

The FSLN's outright victory in July 1979 was not inevitable. The US could conceivably have avoided Somoza's downfall altogether, at least for a time. Had the US acted firmly against Somoza *before* the FSLN achieved its dominant position, there could have been an entirely different balance of forces in the subsequent regime. Then, had the US put itself squarely behind the broadly supported, even if FSLN-led, provisional government, the US could still have influenced the subsequent internal balance, and perhaps external developments, by avoiding an outright military victory in the teeth of US opposition. Instead, the US ended up losing on almost all counts. It had ditched a longstanding ally and backed down from intervening, but not put itself clearly on the side of change. Most of all, the US had visibly tried and – equally visibly – failed to control events in its traditional sphere of influence.

The US Domestic Opposition: 1977–79

From the beginning, there was domestic criticism of Carter's human rights posture in Latin America: for undermining and humiliating longstanding US friends; and for weakening contacts through which to exert positive US influence without establishing the basis for congenial alternatives. There was also alarm at what seemed to be an incautious abandonment of US interests and influence in the region. US public attention had already been drawn to the region as a result of the Panama Canal Treaty process, which continued to be the focus of domestic controversy and had acquired a symbolic importance in the national debate about US policy and power. Prominent in the opposition to 'giving away' the Canal was Ronald Reagan, for whom it was a key issue in his campaign for the Republican nomination in 1976. As one Reagan strategist put it: 'People sense in this issue some way, after Vietnam, and Watergate, and Angola, of reasserting the glory of the country. People once more see a chance for Americans to stand up as Americans.' Many others shared the fear that it would seem 'renewed evidence that the United States is a paper tiger', and 'encourage penny-dictators and minor aggressions everywhere.'[15] With oil-rich Mexico acquiring a new strategic relevance and sensitivity for the energy-conscious US people, and the Panama Canal being a focus of concern about traditional influence, there was a highly sensitised regional context even before the crisis broke. The area was immediately prepared as an issue in domestic debate about US power and policy. There was thus fresh impetus to see events in Central America in terms of their effect on the US global power base and direct US regional interests, and US policy in the region as affecting global credibility.

By June 1979, moreover, conservative sensitivities were particularly high. In the first half of that year, preparations for signature of SALT II had been taking place amid concern about the US strategic position, and revolutions in Grenada and Iran seemed to add new 'losses' to the US list. It was all too easy for the Nicaraguan crisis to be seen in terms of external threat and exploitation, to arouse fears of an uncontrollable spread of revolution on America's southern flank, and for it and the US response to acquire a global significance.

Predictably, reactions tended also to be formulated in terms of the Cuban experience of nearly twenty years before. Indeed, the terms in which opposition to the FSLN by the resurgent US Right would be stated were clear even before the revolutionary victory, when it was still unclear what course the new regime would take and what effect the revolution would have on Nicaragua's neighbours like El Salvador. The Sandinistas themselves were radicals, most were Marxist-influenced, and some were Marxist–Leninists but in June 1979 they were setting up a broadly supported government promising non-alignment, political pluralism and a mixed economy. They certainly had links with Cuba, were unashamedly 'anti-imperialist' and suspicious of the US, but most of their support had come from Latin American countries such as Costa Rica, Panama and Venezuela. Ties to the Soviet Union, which was still dubious about the Sandinistas, were negligible, while Castro could be seen to be urging and acting with caution. A CIA report of May 1979 stated that Castro had been deliberately avoiding any direct military involvement in Nicaragua, and limiting Cuba's role primarily to that of political adviser.[16]

Letters sent to President Carter in June 1979 by a bloc of 125 Congressmen demanding support for Somoza, rejected as folly the acceptance of 'an imposed government coalition that would include totalitarian Marxists who reject the electoral process' and who would inevitably condemn Nicaraguans 'to the same systematic totalitarianism which has denied the Cuban people their basic human rights for two decades.' The US' 'lack of support for its traditional ally, Nicaragua, has been interpreted by the Soviet and Cuban communist leaders as American indifference . . . The result has been greatly increased terrorist activities in Central America, and disturbing

18

political developments in a number of Caribbean nations.' Moreover, 'Cuba was surrounded by water; Nicaragua is not.' It would become 'a Castroite base in Central America, from which the Communists can move northward against other small nations.' 'If the United States takes no action to thwart encroachment by Soviet surrogates in Central America, we will shortly find that the Soviet Union will control an area bordering on two oceans stretching from Panama to the vast oil reserves of Mexico.' 'The people of our country have witnessed the steady retreat of freedom in East Europe, China, Asia, Cuba, Africa and the Middle East. Are Nicaragua and Central America to be next?' The Congressmen urged the President to support Somoza, as 'a signal to the Free World that the United States continues to support its allies against Soviet-backed aggression.'[17]

Subsequent conservative criticisms of Carter's policy, which would give the ideological thrust to Reagan's policy, expanded such views. All tended to accept that regional conflicts and revolutions could not be separated from the global ideological conflict. The Soviet Union was assumed to be ever poised and able to find willing accomplices to take advantage of local problems to further strategic interests ranging from military facilities or client regimes, to the destabilisation of US allies and the undermining of US influence. The very real problems posed by Nicaragua were thus cast primarily, as by Jeane Kirkpatrick in her famous 'Dictatorships and Double Standards' *Commentary* essay of late 1979, in terms of 'dealing with non-democratic governments who are threatened by Soviet-sponsored subversion' and 'the appropriate response to a military struggle in a country whose location gives it strategic importance out of proportion to its size and strength.' Moreover, there was (she wrote) some possibility of moving such governments toward democracy, provided that 'the effort is not made at a time when the incumbent government is fighting for its life against violent adversaries.' There was none of 'a revolutionary "socialist" or Communist society being democratized.' Finally, such regimes were inherently expansionist, and 'create refugees by the million.'[18]

For such critics, Carter had only managed to put in power a government dominated by Marxists, which would fulfil its promises to the OAS to respect non-alignment, political pluralism and a mixed economy, if at all, only if forced to do so. The establishment of a full Sandinista regime would represent an unacceptable challenge to the US' regional and global strength and credibility, an unacceptable change in the regional status quo, and an unacceptable risk to Nicaragua's neighbours. If Nicaragua did not· yet have all the characteristics of a 'second Cuba', it would have, sooner or later, if it was given the chance to do so.

Carter and the Sandinistas

The Carter Administration, however, opted to give the new goverment a chance *not* to do so. Although not without hesitation and internal differences, it now began to apply a new foreign policy toward Nicaragua, hoping it could prevent 'another Cuba' by accommodating and moderating the new regime. The Carter Administration believed that the US could afford to be flexible and patient, given its continued predominance in the region, the moderating influence of the regional powers and Western European countries, and the inevitable Nicaraguan interest in economic relations with the US. It would try to bolster private enterprise and moderate political sectors, and to avoid acting in a manner which would strengthen the position of the more radical and anti-American elements. Economic aid would encourage the regime not to turn to Cuba and the Soviet Bloc, and help to avoid any apparent or politically-presented need for an explicit choice to be made between East and West. At the same time, the US would make clear that it hoped that the regime would fulfil its political promises, and that support for revolutionaries elsewhere would not be tolerated. The US would be understanding of the Sandinistas' revolutionary and anti-imperialist rhetoric, however irritating, and give them both time and incentives to settle down. If successful, such a policy would have not only preventive but positive benefits for the US. As those who supported aid to Nicaragua argued, 'If Nicaragua can make it along democratic lines, other lands needing change from right-wing tyranny will see that the alternative need not be left-wing tyranny.' Moreover, Nicaragua might seem in danger of being 'lost' and thus not to deserve US support, but 'failure to provide the promised American help would all but guarantee that very outcome,' and simply 'concede the game to the Soviets, the Cubans and their surrogates.'[19]

Both Governments, indeed, endeavoured to overcome suspicions, and relations were surprisingly cordial for many months. $62.6 million in US loans, food aid and grants was given during the new Government's first year. A further $75 million aid package put together in August eventually passed through Congress in February 1980, but with a large number of restrictive conditions.[20] These, like suggestions that the prospects of aid would be improved if Nicaragua voted to censure the Soviet Union over Afghanistan, naturally provoked an angry Nicaraguan response. During a further delay caused by debates over the whole Foreign Assistance Act, critics found new causes to oppose aid. In March 1980, a Nicaraguan delegation went to the Soviet Bloc in search of economic aid. In April, the first two moderates on the Nicaraguan Junta resigned, one of them, Alfonso Robelo, amid accusations of betrayal of the original programme. In May, the FSLN acknowledged the presence in Nicaragua of a small group of Cuban military advisers. Even after approval of the package, Carter was obliged to certify that Nicaragua was not exporting revolution to her neighbours, which he did in September 1980.

By January 1981, Nicaragua had received some $118 million in US aid, as would later be emphasised in denunciations of Sandinista ingratitude and betrayal. The FSLN did respond with considerable diplomatic tactlessness, while the aid's effect was somewhat spoilt by its delay and conditionality. However, there was also a fundamental tension in this, as in other aspects of relations. The aid was clearly intended to prevent increased Cuban and Soviet influence. For most Sandinistas, however, relations with Cuba and the Soviet Union were seen ideally less as an alternative than as an addition to relations with the US, and the West in general. Among the motivations for the March trip to Moscow was not only economic need, and a desire to obtain what they hoped would be pointedly less conditional aid, but a positive interest in economic and political diversification. Moreover, given the US' long support for Somoza, its final interventionist efforts, and the strong opposition in the US to Carter's policy, the FSLN never entirely overcame suspicions of the US, nor fears that relations would turn sour, aid be suspended or their regime eventually be attacked. There was thus also a pre-emptive aspect to such tentative steps towards the Eastern Bloc which strengthened the provocative tendencies of many and the ideological proclivities of some. One early consequence was indeed the failure to condemn the Soviet invasion of Afghanistan which so upset the American Right. Many advisers to the FSLN urged Nicaragua to vote condemning the invasion in the UN, on the grounds that to do otherwise would unnecessarily provoke the US at a difficult time in relations. Some FSLN leaders, however, in any case irked by US suggestions as to how they should vote, seem to have preferred to vote against condemnation, on the grounds that they needed to be sure of Soviet support in order to defend the revolution against any eventual onslaught of American imperialism. The result was an abstention. Nicaragua's general behaviour in the UN revealed the ample room for suspicion and misunderstanding. The FSLN claims to have adopted a 'non-aligned' position. The US would claim that 'From the beginning, Nicaragua aligned itself with the Soviet bloc in the United Nations.'[21] Of the 112 votes in the 34th Session of the General Assembly in which Nicaragua participated, it voted against the USSR on 25 occasions, but against Cuba on only 4. Cuba was then leader of the Non-Aligned Movement. The US attitude toward Cuban-style non-alignment was emphasised by the much-publicised 'discovery' of a Soviet combat brigade in Cuba immediately before the

Non-Aligned meeting in Havana in September 1979, a meeting at which the leader of the Nicaraguan Junta, Daniel Ortega, made a speech vehemently denouncing US imperialism. This provocation was only heightened by growing military contacts with Cuba and the Soviet Bloc even in the first year of the Revolution.

Sandinista fears and suspicions grew during the aid debate already referred to, and reached a new level with the election in November 1980 of Ronald Reagan, whose ideological hostility was unmistakeable. For the Republicans and US conservatives, on the other hand, Sandinista actions under Carter seemed only to confirm their own fears and suspicions, and their belief that the policy of aid and tolerance could not work. Carter had pressed ahead with the aid package despite evidence of increasing Nicaraguan contacts with the Soviet Bloc. Moreover, not wanting to be forced to cut off aid and thereby be accused of pushing the Sandinistas into the Soviet camp, he had until the very end, to the anger of the CIA, played down the growing evidence of Nicaraguan contacts with and support for the guerrilla movement which was gaining strength in El Salvador.

Carter and El Salvador

The Nicaraguan Revolution had had an immediate and inevitable effect in El Salvador. Its success directly encouraged the revolutionary groups there, while the crisis also encouraged a variety of attempts to prevent anything similar happening in El Salvador. The US stepped up efforts, begun in late 1978, to force the military president toward reform and dialogue with the moderate opposition. The response of the intransigent military and elite to Left-wing demands and actions became even more violent and indiscriminate. A number of Salvadorean officers and civilians, however, now became convinced that the only way to avoid revolution was to pre-empt it by economic and political reform, and by removing President Carlos Humberto Romero, which they did on 15 October 1979. The US was not involved in the coup, but gave it a cautious welcome. A broad junta – including reformist leaders – was established, only to fall apart within months amid rising violence.

It is highly unlikely that the Junta could have worked even with full US support. Almost before it had begun, the coup had been largely taken over by less reformist officers, who had opposed any inclusion of the Left's 'popular organizations'. Then, with Ministers linked to the economic elite, they blocked proposals for reform. The Right attacked the Junta's reformist members, began to mobilise their ideological base and to re-organise their forces, including the 'death squads'. The infamous rural vigilante organisation ORDEN, banned by the Junta, was re-established as the National Democratic Front (FDN), while Major Roberto D'Aubuisson, tied to the most violent and extreme sections of the security forces,[22] formed the National Broad Front (FAN). The Left was divided in its attitudes to the Junta. The Communist Party welcomed it, and some Communists were given posts in the new government. The Armed Forces of National Resistance (FARN) proposed dialogue with the reformist civilians and officers to create a broad 'anti-fascist front'. The Popular Forces of Liberation (FPL), on the other hand, denounced the coup as a US plot, while condemning as 'suicidal' the insurrectionary actions of the People's Revolutionary Army (ERP). Those actions, indeed, not only weakened the position of reformist officers and ensured that more flexible junior officers stayed loyal to their superiors, but further encouraged the campaign of violent repression. The failure of a December ultimatum by a majority of the Cabinet that the Armed Forces accept dialogue with the popular organisations and submit themselves to the authority of the Junta, led to its collapse in the first days of January 1980. In mid-January, the first co-ordinating body of the popular organisations was formed, showing its strength with a 200000-strong demonstration in the capital, San Salvador. In that same month 309 people died at the hands of the army and security forces.[23]

The crucial point for US policy was thus the turn of the year 1979–80, as the country began to collapse into war and political turmoil. One thing was clear to all. There was not to be another revolutionary victory. The hostage crisis in Iran and the Soviet invasion of Afghanistan sharpened yet further American sensitivities about 'losing' anything else, especially in Central America. With Carter running for re-election in 1980, such sensitivities were all the more important because of their electoral implications. The White House increasingly stressed that it recognised the area's 'extreme strategic importance,' and that the US did 'not intend to abandon the vital Central American region to Cuba and its radical Marxist allies.'[24] The possibility of a guerrilla triumph raised general fears of a chain reaction of instability, international unreliability and Marxist influence spreading northward. Moreover, in El Salvador there was no dynastic US-backed dictator, facing such broad opposition that revolution could be explained as an unavoidable exception. The absence of such a symbolic figure also seemed to give the Salvadorean Left a more clearly ideological commitment to revolution and class struggle than the heirs of Sandino. Although the Soviet-line Communist Party was not the leading force of the contemporary Salvadorean revolutionaries, it was tempting to see them as simply following the tradition of Farabundo Marti, a Communist linked to the Comintern in the 1930s who had attempted to mobilise into armed insurrection those dispossessed by the gross inequities of land and the denial of elections.

However, the military coup and the general turmoil also meant that the US did not have the option of simply propping up a threatened regime. US involvement in the crisis threatened only to associate it with violent repression. One alternative was therefore simply to stop all assistance on the grounds of massive human rights violations by the military and the lack of any real government to give it to. That would probably have led not to an immediate Left-wing triumph, but to an even greater bloodbath and an even more violent military regime facing a broader opposition. The subsequent worst case would have been a collapse into regional conflict, with obvious risks of broader confrontation. The best that the US could hope for would have been a military split and the relatively quick replacement of the repressive regime by a broad coalition government including the Left. But even that would effectively have been 'another Nicaragua', and it was politically impossible at that time for the US to consider standing back and hoping. Another alternative was for the US to try actively to bring all parties, including the Left, into a transitional government of national reconciliation. Although the popular organisations then represented a demonstrable political force, there seemed little immediate prospect of power being taken by the revolutionary groups, who tended to be seen in the US as dangerous extremists lacking in public support. The Administration did not therefore see negotiations including the Left as either necessary or desirable, and even had it decided to try, there would have been formidable problems. The revolutionary Left and radical Right had no desire to compromise with each other, and most of the Christian Democrat Party (PDC) wanted to exclude both. Moreover, the US now had only very limited political influence over either, and the necessary combination of threats and promises to both simultaneously would have had no credibility. US attempts to promote talks before the coup had not only failed but had already brought cries of 'Yankee interventionism' from the Left and anger from the nationalist Right.[25]

The course followed by the Administration corresponded in part to local developments, namely that the only opposition party willing to continue working with the military was the PDC, but also to the combination of domestic pressures. There was strong pressure, for example, for the US to take a more decisive and positive position than it had in Nicaragua. For some, including those who had been alarmed at the demise of a 'pro-U.S. military government . . . which had been economically viable', this implied primarily a restoration of order, rather than further destabilisation by precipitate reformism. Even if they recognised that the turmoil had 'its origins in the historical inequities between the social classes', this group saw the US' priority as defence against Cuban-backed 'Marxist guerrillas'.[26] There was also a strong body which felt, on the contrary, that any solution had immediately to emphasise reform, human rights and a move to democratic processes. This would reduce both the underlying causes of revolutionary conflict and the credibility of the Marxist Left's claim to be the only force willing and able to solve them. Yet others felt that, despite known contacts with Cuba, the revolutionary groups were firstly internal forces with some public support which would have to be taken into account in any peaceful solution, while the forces they opposed were certainly no more attractive.

Thus, although both revolutionary Left and radical Right had some constituency in the US, there was broad support for active US steps to try to strengthen the political centre and moderate forces, before it was forced to make another unpleasant choice between two sides of dubious democratic commitment, and over neither of which the US had much influence. The controversial questions remained, however, as to who in Salvadorean terms was an extremist and who an acceptable or biddable force, and where that left the army, in its majority a body of proved undemocratic bent. On top of all this was concern to prevent hostile 'external exploitation' of the situation in the meantime. By now, of course, the perceived security threat came not only from the Soviet Union across the oceans, or even from Cuba across the Caribbean sea, but very immediately from Nicaragua across the Gulf of Fonseca. The Salvadorean Army, therefore, had to be preserved in order to contain the insurrection. It had therefore to be included in any US-backed government, not only on the internal grounds that without it there could be no stable government to support at all, but also from the external consideration that without it the only means to counter Communist encroachment would be direct action by the US itself. Moreover, the US maintained that the repression and abuses were the work of Right-wing extremists associated more with the internal security forces than with the Army itself.

The US consequently helped to establish a new, Christian Democrat–military junta formed on 5 January 1980. The objectives and predictable problems, both reminiscent of the Alliance for Progress, were clear. The PDC would provide the civilian and reformist component necessary to offer a democratic alternative to armed revolution in El Salvador, and to satisfy liberal opinion in the US. The military, professionalised by the US, would provide the 'security shield' necessary for Marxism to be visibly combatted, for a political centre to be protected against extremes of Left and Right, and for effective social reforms to be instituted to undermine revolutionary appeal. However, the lack of an unequivocal US commitment to the promised PDC reforms, which the Right and most of the elite saw in any case as eminently socialist and which many could not believe that the US really did support, encouraged them to arrange an Army coup against the Junta for late February 1980. The State Department now made absolutely clear that the US' 'willingness to co-operate is predicated on a government committed to these reforms',[27] but the coup was only stopped by a confusing combination of threats, promises and mixed or misunderstood signals to those behind it. The US Embassy threatened the alternative of keeping out, 'warning that Washington would hold its aid and isolate the new regime internationally', but the US went ahead with the provision of non-lethal aid, on the grounds that 'In return for the military aid, the army was willing to listen to us.'[28] The US was committed to the private sector but, to the incomprehension of the traditional elite, seemed to insist on reforms which undermined them. The US stressed the need to restore law and order and to combat Marxism, but complained when 'terrorists' and 'subversives' were eliminated.

At the beginning of March, the PDC divided over its involvement in the Junta. Its Left-wing splinter group (the Popular Social Christian Party), the Social Democrats, the Communist Party and a trade union grouping joined with the popular organisations in April to form the Democratic Revolutionary Front (FDR). It would be the political wing of an alliance with the Farabundo Martí National Liberation Front (FMLN), created in October from the first union of the five guerrilla groups in May.[29] The PDC split also led to Duarte's entry to the Junta. The reforms were now decreed, beginning with the Basic Agrarian Reform Law, shortly followed by decrees nationalising the banks and foreign trade, and then by a further, US-designed, decree giving 'land to the tiller'. The land reforms were not merely cosmetic. For the PDC they were genuinely intended to solve popular problems and, despite insufficient planning and back-up, the Basic Law's provisions were not incapable of making progress in that direction. However, the problems faced were reflected in the simultaneous declaration of a state of siege. It would have been hard enough to carry out the reforms effectively amid Right-wing terror, armed revolution and bitter opposition from those affected, even if the Army to which its implementation was entrusted had been genuinely committed to its success. In fact, the Army was only going along with it at all because of US pressure. While some officers may then have understood the political function of reform in counter-insurgency, many more took direct advantage of the process as a tool of repression, as was predictably emphasised by the Left. The violence grew further, drawing international outrage with the murder on 23 March of the Archbishop of San Salvador by a Right-wing death squad. The government was in practice very weak. The Left denounced Duarte as an ally of repression and as a puppet of US intervention. The Right and traditional elite saw him as socialist, as much of a threat as the armed Left, and as a tool in Carter's aberrant interference. The PDC did have a substantial base, and there was a political centre, but it had already been gravely weakened and was now being discredited, while the chaos tended to drive many toward the social justice or order offered by the organised Left and Right. In mid-1980, the army itself moved further to the Right. In April, D'Aubuisson attempted to organise a coup but was prevented by troops loyal to the remaining moderate military leader, and arrested. The PDC threatened to resign if he was not tried but pressure from eight of fourteen garrisons brought about his release without charge, while the moderate Colonel Adolfo Majano was displaced. The PDC did not resign, and US support continued. It was a critical moment for America's stated policy of supporting the Centre against both extremes, but policy did not seem to be resolved in the centre's favour.

By late 1980, the situation was not stabilising, but seemed to be moving towards civil war. The US had made a political commitment, but seemed to have insufficient political influence to make it effective, especially in the face of a growing revolutionary determination to prevent it. Already it could be feared that, in the pursuit of democratic change, the US would simply be drawn in to the defence of the anti-Communist Right. The election of Ronald Reagan had the effect of exacerbating the US' problems and bringing the crisis to a head. The signals received in El Salvador that he was not enthusiastic about the reforms, and would act much more firmly and with fewer conditions, further weakened the US Embassy's position. The violent Right proceeded to kill five FDR leaders, partly to counter any possible interest in political talks. In December, National Guardsmen killed three American nuns and a Catholic lay worker, and on 3 January 1981 the Head of the Land Reform Agency and two US advisers were murdered. Forced to respond to the churchwomen's death, the US suspended economic and military aid but economic aid was quickly restored after only a government reshuffle. This made Duarte president but the reshuffle also finally removed Colonel Majano and effectively strengthened the political power of the military Right. Restoration of military aid was made conditional on a reduction of violence by the security forces, the transfer of the most brutal commanders and investigation of the churchwomen's murder. That aid was almost the only political lever remaining to the US. In late December 1980, however, the FMLN announced that it had planned a 'final offensive' against the Government, with the aim of winning a revolutionary victory before Reagan took office. The NSC and the

Pentagon urged a resumption and increase in aid, even though the conditions had not been fully complied with. The Human Rights Bureau argued that, with the government in effective control of the country, there was 'no military exigency which requires us to resume military assistance now', and that aid resumption would undermine the credibility of human rights pressure and 'render Duarte irrelevant, [since his] standing with the military is a function of his general ability to obtain US assistance.'[30] By then, however, the changing external context of the conflict made military aid seem almost unavoidable.

The End of Carter's Policy

The Administration had previously acknowledged Cuban influence on the Salvadorean Left, and knew of contacts with the Soviet Bloc and some material transfers from Cuba and Nicaragua. The increase in military aid to the government of Honduras, approved in April 1980, largely responded to the believed use of Honduras as 'a conduit for men and weapons into El Salvador by insurgents with Cuban support',[31] with the importance of Honduran co-operation reflected in US moves to bring about a peace treaty between Honduras and El Salvador. For most of the year, however, such transfers had been small. Carter had also had Sandinista assurances that despite their open political and diplomatic support for the FDR–FMLN in El Salvador, they would not export the material means of revolution. Soon after the September certification, however, US intelligence reported that the FMLN had begun to receive some of the material support promised in the middle of the year from Soviet Bloc countries, and that Nicaragua was becoming 'the center of the clandestine arms flow.' The State Department claims that, in response to strong protests by the US Ambassador in late September, 'the Sandinistas held up transshipment of the arms for one month', only to restart at the end of October once the second tranche of the US aid package had been authorised for disbursement.[32] The amount in question was almost certainly less than the 'nearly 200 tons' claimed in the State Department's February 1981 Special Report,[33] and there is no evidence to support the Report's suggestion that the guerrillas were receiving heavy weapons. However, there is no doubt of Sandinista involvement in the flow of supplies and provision of training and communications facilities to the FMLN.

The general offensive started on 10 January 1981, but the insurrection simply did not happen; there was very limited response even to the call for a general strike. The revolutionaries did have some popular support, but not enough, and the conditions for a national insurrection did not exist. It was already clear that the offensive had failed *before* the Government of El Salvador received any US material support but the decision to restore military aid in some form had already been taken, and not only because of the political effect in El Salvador of an open refusal to do so.

In principle, the US had much the same policy options at the beginning of January 1981 as twelve months before: assist the government; promote negotiations; or keep out altogether. A case for either of the latter two options could still be made, whether on human rights grounds or as being consistent with the policy of non-intervention and flexible response to internal change. But a policy of non-intervention had in general been predicated on the assumption that other powers would also keep out if the US did. The limits beyond which Soviet and Cuban activities would be seen by the US as a failure on their part to keep out were not high in any region of the world. Moreover, US sensitivities and suspicions in this respect had been resurging globally in the latter years of *détente* over developments in South-East Asia, the Middle East and Africa, and had been brought to a peak with the Soviet invasion of Afghanistan. In Central America, those limits had always been low and were already being stretched in Nicaragua while, in American perceptions, the US had been remarkably, even dangerously, restrained during 1980. The growing evidence of guerrilla support from Nicaragua and the Soviet Bloc, even if it could not be expected to be militarily decisive, was enough to tilt the balance within the Carter Administration in favour of military aid to El Salvador, and of an unequivocal commitment to the survival of a US-backed regime. The restoration of military aid was announced on 14 January 1981, and a second $5 million package of lethal aid, and the sending of US military advisers, on the 16th. Ambassador Robert White, previously opposed to military aid, now spoke publicly of its necessity. He claimed that the evidence of external support 'changes the nature of the insurgency movement here, and makes it clear that it is dependent on outside sources.'[34] 'The guerrillas . . . are getting more than we are giving the Government . . . It is unacceptable to the US to let El Salvador fall into the hands of the Marxist–Leninists.'[35]

The basic lines of Reagan's policy in El Salvador were thus set down by the Carter Administration. Honduras' military role in US regional strategy had also begun to be defined. Moreover, it is likely that, had the Carter Administration continued in office for even a few weeks more, it would have made policy changes toward Nicaragua consistent with its stand over El Salvador. The attitude of the incoming Administration was largely based on an ideological reaction to Carter's initial policies. The case can be made that the strength of Republican opposition, and Central American reactions to the prospect of a Reagan Administration, contributed to Carter's problems and failures. The specific situation created by the 'final offensive', of course, would not have arisen had the election gone the other way. But the actual steps taken by his successor were in many respects only a practical development of Carter's final position, coloured by a changed global and ideological vision. Reagan inherited much of the policy and many of the problems. What he brought into the situation did not, for most of his first term, seem to increase the prospects of any kind of success

Notes and References

[1] This was the case, for example, with regard to revolutionary Mexico in the periods immediately preceding the entry of the US into both World Wars.

[2] An inter-oceanic canal in Nicaragua had been considered as early as 1825, and US interest in the potential construction of such a canal continued for a time even after completion of the Panama Canal.

[3] Quoted in Don L. Etchison *The United States and Militarism in Central America* Praeger Publishers, New York, 1975, p. 103.

[4] 1961 US Senate study mission. Quoted in Jenny Pearce *Under the Eagle* Latin American Bureau, London, 1982, p. 53.

[5] Joseph H. Stodder and Kevin F. McCarthy *Profiles of the Caribbean Basin in 1960/1980: Changing Geopolitical and Geostrategic Dimensions* The Road Corporation, Santa Monica, 1983, p. xiii.

[6] Margaret Daly Hayes 'United States Security Interests in Central America in Global Perspective' in Richard E. Feinberg (ed.) *Central America. International Dimensions of the Crisis* Holmes & Meier, New York and London, 1982, p. 91.

[7] Jorge I. Dominguez 'The United States and its Regional Security Interests: The Caribbean, Central and South America' *Daedalus* Fall 1980, Vol. 109, No. 4, p. 119.

[8] *The Military Balance 1979/1980* IISS, London 1979.

[9] Zbigniew Brzezinski, Address before the International Platform Association in convention in Washington, 2 August 1979.

[10] Cyrus Vance, Speech to the American Association of Junior and Community Colleges, 1 May 1979, *Survival* July–August 1979, p. 179.

[11] Zbigniew Brzezinski, loc. cit.

[12] Cyrus Vance, loc. cit.

[13] Zbigniew Brzezinski, May 1977. Quoted in Jenny Pearce, op. cit. p. 116.

14 Quoted in Raymond Bonner *Weakness and Deceit. US Policy and El Salvador* Hamish Hamilton, London, 1985, p. 39.

15 Quoted in Walter LaFeber *The Panama Canal. The Crisis in Historical Perspective* OUP, New York, 1978, p. 190; Hanson Baldwin. Quoted in Walter LaFeber, op. cit. p. 210.

16 Carla Anne Robbins *The Cuban Threat* ISHI Publications, Philadelphia, 1985, p. 247.

17 *New York Times* 18 June and 30 June 1979.

18 Jeane Kirkpatrick 'Dictatorships and Double Standards' *Commentary* November 1979.

19 *Christian Science Monitor* Editorial, 19 October 1979; *New York Times* Editorial, 15 February 1980; Rep. Clement Zablocki *Miami Herald* 24 February 1980.

20 All of it, for example, had to be used for US products, 60 per cent had to go to the private sector, and none to educational projects involving Cuban personnel.

21 Secretary of State George Schultz, Speech before the American Bar Association, 23 May 1985.

22 The term 'security forces' refers collectively to the National Guard, the National Police and the Treasury Police.

23 Jenny Pearce, op. cit. p. 223.

24 *Wall Street Journal* 29 April 1980; *Financial Times* 16 September 1980.

25 Alan Riding *New York Times* 17 September 1979.

26 Roger Fontaine, Cleto DiGiovanni Jr., and Alexander Kruger 'Castro's Specter' *The Washington Quarterly* Autumn 1980 passim.

27 A fifth group, the Revolutionary Party of Central American Workers (PRTC), was formed at the end of 1979.

28 *International Herald Tribune* 24 February 1980.

29 ibid. 18 March 1980.

30 Patricia Derian. Quoted in Raymond Bonner, op. cit. pp. 222-3.

31 Statements of Deputy Assistant Secretary of Defense Franklin D. Kramer to House Subcommittee on Foreign Appropriations, 25 March 1980.

32 *Revolution Beyond Our Borders. Sandinista Intervention in Central America* Special Report No. 132 United States Department of State, September 1985 pp. 6-7.

33 *Special Report on Communist Interference in El Salvador.* Released by the US State Department in Washington, 23 February 1981.

34 Quoted in Raymond Bonner, op. cit. p. 225.

35 *Guardian* 16 January 1981.

2 The Development of Current Policy

The Reagan Administration and Central America

The incoming Administration did not bring with it a clear new policy to deal with the massive problems and multiple dilemmas posed by the Central American crisis. Rather, it brought a new broad approach, strongly influenced on the one hand by the wave of ideological and reassertionist conservative opposition to Carter, with an implicit resurgence of 'traditional' views of the region, and on the other by a much sharpened sensitivity to the current strategic importance and implications of the region. Both factors led to a determination to deal with the crisis with greater and demonstrable firmness, certainly avoiding any further 'losses' and ideally undoing the perceived damage already done to US influence and security in this 'vital and vulnerable' area. There remained a general awareness that the fundamental cause of the instability and conflict lay in the region's deep social and economic problems, recognition of the other dimensions of regional change which had produced an overall decline in US influence, and consequent realisation of the need to address the underlying problems and to find new patterns of regional co-operation. However, the Reagan Administration brought a level of commitment and a vehemence of rhetoric which helped to obscure the fundamental issues beneath polemic and polarisation in the US, and exacerbated the problems in Central America.

The Administration began with outbursts of dramatic rhetoric led by Secretary of State Haig, amid public campaigns reflecting the new approach. The threat was presented in stark and simple terms of communist subversion and external aggression. In El Salvador, the insurgency had been 'progressively transformed into a text-book case of indirect armed aggression by communist powers'[1] in a 'global communist campaign co-ordinated by Havana and Moscow to support the Marxist guerrillas.'[2] Guatemala would be the next 'domino' to fall. Without action there would soon be a ring of hostile powers on the US' southern flank and 'fourth frontier'. The nightmare of a hostile or chronically unstable Mexico was invoked, whether as part of the northward Marxist march to exploit social tensions or of a Soviet plan to control the Mexican oil fields. Communist conquest of the US itself was not ruled out in the most extreme depictions of the threat to the Americas, while promises of waves of refugees from Communism touched US sensitivities, sharp from debates over Mexican migration and the 1980 exodus from Cuba. The historical importance of a secure Central America for US power projection began to be stressed, as did the importance of maintaining US credibility. The US had historically been both willing and able to back friendly local regimes. If it was again seen to be neither, and in an area in which the US could surely expect to prevail, more distant allies under threat would lose confidence in US assurances. Full support for the Salvadorean Government was promised, with hints at an intention to 'go to the source' of the supplies and subversion, in Nicaragua and beyond. The possibility of a blockade on Cuba, or even eventual direct US military action in Central America, was not ruled out. The US would 'draw the line' against Communist expansion, demonstrate its commitment to defend its friends, and show 'Cuba and the other nations that seek to subvert other countries . . . that we have a new Administration, a new national resolve, and we will take the steps that are needed to keep the peace any place in the world.'[3]

Alarmed critics argued that the only vital US security interest was to prevent any establishment of Soviet military bases or strategic use of local facilities. That might be achieved by diplomatic means, through understandings both with local countries and with the Soviet Union itself, in an extension of the 1962, 1970 and 1979 understandings over Cuba. Mexico's stability was seen as threatened more by US intervention than by Left-wing regimes in Central America, which would if anything tend to push the regime more to the Right. Floods of refugees were more likely to come from Right-wing repression and escalating conflict than from revolutionary governments. The Administration's apparent goal of 'a cluster of friendly, stable nations which hold honest elections and respect human rights, welcome U.S. private investment and support Washington internationally . . . is not realistic . . . Hegemony will not easily be reimposed.' Damage to US credibility would be largely self-inflicted after such escalatory rhetoric, and the way to avoid the possibility of setbacks in Central America weakening the US elsewhere was 'not by forcing an unwinnable confrontation, but by seeking a diplomatic solution'. There was no safe and rational alternative but to abandon counter-productive threats in favour of using US economic and regional political influence to moderate the Sandinistas; to ensure prohibition of extra-hemispheric military bases in the region; to support mediation in El Salvador; 'and genuinely to accept profound changes in Central America, even when they diminish immediate U.S. influence'.[4]

The Reagan Administration's approach to Central America was shaped by broad strategic lines entirely opposed to such an outcome. Quite simply, it did not want any more regional regimes regarding which it would have to have any understandings with the Soviet Union. As for those understandings over Cuba, the result seemed only to have been a constant Soviet probing of the limits of American tolerance, and a gradual increase in both the Soviet presence and Cuban strength. Reagan would emphasise the strategic importance of the Caribbean and point out that 'in early 1942, a handful of Hitler's submarines sank more tonnage there than in all of the Atlantic Ocean. And they did this without a single naval base anywhere in the area. Today, . . . Cuba is host to a Soviet combat brigade, a submarine base capable of servicing Soviet submarines and military air bases visited regularly by Soviet military aircraft'.[5] If another regime with Cuban-style non-alignment was consolidated in Nicaragua, on top of Grenada, there would be a potentially 'hostile axis' spanning the Caribbean from West to East with access to the Pacific. It was determined not to let the guerrillas even negotiate their way into power in El Salvador, and not only because it had staked US credibility on their defeat. It also believed that inclusion of Marxist–Leninists in a broad provisional government would, as it thought the case in Nicaragua, lead to the eventual exclusion of all others. Whether or not the Salvadorean Marxists were pro-Soviet now, it could not be guaranteed that they would not seek unacceptable links with them later. Moreover, the Administration saw such criticisms as ignoring the local consequences, which were likely to be continued destabilisation by those ideologically committed to the spread of revolution. It wanted to restore, and be seen to restore, a stable and internationally reliable isthmus.

However, such broad guidelines, and the global and ideological thrust of much of the Administration, could not prescribe specific policy measures and it was somewhat unclear and divided as to what exactly could and should be done in Central America. It took six months even to appoint and confirm a first Assistant Secretary of State

34

for Inter-American Affairs, Thomas Enders, who was, moreover, not of the ideological Right. Moreover, other factors encouraged restraint over Central America. The initial outbursts had sparked off widespread fears that the Administration was marching straight into 'another Vietnam' in El Salvador – and on behalf of a very unsavoury regime. Greater caution began to be urged in order to protect the President's image, and to prevent Congressional alarm from endangering priority domestic and economic policies, or public alarm from endangering Republican prospects in the 1982 elections. The Joint Chiefs of Staff were reluctant to undertake any military action in the region, placing higher priority on other regions, being concerned that such actions might endanger their burgeoning military budget requests, not wanting to become involved in a difficult and unpopular war, and indeed arguing for emphasis on the social and economic dimensions of the crisis. The Administration did not have secure backing on Capitol Hill. The 1980 elections had given the Republicans control of the Senate, and the hardline conservative Jesse Helms the chair of the Western Hemisphere Affairs Subcommittee of the Foreign Relations Committee. In the Committee as a whole, however, Helms was isolated, and even reliable Administration supporters were outnumbered by liberal Democrats and moderate Republicans. Most important, the Democrats retained control of the House of Representatives. The chair of its Foreign Affairs Subcommittee on Inter-American Affairs went to the liberal activist Michael Barnes, while the key Foreign Operations Subcommittee of House Appropriations was chaired by the moderate Clarence Long, and included six liberal Democrats. Moreover, the Administration's February campaign to secure active European support for its policy had had scant success, and Latin America was by no means united in support for the US.

Beneath the rhetoric, the Administration did not actually do a great deal more materially in its first dramatic months than was consequent with Carter's final stand. It sent to El Salvador twenty more military advisers, four more helicopters and a further $25 million in military aid. To Nicaragua it sent strong messages, and suspended wheat sales and what remained of the 1980 aid package. It was unclear and divided as to what more to do, and with what precise objectives. And while it was trying to put together a policy, as opposed to an approach, it was to face strong opposition from those critical, and fearful, of its fundamental position. With more moderate elements in immediate charge of policy, and facing strong opposition in Congress, the Administration was for some two years to prove relatively restrained in practice. However, its rhetoric, and what was or was not done, only contributed to a worsening of the situation in many respects. In El Salvador, elections and the provision of the minimum US assistance required to avert governmental collapse seemed only to deepen the problems, and threatened to draw the US directly into the conflict. In Nicaragua, the loss of opportunities for some reduction of tensions and the limited increase in pressures on the regime, including the beginning of covert support for armed anti-Sandinista groups, only helped to ensure that the elements of suspicion and the potential for conflict would grow and become more intractable.

In the rest of Central America, developments were by no means entirely favourable to the US. In Guatemala, the situation in 1981 remained one of appalling repression and human rights abuse. US military aid to the military regime in its brutal campaign against some 6000 guerrillas remained politically impossible, although US military advisers were still present and contributed to the initiation in the latter part of the year of a new and effective, if still brutal, form of active counter-insurgency. In March 1982, the President was overthrown in a military coup and replaced by General Efraín Ríos Montt, who quickly asserted his commitment to democracy and human rights in the hope of securing a resumption of US military aid, as was indeed sought by the Administration. Public and Congressional scepticism about the asserted human rights improvements, however, prevented even authorisation of military sales throughout 1982, thus creating considerable tensions in US–Guatemalan relations.

In Honduras, the military government allowed elections to be held in 1981, and a civilian government took power at the beginning of 1982. The positive effect of this example of democratisation was, however, weakened by the evident real power wielded by the Armed Forces and the increase in human rights abuses during this period as the regime tightened internal security and clamped down on the few small revolutionary groups in the country. Deeper involvement in the regional crisis, as well as serious economic problems, seemed to threaten only to increase the obstacles to development of a full and free democratic process. In Costa Rica, deep economic troubles threatened to undermine the country's existing stability and political democracy, while regional tensions increased internal frictions.

By 1983, increasing problems for Administration policy both in Washington and in Central America would bring a new phase. On the one hand, those in the Administration pressing for a tougher approach came more to the fore. On the other hand, there was a need to secure greatly increased funding from Congress, to establish greater bipartisan support for Central American policy, and to take into account the diplomatic initiatives of the Contadora Group, formed by Mexico, Venezuela, Colombia and Panama in January 1983. There was thus not only an increase in Administration confrontation with both

Congress and the Sandinistas, but there was also an increase in the US commitment in El Salvador and Central America as a whole. There was also some attempt to present a more coherent policy capable of receiving minimum bipartisan support, defining US concerns and objectives and compromising more with Congressional critics. The principal vehicle for this effort was a National Bipartisan Commission on Central America, established in July 1983 under the chairmanship of Henry Kissinger, which presented its report in January 1984.

In the case of El Salvador, this process of debate and confrontation did not lead to much change in stated policy objectives. Those were indeed to remain very much what they had been under President Carter. Rather, the Administration eventually succeeded in securing sufficient resources to support the military dimension of the policy, while being forced by Congressional insistence to address the problems of the political dimension with some of the same firmness. By 1985 there was a relatively clearly defined policy, enjoying broad consensus and with some prospect of success.

With regard to Nicaragua, a specific policy had also emerged by mid-1985 in the form of an explicit political commitment to the anti-Sandinista forces but it enjoyed only tenuous support, and had been achieved largely by the apparent failure, or closure, of most alternatives. It was defined primarily by negatives – prevention of consolidation of the regime without the use of direct US military force. It did not seem certain that US policy would achieve either that or the stated positive goal of forcing negotiation between the regime and the armed opposition as the basis for construction of a new political system. It did seem certain that intra-regional instability and tensions would be prolonged, raising fears about the prospect of escalating conflict, and the consequences of continued regional polarisation and militarisation for the stability, and democratic processes, of neighbouring Costa Rica and Honduras. By 1986, those two countries had not suffered negative effects to the extent feared by many, but there remained cause for concern, especially since the continued tensions further impeded genuine economic recovery and development, without which there could be no basis for long-term stability. Moreover, although developments in Guatemala seemed on the one hand to represent a positive step for the US' policy of the promotion and protection of democratic civilian structures, that step was both tenuous and likely again to draw the US directly into the Guatemalan situation, for better or worse. Much depended not only on whether the apparent success in El Salvador could be translated into stable progress, but also on how much the Administration had learnt from the long and painful process it had been forced to go through there.

Reagan and El Salvador

The Administration's central objective in El Salvador was continued military aid to the Government against guerrillas numbered by a Pentagon study in February 1981 at 3700 full-time and 5000 part-time combatants, and likely soon to grow stronger.[6] The Pentagon did not expect a lack of aid to produce immediate or outright revolutionary victory. It did fear that lack of aid might allow the guerrillas to put the 14000-strong Government forces at such military disadvantage that the Government would find it almost impossible to recover, while a clear lack of US support for the Government would demoralise the Armed Forces, and increase active popular support for the rebels. There was also fear of a consequent bloodbath by the far Right which would devastate the political centre and strengthen the Left in the long term. The dilemma for the US was how to balance the function of aid of giving military advantage and external reassurance with that of providing sufficient internal political leverage to assure the promised progress toward moderate democracy. The incoming Administration, however, was unclear as to how to approach the political problems in El Salvador, the depth and nature of which it partly seemed unable or unwilling to appreciate beneath the ideological resolve of its firm approach. It was forced to clarify its position by a strong debate with and in Congress which centred on the question of conditionality of aid.

The Administration's initial reaction was to cease aid conditionality entirely, and to remove such ill-timed obstacles to effective local action against the forces of international Communism. In February, it lifted all conditions on the grounds that aid was of vital necessity to save the Government from defeat. The decision also corresponded to the initially predominant, and insufficient, view of the priorities for success in El Salvador. This went beyond the assertion that the problem of security was immediate while the process of reform and development was long-term, or the Administration's general lower priority on human rights. Simple identification of the FDR–FMLN with a hostile external threat permitted the Administration to find a satisfyingly simple answer to the basic dilemmas presented: that socio-economic development required political stability, but political stability required socio-economic improvements, while solution of the internal conflict depended upon ending external involvement, which depended upon solving the internal problems which attracted it. For the Administration, priority defeat of the insurgency was not only in US security interests, but necessary to restore the conflict to internal dimensions (implicitly including the US as a natural and beneficent influence), and to remove a deliberately destabilising political force which prevented socio-economic development. On that basis the US could, as Reagan's first Ambassador in San Salvador put it, 'Save the economy, stop the violence, have the elections, and ride into the sunset.'[7]

However, the Special Report on Communist Interference in El Salvador had certainly not produced a majority in favour of unconditional support to a Government under which massive abuses by the Army and Security Forces were being perpetrated in El Salvador, and widely publicised in the US by human rights organisations and the Catholic Church. Opposition to an unconditional US commitment, with increasing US military involvement, was strengthened by doubts about the prudence of staking US credibility on the survival of a dubious and shaky regime. Initial moves to suspend all military aid until the Government controlled the Security Forces failed, most of those sceptical about aid being still reluctant to risk a revolutionary victory and accusations of having 'lost' El Salvador. However, Congress did limit the actual amount of aid sent. Administration requests were cut in the authorising bills and, after stiff resistance in the House Appropriations Subcommittee on Foreign Operations in March 1981 to the reprogramming of $5 million, the President resorted more to his emergency drawdown authority. The greater part of the military aid sent in the first two years had in fact to be sent through this means: $25 million in fiscal year 1981 and $55 million in 1982, out of totals of $35.492 and $86.5 millions respectively. The result with regard to conditionality was an amendment to the 1982 Foreign Aid Bill, first proposed in April and made law in December against Administration resistance. The President was required to certify every six months for the following two years, before providing aid, that the Salvadorean Government was 'achieving substantial control' over the Armed Forces to end 'indiscriminate torture and murder', 'implementing essential economic and political reforms, including the land reform program', carrying out free elections, and showing willingness to find a political solution to the conflict. Efforts by liberal Democrats on the House Foreign Affairs Committee to give Congress the power to veto a presidential certification failed to win sufficient support. Since the President's commitment in El Salvador practically ensured that he would not deny certification, even if to do so might have allowed him to blame policy failures on Capitol Hill, the predictable result was a highly dubious and mutually fraudulent process which sent unclear messages to El Salvador.

Despite the strength of opposition to Reagan's line, the debates did not reveal many clearly articulated or supported policy alternatives to construction of a moderate government. The issues and options were indeed often lost in rhetoric. The exaggerations, distortions, and even misrepresentations by Administration figures created a clear 'credibility gap' with many in Congress and the public, and helped to provoke a wave of counter-rhetoric, none of which made policy formulation or implementation any easier. Moreover, demands to give priority to the socio-economic roots of the conflict, rather than play up the security dimension, were often as evasive in their implications as the Administration's view was insufficient in its scope. Many of those who played down the security dimension, and did not see the incumbent government as either stable or legitimate, either failed to address the problems posed by the war, or balked at the alternative of negotiations leading to a new interim government of broad participation and national reconciliation, as was since early 1981 the proclaimed objective of the FDR–FMLN. There was massive public support for the broad notion of a political settlement, reflected in Congressional resolutions such as that passed almost unanimously by the House in March 1982, calling for 'unconditional discussions between the major political factions in El Salvador'. There was some support for a negotiated settlement, encouraged by mediation offers from the West German Government and the Socialist International, and by the Franco-Mexican Declaration of August 1981 calling for talks to be held with the FDR–FMLN as a representative political force. Critics continued to stress that, despite the presence of committed Marxist–Leninists and the receipt of external support, the importance of which was disputed, the FDR–FMLN was not a creation or repetition of either Cuba or Nicaragua, and did include political moderates. However, the rebels' attraction was in most cases a function more of the unattractiveness of their opponents than of their own democratic appeal, while the attraction of negotiations was mainly a function of the perceived unviability of alternative paths. Moreover, few detailed proposals were given as to how to overcome the immense problems that would be faced by negotiations on the ground. A 'political', as opposed to a 'military', solution was most broadly seen as the establishment of a functioning democratic system and the incorporation into it of those revolutionaries willing to participate, as opposed to the simple annihilation of the Left. Concern at perceived military emphases mainly reflected the feeling that in the current circumstances elections alone could not solve the political problems, and that it was unrealistic to expect rebel representatives to participate when they would face almost certain death at the hands of Right-wing death squads or the security forces themselves. The March resolution, indeed, did not call for unconditional 'negotiations', but discussions 'in order to guarantee a safe and stable environment for free and open democratic elections'. As such, it was not opposed by the Administration, and could be supported by almost everyone – from those who did want negotiations to those who simply wanted to avoid political confrontation in election year.

There was a broad consensus as to the ideal for US policy: the containment of the insurgency without drawing the US into military intervention, and the construction of a genuine democratic system, through support for a moderate centrist government capable of controlling the Army and Security Forces and of carrying out reforms. The debate was mostly about whether such a policy could, rather than should, work, and whether the Administration was seriously and sufficiently tackling the social and political aspects of the situation. Without progress in that regard, military support and involvement would be dangerously futile and counter-productive. The simple approach of military aid and elections did not seem sufficient, and seemed to threaten only to prop up those groups most opposed to change and justice, while more provision of such aid might actually decrease rather than increase US influence over developments.

The US seemed to be making very little progress in human rights and political issues. The Right-wing death squads persisted with their campaign of overt terror, believing (correctly) that they were acting with the connivance and under the protection of the Armed Forces. The Security Forces continued to kill and torture. The Army seemed to remain tied to the political Right and the traditional economic elite, and was responsible for continued indiscriminate violence in the countryside. It was hoped that elections in March 1982 would put in power the PDC, as a moderate government committed to the reform process, which would satisfy domestic critics and appear a plausible centrist alternative in El Salvador. The Administration was quick to point to the large official turnout figures as evidence of the guerrillas' lack of popular support, but the PDC did not win a majority, the elections revealing continued polarisation as many despairing of the war and of Duarte's promises turned to the Right. The prospect of a Right-wing coalition government, presided over by the infamous D'Aubuisson, and likely to reverse the reforms, was only averted by a burst of proconsular activity by the US Embassy and a letter from Haig threatening to cut off aid. However, the Constituent Assembly was dominated by the Right, and would be presided over by D'Aubuisson. The US did win agreement to include the PDC and to appoint as Provisional President the independent businessman Alvaro Magaña, and won also promises by the Right to respect the existing reforms, protect human rights and move to hold presidential elections. But the killings continued. The Assembly soon suspended the third phase of the agrarian reform, which had mainly been inspired by the American Institute for Free Labor Development (AIFLD). The far Right had already murdered two American AIFLD officials in January 1981, one of many notorious killings for which justice was being seen not to be done, and the PDC was now denouncing a fresh wave of assassinations of its own officials.

The US Embassy did attempt to curb the violence, especially in the periods immediately preceding 'certification.' The problem was not only that it did not try to do enough. The fundamental problem was that US threats carried only limited weight. The Administration's lesser general emphasis on human rights, its evident lack of real enthusiasm for the Salvadorean reforms, which went against its own ideological beliefs, and its vociferous commitment to 'drawing the line' against Communism in El Salvador, had an inevitable political impact in the country itself. If in early 1980, many of the far Right, intransigent elite and military had found it hard to believe that the Carter Administration really meant what it said about reform and human rights, they found it doubly so with Reagan in 1981. Indeed, part of the Salvadorean Right fully expected that Reagan would go along with a coup against Duarte, the threat of which quickly arose in March. The credibility of State Department assertions of the need to end abuses, and of Embassy pressures on local anti-Communists was further undermined by statements by some Administration officials about the mistake of excessive conditionality, the vital importance of aid, and the need to avoid the mistake of treating El Salvador 'in its own local terms . . . and to deal with this issue as a global problem'[8] of International Communism. Ambassador Hinton's statements during the election problems seemed only to confirm the weakness of his demands: 'It is true that we indicated a belief that some actions could be more helpful to El Salvador and to support for aid for El Salvador, *which will continue in any case*, than others'[9] (Emphasis added). Supporters of the new, extreme Right-wing Nationalist Republican Alliance (Arena), led by D'Aubuisson, were therefore convinced that there would never be a real cutoff of aid: 'Reagan will never let the communists win here. It's just a complete bluff.'[10] As the problems continued, and the officer believed responsible for the murder of the American land reform officials was freed, the exasperated Ambassador was forced in late 1982 to spell out that if there was no substantial progress, 'the United States, in spite of our other interests, in spite of our commitment in the struggle against communism, could be forced to deny assistance to El Salvador.'[11]

There was indeed a real dilemma involved. Salvadoreans would seem to be the more likely to respond to aid restrictions and threats, the greater the insurgent threat, and thereby the greater the importance to them of the aid. But the greater the insurgent threat, the less likely the US would seem to be to cut off aid, and thereby the less convincing the pressures. In 1981 and 1982, outright military victory by either side did not appear imminent. The Salvadorean military did not then believe that the guerrillas posed a threat to their survival, and some shared the view of the far Right that, if it was not for all the political confusion and constraints, they could simply wipe out subversion in a matter of months. However, they were aware of the dangers of international isolation and material vulnerability in particular. El Salvador, like most of Latin America, had in the 1970s increasingly acquired military equipment from sources other than the US. The core of the Air Force consisted of old French-manufactured jet aircraft bought from Israel, from which El Salvador had purchased some 80 per cent of its arms imports between 1972 and 1980. The military was having difficulty in finding spare parts and armaments for the aircraft and West Germany would now not supply spare parts or muzzle-launched grenades for the G3 rifles which had become standard issue for 75 per cent of the Armed Forces. In 1982, therefore, there was sufficient incentive for the Armed Forces to tolerate the PDC, but by no means enough for the High Command to take any active steps – especially against its own – to bring substantial changes, or fundamentally alter its political position.

After the March 1982 elections, the US Administration began to give more attention to the political challenges. Efforts to overcome the divided government's virtual paralysis, and to present a convincing appearance of progress toward peace and democracy, led to a pact in August 1982 between the three ruling parties: the PDC; the National Conciliation Party (PCN) (which had long represented the army and traditional elite); and D'Aubuisson's Arena. The seven-point agreement established political, human rights and peace committees to supervise its execution. A new constitution was to be ready for 1983, and presidential elections held in 1984. The Administration had sent only enough military aid to fend off the guerrillas, and had not fought very hard to secure more from Congress, partly because it could turn to its drawdown authority. By the end of 1982, however, the President was receiving strong Congressional warnings not to over-use that. The House had refused to include any military funds at all for El Salvador in the supplementary money bill of September 1982. More aid would soon be needed militarily, and it would have to be won from Congress.

In early 1983, the Army continued to appear brutally ineffective. It seemed reluctant and incompetent to carry out assertive counter-insurgency operations and to move from its overall 'nine-to-five war' approach. Its reliance on massive sweeps backed by artillery and the A-37 ground attack aircraft supplied by the US in 1982 brought large numbers of well-reported civilian casualties and more new recruits than losses to the guerrilla forces. Morale in the Salvadorean Armed

Forces remained very low, as a result of inadequate training and leadership, high casualty fatality rates and a guerrilla policy of good treatment and release of those surrendering. The Armed Forces were expanding rapidly, from some 16000 in mid-1982 to around 25000 in mid-1983. However, US training, already being carried out also at bases in the US and beginning to be carried out in Honduras (to compensate for the limits created by the ceiling of 55 US advisers in El Salvador itself) had not caught up with this expansion, and the number of effective combat leaders remained low. Dissatisfaction with the corrupt and ineffective High Command led at the beginning of 1983 to open mutiny by a senior garrison commander – Colonel Sigifredo Ochoa – who had carried out a devastatingly effective campaign in his department, and demands, led by the Head of the Air Force, Colonel Juan Bustillo, for the resignation of the Defence Minister, General Jose García. The episode was particularly awkward for the US. Colonel Ochoa was at the same time a prominent example of the effective new counter-insurgency officer it wished to promote, and a politically sensitive figure because of his toughness and apparent association with the Salvadorean far Right which the Embassy was trying to isolate. As Defence Minister, on the other hand, General Garcia had proven militarily disappointing, failing notably to make effective use of the new US-trained Immediate Reaction Battalions, but he had been relatively compliant politically. In the event, Ochoa was sent to attend a course in the US, but Garcia was replaced by National Guard Commander General Carlos Eugenio Vides Casanova, in the first stage of a reorganisation of the military command structure which would in November of that year bring in as Chief of Staff, Colonel Adolfo Blandon. The guerrillas, on the other hand, were growing fast and by the end of 1983 reached perhaps 12000 combatants. In certain areas – at the peak equivalent to nearly a quarter of the country's territory – they exerted general control and had relatively stable support structures. Supplies were still coming in from outside El Salvador, but a significant proportion of the guerrillas' arms and ammunition was being captured, or otherwise secured, from government forces and internal sources. They had gained considerable combat experience, and had generally high morale. They were also beginning to move and attack in large units, and were forming their own elite battalions. Their increasing military effectiveness was reflected in the government forces' mounting casualties: 3801, including 1073 dead, between 1 July 1981 and 30 June 1982; 6815, including 2292 dead, in the next twelve months.

In February 1983, UN Ambassador Jeane Kirkpatrick visited El Salvador, and returned with a pessimistic assessment and reports that the Government and Armed Forces not only needed substantially more assistance, but were suffering from the uncertainties about the provision of military aid. The President now decided fully to confront the Congress. On 27 April, he gave an address to a Joint Session of Congress intended to secure immediate support for a dramatic raising of the military aid requested for El Salvador in fiscal year 1983 from $61.3 million to $136.3 million, of which $60 million was to be reprogrammed. In this key address, he spelled out his Administration's view of the strategic stakes in the area with a powerful, traditional anti-Communist rhetoric. The Salvadorean revolutionaries were dismissed as 'Marxist–Leninist bands', 'a small minority who want power for themselves and their backers . . . The goal of the professional guerrilla movements in Central America is as simple as it is sinister: to destabilize the entire region from the Panama Canal to Mexico', to impose totalitarianism on hemispheric nations and integrate them 'into the most aggressive empire the modern world has seen . . . If the Soviets can assume that nothing short of an actual attack on the United States will provoke an American response, which ally, which friend will trust us then?' The military aid was vital 'so that the people of Central America can hold the line against externally supported aggression.' The objective of this part of the speech was to pressure Congress into releasing the funds. The President challenged his critics with charges of irresponsibility: 'I do not believe there is a majority in the Congress or the country that counsels passivity, resignation, defeatism in the face of this challenge to freedom and security in our hemisphere.' He ended with a barely veiled threat to the Democrats that, if his policy failed, it would be for their denial of resources and they would be blamed by the nation, and the electorate, for 'losing El Salvador': 'Who among us would wish to bear responsibility for failing to meet our shared obligation?'

At the same time, however, the President went beyond simple assertions of the need to hold or draw lines in Central America, claiming to offer 'a program that prevents communist victory in the short run but goes beyond to produce, for the deprived people of the area, the reality of present progress and the promise of more to come'. He stressed that security assistance was not seen as 'an end in itself, but as a shield for democratization, economic development and diplomacy. No amount of reform will bring peace so long as guerrillas believe they can win by force. No amount of economic help will suffice if guerrilla units can destroy roads, bridges, power stations and crops again and again with impunity.' He acknowledged 'major problems regarding human rights, the criminal justice system and violence againt non-combatants'. The first of his four basic goals in US policy implied a promise to address them more actively: 'in response to decades of inequity and indifference, we will support democracy, reform and human freedom. This means using our assistance, our powers of persuasion and our legitimate leverage to bolster humane democratic systems where they already exist and to help countries on their way to that goal complete the process as quickly as human institutions can be changed. Elections in El Salvador and also in Nicaragua must be open to all, fair and safe . . . We will work at human rights problems, not walk away from them.' The President had now, beneath the anti-Communist rhetoric, moved towards compromise with his moderate critics, at least in words. Many Democrats remained unconvinced, however, and demanded greater progress in practice before approving such a large increase in US military aid and involvement. Moreover, the President remained under pressure from the Republican Right to give unconditional priority to the military defeat of the guerrillas, and, from some, not to rule out the use of US forces in the case of imminent governmental collapse. The alleged interest of Thomas Enders, Assistant Secretary of State, in a negotiated settlement was indeed one factor contributing to his removal in June at the instigation of those urging a tougher approach. In response to Congressional demands for more diplomatic efforts, President Reagan appointed a Special Envoy, Richard Stone, who did meet with rebel representatives, but his mandate was made clear in the presidential address: 'The terms and conditions of participation in elections are negotiable.' There was also suspicion from the Right of the US Embassy in San Salvador, officials of which were already complaining that their reports were being ignored by some in Washington who did not want to recognise the realities of the situation, while Ambassador Hinton was coming under criticism for his outspoken attacks on the violent Right. He too was replaced.

Local circumstances and pressures in Washington made it imperative that there be both military and political progress in El Salvador in order to justify continuation of current policy. The fundamental challenge was whether the Administration could bring about sufficient political improvement to secure sufficient military resources, and then genuinely use the provision of those resources to ensure durable political progress. The Administration, however, was still somewhat hesitant and divided over the question of political conditionality and pressures, with the result that unclear signals about its objectives and priorities continued to be received in El Salvador. By the Autumn of 1983, the war seemed to be going worse than ever, while political problems seemed only to be growing. A rebel offensive in September revealed the weakness of the showpiece pacification and resettlement campaign in the province of San Vicente. It also prompted a number of indiscriminate military responses, including the bombing of the small town of Tenancingo with some 50 civilian deaths, which was taken by many Administration critics as indicating the impossibility of reforming the Salvadorean Armed Forces. It also contributed to a surge in death-squad activity of the most overt type. Responsibility for many deaths was acknowledged by the Secret Anticommunist Army (ESA), which invoked the need to act against 'communists' who advocated a negotiated solution to the conflict.[12] The killings were also associated with the protracted battle in the Constituent Assembly between the PDC and the Right, who were attempting to include clauses which would set back the land reform process, thus provoking protest marches by workers and peasants. The military were growing openly frustrated with the Constituent Assembly's failure to have met three promised deadlines, and Duarte was talking openly of a possible coup. Through November and December 1983, both the military and human rights situations continued to deteriorate. The rebels' strength was dramatically revealed at the turn of the year with their over-running of the El Paraiso barracks, killing over 100 soldiers and capturing large quantities of military supplies. Meanwhile, meetings between the rebels and both government representatives and the US Special Envoy had brought no results. Neither the Government nor the US had any desire for the type of negotiated power-sharing settlement proposed by the rebels, while the practical obstacles to such a solution remained immense. Given the violent opposition of the Right to any such idea, it would almost certainly have required a greater and more forceful external presence than the mediators and 'international witnesses' suggested by the FMLN–FDR in their January 1984 'Proposal for the creation of the Provisional Government of Broad Participation'. The conditions and objectives of the rebels' proposals seemed to be becoming more moderate, but they rejected offers of amnesty in order to participate in the existing electoral process as entirely insufficient, arguing that it would be suicidal to attempt to do so in the current climate of political violence. The Government's failure to make progress in reducing human rights abuses and death-squad activities only seemed to support that argument and give added weight to pressures within the US to accept, and push for, some sort of negotiated solution. The US media pointed to Reagan's staking of US credibility on success in El Salvador, and argued that 'as the Salvadorean military unravels and the death squads continue their bloody work, the realities on the ground in El Salvador may face him with a very unpleasant choice: go in – or back out.'[13]

The Administration had achieved a limited increase in military aid for 1983: $81.3 million as compared with an initial request for $61.3 million, although still much less than the total $136.3 million requested over the year. In November, Congress cut the $86 million requested for fiscal year 1984 to $64.8 million, with a new condition attached that

30 per cent would be withheld until those accused of the 1980 murder of the four American churchwomen were brought to trial and a verdict given. The certification process was renewed separately after the failure to enact an alternative process through the proposed 1984 Foreign Aid Authorization Bill. Under strong pressure from Congress, and itself now frustrated and annoyed by the Salvadorean failure to control the death squads, the Administration began to take new steps to address the issue. Senior Defense and State Department officials visited El Salvador in November to stress to the military that unless they took measures to curb the rightist violence there would be serious problems in securing military aid. Their somewhat diluted threats had no immediate effect. Moreover, the Administration was still hesitant about pushing too hard. The conflicting views were reflected in the relevant sections of the Kissinger Commission's report. It was agreed that much more aid was needed – some $400 million over 1984 and 1985 – to break the military stalemate, and even to avert the 'collapse' which was not 'inconceivable', and also to provide sufficient resources to carry out a more humane campaign than the 'brutal alternative methods of counter-insurgency which wreak intolerable violence upon the civilian population'. An enforced cut-off of aid would be 'unacceptable' given the vital nature of US interests involved, but without 'credible' US insistence on improvements in human rights, the crucial political progress could not be ensured. In the end the Commission recommended 'serious enforcement' of conditions on which aid should be 'made contingent': 'demonstrated progress toward free elections; freedom of association; the establishment of the rule of law and an effective judicial system; and the termination of the activities of the so-called death squads, as well as vigorous action against those guilty of crime and the prosecution to the extent possible of past offenders'. Kissinger and two fellow Commissioners, however, added a note recording their 'strong view' that conditionality should not be interpreted 'in a manner that leads to a Marxist–Leninist victory in El Salvador'. Moreover, it was clear that there were some in the military and on the far Right who did not seem particularly concerned about a possible cut-off of US aid, which might in fact permit them to conduct the war in their own way, as the Guatemalans had been doing. If the Government and High Command were to crack down, a possible backlash was feared leading to an enforced cut-off of aid and a total loss of US influence in the country. The Administration's position remained confusing. On the one hand, the new US Ambassador, Thomas Pickering, made a speech vigorously denouncing the death squads, and D'Aubuisson was refused a US visa. On the other, the President exerted a veto over the certification process at the beginning of December, once Congress had adjourned.

That move did not, however, reflect a lack of Administration interest in progress in most of the areas covered by the certification requirement, so much as a decision not to go through with another embarrassing certification at a crucial moment for US policy. There may also have been a feeling that further certifications of improvements which had not fully taken place would only prolong the conviction in El Salvador that the Administration did not really mean what it said. Until the Administration took other steps to convince the Salvadoreans that it was serious, however, the move could only have the opposite effect. With the wave of Rightist violence continuing in December 1983 as the campaigning was opened for the presidential elections to be held in March 1984, Vice-President George Bush went to El Salvador. He demanded an end to the practice of 'disappearances', presented two lists of military officers and civilians known to be involved in death-squad activities who should be transferred out of the country, announced that the US Government would be taking measures against Salvadoreans in the US involved in financing those activities, and made clear that unless there were improvements and specific actions taken, Congress would not approve continued military aid to El Salvador and the Administration would not even try very hard to secure it. It seemed that the Administration had finally begun to confront the far Right. There was an immediate reaction of anger and incomprehension from the Right. There were indications that many in the High Command were willing to respond, but there was limited visible progress in the first months of 1984. A small number of the most notorious figures named were shifted from their posts in the Security Forces. The trial of the National Guardsmen who carried out the killing of the American churchwomen was set in motion, but the officer known to be responsible for the murder of the Salvadorean and two American land reform officials continued to evade prosecution. Congressional resistance to increased military aid continued. Additional aid still had to be sent by discretionary channels.

The next step came with the presidential elections in El Salvador. There is reason to believe that some within the Administration did not see Duarte as the most desirable PDC candidate, or even see the PDC as the only desirable alternative to Arena and D'Aubuisson. There were fears that the political Right and the business sector, and some in the military, might not only refuse to co-operate with a Duarte Government, but could even act directly against it. In the event, however, the presidential choice came down to Duarte and D'Aubuisson, and in that contest the US had to be on Duarte's side. Allegations by D'Aubuisson, and his American friends, of US participation in a fraud are exaggerated, but the US Government seems to have taken some measures to assist his prospects, including some indirect channelling of funds, and it did not fully disguise its preference. As soon as Duarte was elected on 6 May, the Administration lavished praise upon him, endeavouring to convince dubious Congressmen that he deserved full support, and dubious Salvadorean Rightists and businessmen that he must be tolerated. President-elect Duarte was quickly invited to the US, where he promised Congress that he would take firm action to end human rights abuses and to investigate past cases. Most opted to give him the benefit of the doubt and, in the wake of his visit, Congress approved $62 million in supplementary military aid for El Salvador. In May also the five National Guardsmen were tried and sentenced, thus releasing the $19.4 million that had been held pending a verdict. There remained considerable scepticism as to Duarte's capacity to carry out his promises. Although he quickly succeeded in replacing the Chief of the Treasury Police and was to disband its notorious intelligence section, there was little further evidence of military willingness to go along with Duarte's investigative commissions. Moreover, Duarte still faced a Right-wing majority in the National Assembly, which quickly rejected his nomination for the post of attorney general and his list of candidates for the Supreme Court. Duarte was, however, quickly winning greater international legitimacy, and in another visit to Washington in July succeeded in further convincing Congress that there was at last a real hope of moderate democracy taking root in El Salvador. In early August, General Gorman, Head of Southern Command, appealed to Congress by stating that, if Congress provided aid at the levels recommended by the Kissinger Commission, the guerrillas could be brought under 'effective control' within two years. After a considerable battle in the House, Congress even approved a further $70 million in military aid for the remaining weeks of fiscal year 1984, thus bringing the total for the year to $196.5 million. An initial $128 million in military aid was approved for fiscal year 1985.

The Administration had now secured the minimum conditions for its policy to have some prospect of success. Military aid was not at the levels recommended by the Kissinger Commission, but had increased massively and, although the military corner had not been turned, fears of governmental collapse had gone. There had been some improvement in the human rights situation, and there was a government in place with sufficient legitimacy to receive broad backing from Congress. By the end of the year, the Administration would also be able to point to President Duarte's October agreement to hold talks with the rebels as evidence of its own interest in finding a peaceful solution to the conflict. The failure of the second round of the talks in November 1984, moreover, could with some credibility be attributed to the rebels' insistence on full power-sharing even though a functioning electoral system had begun to be established.

Reagan and Nicaragua

1981: The failure to avert confrontation

The July 1980 Republican Party platform stated openly that 'We deplore the Marxist Sandinista takeover of Nicaragua . . . [and] will return to the fundamental principle of treating a friend as a friend and self-proclaimed enemies as enemies'. Even Nicaraguan moderates were alarmed by such language, quite apart from conservative suggestions that the remnants of Somoza's National Guard in Honduras could be made into 'a genuine fighting force' as there was 'no alternative to a removal of the current government'.[14] A prominent businessman who had been an initial junta member, Alfonso Robelo, in late 1980 expressed fears that Reagan's 'myopia', provoked by FSLN rhetoric, might lead him to take steps which 'could bring a hardening of the regime', and an escalation of tensions which would make it even harder for Nicaraguans to settle on a moderate course.[15] Indeed, whereas Republican rhetoric convinced most Sandinistas that a Reagan Administration would be committed to their downfall, their own anti-imperialist rhetoric, together with various military and diplomatic moves, only served to provoke and strengthen the conviction of their ideological opponents. Almost all the elements for a serious escalation of suspicions and tensions were in place before Reagan's inauguration. The initial question was whether those elements could be prevented from developing into confrontation.

The Sandinistas acknowledge that the decision to build up their military forces dates back to 1979. Somoza's National Guard had been internally oriented and surrounded by either friendly military governments or non-military Costa Rica, and could therefore be relatively small. The FSLN, according to Defence Minister Humberto Ortega, faced after its victory 'the probability that they would be surrounded by neighbors who were opposed to their political philosophy, . . . and . . . a concern over internal security to protect their revolution.' They turned to the Soviet Bloc and Cuba 'chiefly because of ideological agreement and low cost weaponry' but also because of distrust of the US. Defence was seen to require expansion of regular forces to between 20000 and 40000,[16] with a much larger popular militia, and also, given the relative strength of the Honduran Air Force, the establishment of air defences. In early 1981, the build-up remained relatively limited. Honduras then had regular forces of 11200 and paramilitary forces of 3000, with some 17 *Scorpion* reconnaissance vehicles armed with 76 mm guns, and 27 combat aircraft. Guatemala had total forces of some 18000 and El Salvador some 17000. Nicaragua's regular forces were estimated at 6700, with paramilitary forces of 8000, while the only confirmed delivery of Soviet heavy equipment was of three PT-76 light tanks.[17] It could not be considered to pose any military threat, or to be disproportionate to the country's needs. However, it was already a source of potential concern, most of all because of the military ties being established with Cuba and the Soviet Bloc, and any much greater expansion would predictably increase suspicions in Nicaragua's neighbours and in the US. It was largely conceived as a defensive precaution but, if insufficient reason was seen not to go ahead with the build-up, it would only contribute to an escalatory spiral of military preparation.

As the prospect of a Reagan Administration came closer, the FSLN did not take the pre-emptive measure of holding elections at the end of 1980, once their generally admired literacy campaign was finished, as was not only demanded by Nicaraguan moderates but reportedly counselled by Fidel Castro, which would have strengthened their position both internally and internationally. They did give assistance to the FDR–FMLN in El Salvador and their pre-emptive 'final offensive'. To the extent that this did not only reflect revolutionary euphoria and a sense of moral obligation, the decision corresponded to the belief of many Sandinista leaders that Reagan was out to get them anyway, and that such support would not be determinant in the development of relations with the US. The US had not let its relations with Venezuela, Panama or Costa Rica be determined by those countries' practical support in the struggle against the universally discredited regime in Nicaragua. The current Government of El Salvador did not then have much internal or international legitimacy, while the revolutionary alliance hoped to receive the same broad support as had the anti-Somoza forces. Consequently, a Sandinista decision openly to deny all support to the rebels did not seem certain to avert US hostility, but would definitely reduce the chances of the rebels' success in their offensive. Not all Sandinistas, or indeed Cubans, may have shared the confidence of many Salvadorean groups in that success[18] but the clear benefits for revolutionary Nicaragua of a rebel victory in El Salvador must have seemed to outweigh both the doubtful benefits of denying support and the apparent costs of giving it. For most Americans, however, whatever the scale of the support and however unattractive the Salvadorean Government, it could only seem a breach of Sandinista promises not to get materially involved in the conflict. For the incoming Administration, it was confirmation of the new regime's unacceptable behaviour, and for some, of its unacceptable nature.

The first few months of 1981 were crucial for determining subsequent US relations with Nicaragua. Despite its unmistakeable dislike and distrust, the Administration was in fact hesitant, unclear and divided as to precisely what to do about the Sandinistas. On the issue of support for the FMLN, however, the Administration was united; it expected broad domestic and international support; and it made strong representations to the Nicaraguan regime. The failure of the Salvadorean offensive and the attitude of the new US Administration had led to serious concern among the Sandinistas, to the realisation that the Salvadorean conflict could not be won militarily, and to the desire to prevent that conflict from jeopardising their own survival. According to the State Department, they responded to US demands with assurances that 'they understood U.S. concerns about El Salvador, would not "risk the revolution for an uncertain victory in El Salvador", and had taken a firm decision not to permit Nicaraguan territory to be used for transiting arms to El Salvador.' However, the State Department claims that intelligence showed that 'arms traffic through established routes, particularly by air, from Nicaragua to El Salvador had slowed if not stopped, but that other routes were being sought . . . the FSLN was engaged in continuing supply efforts as well as accumulating in Nicaragua arms for the FMLN'.[19] If the Sandinistas had consciously sent a signal of serious intentions to the US by reducing their support for the FMLN, it had not been sufficient, not been received, or not been believed. Since Reagan felt he could no longer certify 'that Nicaragua was not engaged in support for terrorism abroad',[20] disbursement of the remaining $15 million of Carter's aid package was formally suspended on 1 April 1981.

To some extent, the failure to reach any agreement reflected a continued fundamental difference with regard to El Salvador. The US wanted nothing less than the surrender of the guerrillas. The Sandinistas did not now expect them to win an outright victory, but they did see their access to power in El Salvador through a negotiated settlement as being in Nicaragua's interests. Their outright defeat would be seen as a positive setback and a potential threat. Another possible reason for not cutting all ties was uncertainty as to whether the US would respond. Whereas support for insurgents was for the US a simple wrong which should ideally be stopped unilaterally, the Sandinistas saw support for those combating a repressive regime as an act of moral rectitude which should be reduced only in exchange for some concession by the US. US economic aid, moreover, did not seem to them so much an act of exceptional generosity and political goodwill as the duty of a rich nation to a poor one, and a particular moral obligation on the part of the country which had given them decades of dictatorship. It would also have been politically difficult for the Sandinistas fully and openly to divorce themselves from the FDR–FMLN in El Salvador in the hope of continuing to receive US aid, and thus appear to bow to 'imperialist' demands. Even if they had done that, however, it is not certain that that alone would have led to a continuation of aid, or prevented subsequent tensions. Although the Salvadorean issue was more than a pretext for hostility, it was certainly not the only issue on which the Administration would want change before it could, if at all, live with Nicaragua in peace and confidence. To have reached what would have constituted a positive agreement with the Sandinistas based only on cessation of support for the Salvadorean guerrillas would have been to surrender US leverage on other issues such as military force levels and ties to Cuba and the Soviet Bloc. Moreover, the Administration had come into office on a platform of opposition to aid to Nicaragua and to the Nicaraguan regime itself, amid criticism that it was preparing a policy of unreasoning confrontation. It would therefore have been politically advisable in any case to delay suspension of aid, so that the Administration could plausibly claim to have tried to reason with the Sandinistas. But it would not have been politically attractive to be seen within months to continue aid, and thereby seem to recognise the legitimacy of a regime decried as a Marxist–Leninist intrusion into the hemisphere. It is not certain that the Sandinistas would have responded to a continuation of aid by making a full break with the FMLN and refraining from further strengthening their military forces and ties with Cuba and the Soviet Bloc. Nor is it certain that that would have guaranteed normal relations with the US. Nevertheless, a first, perhaps crucial opportunity to avoid confrontation was certainly missed, thus increasing the mutual distrust, and leaving both sides with the feeling that the other had failed to respond and was not interested in serious negotiation.

That feeling was only confirmed by talks held in August 1981. At the request of departing Ambassador Pezzullo, the US Assistant Secretary of State, Thomas Enders, flew to Managua, and there was discussion of a possible deal. Managua would stop the flow of arms to El Salvador and limit its military build-up, while Washington would not permit training of anti-Sandinistas in the US and would give assurances that it would not attempt to overthrow the Nicaraguan government. According to Pezzullo, 'The concept was agreed in general terms . . . They said they could see our interests. We could see their concern about security'.[21] The talks ended with an agreement to exchange proposals in five areas. However, even during the Managua talks, two sorts of persistent obstacle to negotiation were evident. First, the Sandinistas made clear that internal politics were not negotiable. Second, Enders' demands for a complete end to Nicaraguan support for the Salvadorean rebels seem to have been presented, and were certainly perceived, as a precondition for serious dialogue. Again, in US perceptions, a unilateral end to an unjustified act did not necessarily seem unreasonable. But the Sandinistas wanted it, if at all, to be part of a broader bilateral agreement. Moreover, those things which the US would agree not to do on its own part – particularly to overthrow them but to some extent even to deprive them of economic aid – could seem to the Sandinistas to warrant unilateral ends, as unjustified acts, as much as anything they were doing. On 8 September, the Administration did send a draft declaration unilaterally promising vigorous enforcement of US neutrality laws concerning Nicaraguan exiles and, on the 16th, Enders sent a draft of a proposed joint declaration of non-intervention in Central America. But although the US claims to have made, and was certainly preparing, a '5-point proposal', the draft papers on other areas do not appear to have been formally presented. The content of the proposal on security issues was, however, communicated to the Nicaraguan Ambassador. Among other things, it asked that Nicaragua should freeze acquisition of heavy weapons, return to the country of origin arms systems not possessed by other countries, limit its army to between 15000 and 17000 men and eventually reduce it to less than 10000, all under international supervision.[22] Ambassador Arturo Cruz said that it 'sounded like the terms of surrender' and that it did not make clear what the US would do in return.[23]

The Nicaraguans' own attitude did not increase the chances of negotiations' success. Over-reaction to a small US–Honduran naval exercise in early October led them to break the tacit understanding to lower the level of rhetoric with a strong attack on US policies at the UN. Complaints about naval exercises and demands to close the Florida training camps effectively became preconditions of their own. They further weakened the position in the US of those prepared to support negotiation on external issues with the repeated closures of the opposition newspaper *La Prensa*, tensions with the Church and the imprisonment of four business leaders who had accused the Government of a drift toward Marxism–Leninism. By the end of October 1981, the negotiations were over. So too was the period of any attempt at diplomatic settlement based only on talks and the offer of positive incentives and only on external issues.

By November 1981, there was little disagreement in the Administration that something new had to be done, and quickly. Administration officials pointed to Sandinista support for guerrillas in El Salvador and elsewhere, the build-up of arms in Nicaragua itself and plans believed to aim at a standing army of some 50000, the training in Bulgaria of Nicaraguans to fly MiG aircraft and the apparent preparation of airfields to receive them, the presence of Cuban security and military advisers estimated by the US to number over 1000, growing political and economic ties with the Soviet Bloc, and what Secretary of State Haig publicly termed the 'totalitarian trend' in Nicaraguan politics.[24] Haig warned that 'the hours are growing rather short' to prevent another Cuba, publicly refused to rule out the possibility of US moves to overthrow the Sandinistas, reportedly asking the Pentagon to study military options,[25] and hinted to the OAS in December at the possibility of action under the Rio Treaty. However, adverse domestic and international opinion, and an element of fear as to its possible encouragement of direct Soviet action in Poland,[26] rendered almost impossible any direct US military action against the Sandinistas. Navy Secretary John Lehman publicly stressed that even the blockade of Nicaragua suggested by some would draw down US forces needed elsewhere and would be 'an act of war under international law', adding that 'never again will we get in any military action without the solid support of the government and the people'.[27]

The natural next step for the Administration was to increase the pressures on the Nicaraguan regime, but in ways which would not provoke great domestic and international opposition and endanger support for policy in El Salvador, on which its attention was primarily focussed. A full economic embargo, or anything stronger, would have been hard to justify and undeniably have pushed Nicaragua even closer to the Soviet Bloc. Instead, the US began to work against Nicaraguan access to loans from international financial bodies. The US did not break diplomatic relations, but Ambassador Pezzullo was not replaced for seven months. There was not much more of an open nature that the Administration was then able or prepared to do. The CIA, however, had been pressing for covert activity to be stepped up to include support for armed anti-Sandinista groups being trained by Argentines in Honduras. At an NSC meeting on 16 November, President Reagan authorised a $19 million dollar CIA programme to build a popular opposition front to the Sandinistas, and to train a force, initially of 500 men, to carry out political and paramilitary operations against the 'Cuban presence and Cuban–Sandinista support infrastructure in Nicaragua and elsewhere in Central America'. After the presidential finding on 1 December that the move was in the national interest, the Intelligence Committees were duly informed. In the House Committee, many questions were asked about the possible risks, one Republican member subsequently saying that it was obvious that the Director of the CIA, William Casey, had not thought through all the potential repercussions, while some concern was expressed in the Senate Committee about the ultimate direction of the programme.[28] It was, indeed, not to be clear what the objective really was. It was said to be the practical interdiction of the arms flow to El Salvador, combined with pressure on the Sandinistas to 'look inward' rather than continue to 'export revolution', and then, more generally to put pressure on them to negotiate seriously on the issues of concern to the US and Nicaragua's neighbours. But it was in part a readily available means to do something, which was taken up as much because of the apparent lack of anything better to do as because it offered a particularly appropriate means to achieve clear policy goals.

The US did not entirely create the rebel forces. Those elements from Somoza's National Guard, which were to constitute the core of the military leadership of the Nicaraguan Democratic Force (FDN), formed with a number of civilian opposition figures in 1982, had been active since 1979. Most of the Misquito Indians on the Atlantic Coast who joined armed anti-Government groups did so because of grievances with the Sandinistas. Those opposition figures who went from 1982 onwards to form the anti-Sandinista forces operating on the southern border did not do so at the bidding of the CIA, and indeed for a long time refused to co-operate with the CIA-backed forces in Honduras, because of the latter's strong ex-Somocista elements. However, the fact that the US did not entirely create, or control, the forces it came to support did not alter the doubtful internal legitimacy of those associated with the Somoza regime, which tended to be further weakened by CIA support. Moreover, it did not make those forces any more appropriate as an instrument in US policy. Former CIA Director Stansfield Turner warned in 1983 that 'the people the CIA enlists to do the covert work will not always have the same purpose as the United States [and usually] gain sufficient momentum of their own at some point to go on without us if necessary,' with the likelihood that 'our own purposes change from those originally set.' Another risk was that 'the CIA people operating them can get carried away with their dedication to getting the job done'.[29] By 1983, President Reagan's argument that he was 'simply trying to interdict the supply lines which are supplying the guerrillas in El Salvador',[30] was wearing very thin. The rebels had not directly interdicted a single bullet, and Enrique Bermudez, military attaché to Washington under Somoza and now military head of the FDN, had openly stated in

December 1982 that they 'would never accept the role of American mercenary. It is not acceptable to us to carry out missions to interdict Cuban and Russian supply lines to El Salvador. We are Nicaraguans and our objective is to overthrow the Communists and install a democratic government in our country'.[31] The anti-Sandinista force which was originally supposed to be only 500 strong grew rapidly, according to CIA figures, to 1000 by February 1982, to 4000 by December 1982, 5500 by February 1983, 7000 by May 1983 and 8000 by June 1983. There was a danger that the covert action might get out of control, with risks of escalation and direct confrontation. And the probability was high that the counter-revolutionary forces, which would help preclude other options for settling US–Nicaraguan relations and might not easily be 'called off' even if the Administration so desired, might end up by defining US policy.

The escalatory spiral

The process of escalating tensions and suspicions had now been set firmly in motion. The Administration was applying pressures in order to bring about serious negotiations. However, the pressures could not be separated from, and thereby increased independently of, the issues on which concessions were to be secured through talks. Nor would they be certain to discourage the Sandinistas from taking steps which would contribute to the escalatory spiral. Without any mutual trust or any mutually accepted mechanism of guarantees, greater pressures were likely to contribute to an increase in the perceived dangers and undesirable developments, and thereby to demands for greater concessions and yet greater pressures.

In the case of Nicaragua's military build-up, the Sandinistas certainly took some unnecessarily provocative steps. However, the Administration's vehement rhetoric and moves which helped to increase both internal insecurity and tensions with Honduras, such as support for armed attacks from across the border, could only encourage the Sandinistas to maintain their military build-up. Any political incentive to cease the military build-up, as suggested even by the friendly Mexican Government, was outweighed by perceived demands of security. By mid-1982, the process of military organisation and equipment had taken place at a rate undeniably faster than that of the other Central American countries. Nicaragua's regular forces had grown to an estimated 21500, with reserves of 60000, a border guard of some 5000 and militia of perhaps 50000. The inventory had also expanded.[32] Much of the new equipment could be justified as giving an appropriate defensive capability. The Soviet SAMs and anti-aircraft guns, and even the desired interceptor aircraft, caused an alarm that was related much more to the strategic implications of their origin and the political character of their recipients than to any local military threat. However, Nicaragua was to receive not only armoured personnel carriers, but main battle tanks, which were not possessed by any of its neighbours, not least because of their inappropriateness to local conditions. Some 25 T-54/-55 tanks had already been received, and more were on the way. It may be that the Soviet Union simply preferred to give these obsolete machines as a source of heavy practical reassurance rather than the even more provocative MiG-21s requested by the Sandinista leadership. It seems highly likely that they were acquired not with any thought of offensive action but for 'mobile defensive firepower and shock-action riot control of feared urban counterrevolutionary uprisings'.[33] They did not by themselves pose a serious threat to Nicaragua's neighbours, but they did seem inappropriate to its needs, and an unnecessary provocation to everyone. Moreover, the expansion of troop numbers and new technical demands brought a substantial increase in the number of Cuban and Soviet Bloc military personnel in Nicaragua, which likewise strengthened strategic and political suspicions. In response, the US began in 1982 to further strengthen Honduras' military capability, and to increase its military presence in Honduras. In May 1982, an agreement was negotiated with the Honduran Government and a $21 million military construction programme approved by Congress. The US would improve the Palmerola and Goloson airbases 'in return for US access for various contingency uses including transit, search and rescue, and reconnaissance'.[34] In 1983 these bases, and other facilities established, began to be used in an active supportive military role, particularly as a base for intelligence overflights of El Salvador and Nicaragua. Only one small joint exercise took place in 1982, but in February 1983 a series of much larger exercises began with *Ahuas Tara I* (Big Pine I), involving a total of 1600 US personnel. US military assistance to Honduras grew from $9.1 million in 1981 to $31.3 million in 1982 and $37.3 million in 1983. By mid-1983 the Honduran Armed Forces had grown to some 15200, with 4500 paramilitary. Nicaragua's total armed forces, however, were by then estimated at around 48800, including reserves on active duty, with a growing militia of perhaps 30000, and an expanding inventory of artillery and armoured vehicles, including some 45 Soviet T-54/-55 tanks.[35] In May 1983, the Administration moved to a new level of direct pressures. It was announced that Nicaragua's sugar import quota was to be virtually ended. Partly as a new political step and partly in response to the arrival in Nicaragua of a large new contingent of Cuban advisers, including one senior general, and of large shipments of military equipment, the decision was also taken to begin a new level of US military presence in the area. In late July, shortly after reports that the CIA was planning to support a force of 12000 to 15000 rebels, and while the Ranger carrier task force took up position off Nicaragua's Atlantic coast and the battleship New Jersey and six other vessels moved to take position off its Pacific coast, reports appeared of the new military plans. A large joint exercise, *Ahuas Tara II*, was to be held in Honduras from August 1983 to February 1984, involving between 3000 and 4000 US combat troops. The naval forces were also said to be practising for a possible military quarantine around Nicaragua. Officials said it was 'a program for a significant and long-lasting increase in the U.S. military presence in Central America', involving preparations so that US forces could be swiftly called into action if necessary, as well as a deterrent show of force intended to convince the Soviet Union and Cuba to cease their interference in the region, and the Sandinistas to cease their support for the Salvadorean guerrillas.[36] In early August, as the exercises got under way, military leaders of El Salvador, Honduras and Guatemala met on the USS Ranger to discuss the reactivation of the Central American Defence Council (*Condeca*). Two days later, the Guatemalan Defence Minister who had attended that meeting overthrew the President, who had been reluctant to adopt any aggressive posture against the Sandinistas. Nicaraguan alarm at this move only grew when, shortly after the US–Caribbean action in Grenada and as US Marines and Honduran infantry practised a seaborne landing, it was reported that *Condeca* was considering the legal basis for collective action with direct US participation against Nicaragua. Meanwhile, the Nicaraguan rebels had launched a large new campaign, and by October 1983, as saboteurs hit oil and industrial facilities, real pressure began to be felt. One predictable element in the Sandinista response to these developments was to strengthen their military capacity, and to increase the militarisation of the country. In August 1983, the introduction of conscription was announced. By mid-1984, the Nicaraguan armed forces had grown to an estimated active total of 61800, with a militia of perhaps 40000. They had some 60 T-54/-55 main battle tanks, 10 PT-76 light tanks and 120 armoured vehicles, perhaps 12 multiple rocket launchers and at least 90 heavy artillery pieces. The Honduran forces, openly relying on the US for security, grew in the same period only to 17200, with paramilitary forces remaining at 4500, with little increase in their relatively small armoured inventory, but they maintained a relatively large air force.[37] By the end of 1983, the Nicaraguan build-up had reached the point at which it was a source of concern to almost everyone. The Sandinistas still did not have the military capacity, or any apparent incentive, to invade their neighbours, and it is doubtful whether many people, in Honduras or Washington, really believed in the threat of conventional invasion widely invoked in 1983. But the forces were disturbing in their size, in their ties with Cuba and the Soviet Bloc, and in their appearing to be an army at the service of a hegemonic political party. It was the Popular Sandinista Army (EPS).

In the case of guerrilla support, an increase in pressures confirming the belief that Reagan was implacably opposed to the Sandinista regime would not necessarily increase their willingness to make a unilateral break with the rebels in El Salvador, given their feeling that anything less than a negotiated settlement in El Salvador would increase their own isolation and vulnerability. The relative importance for the guerrillas' military capacity of supplies moving from Nicaraguan territory to El Salvador appears to have diminished between early 1981 and late 1983. There was certainly a decrease in the flow across Honduran territory, partly as a result of US-assisted improvements in the Honduran forces' interdiction capability. But the flow was not halted, and Nicaragua remained significant in providing command, control and training facilities, and in the movement of personnel for training and support activities elsewhere, including Soviet Bloc countries. However, Sandinista leaders not only continued to give some support to the FDR–FMLN. There had been contacts with Left-wing Honduran groups since 1979. Now, perhaps tempted to respond in kind to the sending of subversives and saboteurs across the northern border, they did not stop, and may have encouraged, a column of would-be Honduran guerrillas which crossed the frontier from Nicaragua in July 1983. As this spiral of covert action and counter-action progressed, the Nicaraguan government only seemed to confirm that it was indeed committed to the 'export of revolution'.

US pressures did not determine the fundamental structure of the internal system in Nicaragua, although it can be argued that the legacy of past US policy in Central America was partly responsible for the widespread Sandinista association of US interests and demands with domination and social injustice. This strengthened the belief in the need for political control against predictable counter-revolutionary moves, and the tendency to subordinate traditional forms of electoral democracy to structures protecting the pursuit of social justice. The Administration's accusations of brutal totalitarianism were exaggerated. Despite some abuses and bad handling of the ethnic minorities, Nicaragua's record on physical human rights abuses remained incomparably better than that of El Salvador and Guatemala. In Nicaragua, many officials responsible for abuses were judicially punished. The Sandinistas had not done away with political pluralism and the mixed economy. Some 55 per cent of GNP was still generated by the private sector, and the 1981 agrarian reform law envisaged considerably less land distribution than the 1980 Salvadorean law. Opposition parties and private interests were given representation in the Council of State. Not all the *Comandantes* were orthodox Marxist–Leninists, and the Sandinista Front and its allies contained many who were not Marxist at all. However, the revolutionary national project to which they were all committed was based on principles of 'Popular Power' and a radical priority was given to the basic needs of the population, in which the 'bourgeoisie' and their representatives would play a subordinate role. The political system continued to be one in which the Party held hegemonic power and control at all levels, and with the exception of the Supreme Court, it seemed to be a Sandinista State. It seemed probable that the Sandinistas would 'not consent to a parliamentary democracy that offers the opposition parties and the allied bourgeosie any chance to come into power. The fact that the entrepreneur and the government of the United States so vehemently demand the establishment of a parliamentary democracy is taken as proof by the FSLN that this form of democracy must be understood as the political order designed to assure the dominance of the class opposition'.[38] As the Sandinistas began to define the political system, however, US actions had a direct effect in shaping their internal behaviour. Although pressures were supposedly intended to bring about Sandinista concessions to the domestic political opposition, an increase in internal insecurity and instability, especially if tied to external threats, was likely only to weaken moderates within the regime and to strengthen those ideologically inclined toward State control. By associating domestic political opposition with armed counter-revolution and US destabilisation, it might restrict the freedom and undermine the legitimacy of Nicaraguan moderates. In March 1982, with a US destroyer sitting in the Gulf of Fonseca, leaks about the November NSC meeting were picked up by the Managua press. The reported intention to 'Build support . . . for an opposition front'[39] became headlines of 'CIA Millions to Nica "Moderates".'[40] Days later, two bridges near the Honduran border were blown up by saboteurs. The Government declared a state of emergency and suspended various constitutional guarantees. No change took place in the structure of the political system. Strong censorship was kept up, and political and social control maintained. By 1983 a number of prominent Nicaraguan figures, including Alfonso Robelo, Arturo Cruz and the Comandante Cero, Eden Pastora, had left the country amid allegations that the FSLN had sold out the Revolution to Cuba and Marxism–Leninism.

The rather confusing public position of the Administration, largely reflecting the political demands of the debates over military aid to El Salvador, did not help. On the one hand it tended to be all the more vehement in its rhetorical assaults upon the Sandinistas in order to convince sceptics of the unacceptability of the alternative to aid. At the same time, the need not to jeopardise that aid through fears of direct US military involvement in Central America encouraged it to promise that it would not intervene in Nicaragua, or support indirect moves to overthrow the Nicaraguan Government. The bitter rhetoric helped to convince many in Nicaragua of the Administration's implacable hostility, and thereby of the imprudence of unilaterally ceasing the build-up of external defence and internal control. The feeling that Reagan 'didn't really mean it', or that domestic opposition would always prevent it, might encourage some in the Sandinista regime to believe that greater concessions and flexibility could secure an agreement. On the other hand, it might encourage others to believe that they could get away with further militarisation and State control, and be able to point to US threats as a justification. But the possibility of direct intervention, and the reality of indirect attack, could only encourage a continued build-up just in case. Intimidation and isolation without a credible prospect of either diplomatic settlement or overthrow was likely only to produce a more politically controlled, heavily armed and Soviet-reliant Nicaragua.

Insistence on internal change

The developments of 1981 had weakened, or changed, the position of those willing to consider containment, or 'Finlandization', of Nicaragua. By the Spring of 1982, it was already becoming clear that the *sine qua non* for normalisation of relations was henceforth to be the establishment of a regime in Nicaragua considered by the Administration to be democratic. Proposals presented in April, while in some respects more balanced in their treatment of security issues, had a new emphasis on internal democracy. Almost all within the Administration came to share Enders' concern of August 1982 as to 'what assurance . . . any of us [can] have that promises of non-interference will be kept if the Nicaraguan state remains the preserve of a small Cuban-advised elite of Marxist–Leninists, disposing of growing military power, and hostile to all forms of social life but those they dominate?'[41] By late 1983, the Administration was openly committed to achieving internal political change in Nicaragua, or at least to preventing consolidation of the Sandinista State, and the terms were established in which it would present its case and act toward initiatives for diplomatic settlement.

Beneath Reagan rhetoric about Soviet beachheads for conquest of the Americas, there had developed a strategic rationale for preventing consolidation of the internal regime even if external issues might otherwise seem to be solved. This was in many respects similar to the

Administration's strategic concerns about revolutionary Grenada. The argument was that, even if no Soviet advanced weapons were imported, no port or airfield access granted and no personnel left stationed, the infrastructure would have been established for possible use in case of Soviet opportunity or need. The Punta Huete airfield can handle anything in the Soviet air inventory, and could, like San Francisco los Baños in Cuba before it, end up as an important Soviet asset. Access to Punta Huete as well as to Cuba would give some additional advantage for long-range reconnaissance. At present, Soviet TU-95 *Bears* are able to fly down the eastern side of the United States, refuel in Cuba and return through Angola. The intelligence value to the Soviet Union of flights along the west coast of the US might be considerable. The *Bear* could easily make the easterly flight from Kamchatka, or even Vladivostok, to Nicaragua, refuel there and return to the USSR by way of Angola. Even if it could go directly to Cuba, there would be an advantage in being able to overfly Nicaragua, and with a diversion airfield available. Much the same applies to potential Pacific reconnaissance. In view of Nicaragua's distance from the Soviet Union, and its proximity and vulnerability to the US, Punta Huete, like the port of Corinto, would be of little or no strategic utility in the case of global war. It has some hypothetical utility for missions against sea lines of communication (SLOC), but only if the USSR were to risk putting in aircraft with such capability. Even MiG-21s, if they got to Nicaragua, would pose a very limited potential threat in that respect. The bottom line of US concern is simply the presence of a regime in Nicaragua believed to be sympathetic to the Soviet Union. Nicaragua does not, as does Cuba, currently possess or house the military means to pose a threat to the SLOCs. Its behaviour, even if it acquired the means, could not be considered certain, as Cuba's is not. However, the very possibility is an unwelcome distraction of US attention and resources. Moreover, the nature of the Soviet Union's strategic interest in the region is not entirely predictable. If as a result of developments in global relations or other regions, the Soviet Union were again to see a necessity for a direct strategic presence or some assertive action, and to have a compliant or dependent local regime, a highly dangerous situation could arise. Such fears arose in April 1983 when, after Soviet officials had spoken of the possibility of stationing intermediate range nuclear missiles somewhere close to US borders if *Pershing* 2 and cruise missiles were deployed in Europe, Nicaraguan Defence Minister Humberto Ortega made a public and apparently unsolicited statement that if the Soviet Union put forward the idea, Nicaragua would consider it. However unlikely such a move may have appeared at that time, the very possibility seemed to the Administration to demonstrate 'the importance of not having Communist-supplied, Communist-led, Communist-supported clients so close to us in the region'.[42] The consolidation of such a political regime, especially if allowed to become 'fully armed' but even by virtue of its existence, seemed to raise the risk of 'some variant of the Cuban missile crisis' [43] in the future.

At the regional level, the Administration shared the belief of Nicaragua's neighbouring governments that a change in the internal regime was necessary for long-term security, stability, and co-operation. It was felt that while Nicaragua remained as it was, democratic Costa Rica could not remain as it was, and that the others could not become closer to what Costa Rica was, which is what the Administration ideally wanted: 'a Central America more like Costa Rica than Cuba'.[44] No diplomatic agreement which protected the internal regime was desirable. As the Kissinger Commission reported, 'the consolidation of a Marxist–Leninist regime in Managua would be seen by its neighbors as constituting a permanent security threat. Because of its secretive nature, the existence of a political order on the Cuban model in Nicaragua would pose major difficulties in negotiating, implementing and verifying any Sandinista commitment to refrain from supporting insurgency and subversion in other countries. In this sense, the development of an open political system in Nicaragua, with a free press and an active opposition, would provide an important security guarantee for the other countries and would be a key element in any negotiated settlement.' For the Administration, there was special concern that, without an open political system, the Sandinistas could return to support for revolutionary movements overnight, while it might have to go through another lengthy battle with Congress before being able to respond effectively. With regard to any diplomatic settlement, effective external verification was only part of the problem. What the US Administration, and Nicaragua's neighbours, would seek also was a 'self-guaranteeing' system in Nicaragua: what Reagan would term 'a legitimately pluralistic democratic political structure which will assure that Nicaragua will not continue activities threatening to their (sic) neighbors'.[45]

The lines are laid

Many of the Administration's critics pointed to the escalatory spiral and argued that its policy was simply counter-productive and self-fulfilling: it was forcing Nicaragua closer to becoming what it claimed to be trying to avoid, another Cuba. It would then have to tolerate 'another Cuba' or invade. The situation was not only one of self-fulfilling prophecy on the part of the US Administration. The

Sandinistas bear considerable responsibility for the fulfilment of their fears about the US. For most of the Administration, moreover, that argument simply reflected both a mistaken view of Castro, who for them had not been pushed but had always been heading towards Marxism–Leninism and the Soviet camp, and a failure to see the true nature of the Sandinistas and the full extent of the dangers posed by their regime. It predominantly believed that the Sandinistas' maintenance of some political pluralism and private enterprise had been no more than a facade designed to dupe European Social Democrats and American liberals into giving them support and protection while consolidating their power, prior to establishment of a full Marxist–Leninist one-party State.

The process could be seen as a simple result of the Administration's fundamental assumptions and parameters. Consolidation of Sandinista power was unacceptable. Direct military action to remove them was impossible. Therefore indirect action to prevent consolidation, and if possible to establish a new system, was the logical alternative, but a full and open move to that course would have to be delayed until El Salvador was won, the forces for indirect action built up and sufficient domestic support generated. It would therefore not be entirely counter-productive that under pressure the Sandinista Government should harden internally, as it would only be 'revealing its true colours'. Nor was it entirely regrettable that it should increase its military strength and ties to Cuba and the Soviet Bloc, to the extent that this might help alert those suffering from the 'Vietnam syndrome' to the dangers of a 'second Cuba', and those reluctant to support immediate indirect measures. Whether or not the Administration was consciously and unanimously pursuing such a course, the result was the same, and was not unwelcome.

Circumstances were allowed, perhaps encouraged, to develop which would first ensure escalating confrontation, and then define the course of US policy by a process of elimination of alternatives and agreement of negative objectives. The failure to prevent the sources of serious tensions from developing, partly as a result of the Administration's failure to convince the Sandinistas that it would be prepared to live with them so long as they posed no external problems, fully convinced the Administration of the necessity of internal change in Nicaragua. Its consequent reluctance to move toward forms of immediate settlement with the Sandinista Government ensured further escalation of those tensions, and this in turn increased belief in the US in the desirability of internal change. The setting in motion of US-backed anti-Government forces directly contributed to the preclusion of other options, and helped to put in place a seemingly inevitable course for when all else would be claimed to have failed. One effect of armed opposition and external destabilisation would be to encourage a tightening of political control in Nicaragua, and strengthen the resolve of Sandinista supporters. That would both reduce the effectiveness of legal political opposition and encourage some internal opponents to join the armed opposition. The options for achieving an end to Sandinista dominance might increasingly seem to be reduced to support for the armed opposition, even though the growth in Nicaragua's military strength and political control might increase its capacity to contain rebel activities militarily while suppressing the discontent arising from the effects of the war. A dynamic was established which seemed inexorably to lead to a policy of open US political commitment to the anti-Government forces, almost whatever their nature and prospects of success.

However, the demands of El Salvador and a number of other factors, including long and strong resistance from the US Congress and public, led to considerable delay in reaching even the minimum level of support for such a policy achieved by mid-1985. In 1983, even as tensions with Nicaragua escalated to new levels and the rebel forces began to inflict serious damage on the Sandinistas, the US Administration had to adapt its position to take into account both domestic opposition and the emerging framework of regional diplomacy.

The emergence of Contadora

The Administration had since 1981 given some response to the urgent need for regional programmes to help bring economic stabilisation and recovery in order to prevent the spread of conflict and crisis, and to lay the basis for stable democratic development. The area's economy remained in serious trouble, as a result of armed conflicts, shrinking demand and growing tensions within the Central American Common Market, debt burdens, global recession and low prices paid for the region's traditional exports. The first result was the President's Caribbean Basin Initiative (CBI), presented in early 1982. Although partly a means to send more funds to El Salvador, its proposed combination of economic aid, investment incentives and tariff concessions constituted a limited step toward a regional policy addressing some of the fundamental problems. External economic aid alone, however, even in the massive amounts subsequently proposed in the Kissinger Commission's report, clearly could not solve the internal conflicts or reduce the intra-regional tensions which impeded economic recovery by maintaining a climate of uncertainty and instability discouraging foreign investment, and weakening the sub-regional co-operation essential for real development of these five small economies. Regional stability would require both regional security and regional development.

The regional question for the US was analogous to that in El Salvador: whether to give priority to negotiation and conciliation; or to containment and neutralisation of a force seen as committed to revolutionary destabilisation. The two levels could not be dissociated from each other, nor from the broader international tensions surrounding the crisis, in particular the question of the Cuban presence. The various tensions tended to be mutually reinforcing. The thrust of US policy was to be isolation and exclusion of revolutionary forces at all levels, with the possibility held out of reincorporation subject to political conditions in the case of the FDR and the FSLN, but not of Cuba's presence. The CBI thus excluded Nicaragua on political grounds. This approach was supported by many Latin American nations, particularly Nicaragua's Central American neighbours. From the beginning, however, the Administration also encountered regional opposition, particularly from Mexico, to its approach to the crisis.

The Administration's posture at the beginning of 1981 had to some extent reflected a reassertion of US influence and power with regard to the regional powers, including a strong reaction to any notion that Cuba should be treated as such. It did not generally share the view that the regional powers could or should be relied upon to exert a moderating influence and provide international guarantees which might partly substitute for direct US influence. Many in the Administration already thought that they had been revealed as impotent or imprudent by failing to ensure Sandinista compliance with what was seen as a political agreement conditionally allowing the Sandinistas to take power. Nevertheless, the Administration did not want the crisis to prevent improved relations with the region and key countries within it, and did want multilateral backing for its policies.

In early 1982, Latin American opposition remained relatively limited. Mexico remained virtually isolated. Very few countries had supported the Franco-Mexican Declaration, and the OAS had endorsed the electoral path in El Salvador. Cuba's relations with the rest of Latin America were being strained. Although a number of Latin American Governments, including the Christian Democratic Government of Venezuela, continued to give help to the Sandinistas, Mexico was alone in its public enthusiasm and optimism about their regime, while Argentina was actively helping the armed anti-Sandinista groups in Honduras. In February 1982, shortly after a Sandinista peace proposal, the Mexican President, José Lopez Portillo, attempted to go further toward satisfying US concerns without losing the Sandinistas' confidence. He publicly praised their moderation thus far, but Mexico's own concern about political developments, and implicitly its capacity to exert a moderating influence, was illustrated by the fact that Nicaraguan business leaders who had been imprisoned in October 1981 for criticising the regime were released shortly before his arrival in Managua. His proposals also included a Nicaraguan arms reduction, and he suggested that Mexico and other friendly and allied countries could serve as guarantors that the wave of change sweeping Central America would not threaten US security interests. However, he also suggested that a reduction of tensions between the US and Nicaragua realistically required talks between the US and Cuba, and talks between the warring parties in El Salvador. The US had no interest in Salvadorean mediation. Haig had already met the Cuban Vice-President at Mexico's arrangement at the end of 1981, and further contact took place in early 1982, but with no positive result. Moreover, the Administration did not share the view of some that Mexico's good relations with Castro, or with the Salvadorean rebels, made it a very suitable moderator or mediator in the region.

The Administration clearly preferred, and encouraged, an alternative line of regional diplomacy corresponding to its own policy. In January 1982, Costa Rica, Honduras and El Salvador formed a Central American Democratic Community which effectively increased Nicaraguan isolation but was open to all regional countries 'which share and practice its democratic principles and objectives'.[46] Support for that line did not, however, increase during 1982 as the Administration must have hoped. Venezuela's position was modified during the year. Its enthusiasm for US policy in El Salvador fell as the PDC went into harassed opposition. The position of the US during the South Atlantic crisis increased frictions and doubts about US policy, while the position of Cuba helped to improve Venezuelan relations with Havana. Nor was Venezuela impressed with the amount of US aid offered through the CBI, which was about the same as that given by Mexico and Venezuela to regional countries through their 1980 programme of concessional oil sales. The vehemence of US rhetoric, reports of US covert rebel funding and increasing tensions on the Honduran–Nicaraguan border brought concern in both Mexico City and Caracas that regional conflict or US intervention was likely in the absence of greater efforts toward peace. In September 1982, Mexico and Venezuela joined in making peace proposals for a reduction of tensions between Nicaragua and Honduras. Largely in response, the US joined Costa Rica, Honduras, El Salvador, Belize, Colombia and Jamaica in a declaration from the Democratic Forum held in San Jose in October 1982. Behind this meeting was the potentially positive intention of discussing the basic principles on which a durable reduction of regional tensions might be reached. The Declaration thus proposed in general terms the withdrawal of foreign military advisers, an end to the importation of heavy weapons and support for insurgencies against neighbouring regimes, international surveillance of borders, and the establishment of democratic institutions. However, the meeting also corresponded to the US approach of presenting an isolated Nicaraguan Government with a set of conditions, including change in its internal policies, for its toleration. In that context, the US did not want any simple reduction of the various bilateral tensions, which served to maintain pressure upon the Sandinista regime. The exclusion of Nicaragua, and of the unpredictable Guatemalan Government, led Mexico and Venezuela not to attend at all, and Panama and the Dominican Republic to send only observers. Even some participants were subsequently to show appreciation of the political awkwardness of discussing supposedly regional principles for co-operation with the US but without the regional country most affected. At the end of 1982, a more coherent Latin American diplomacy began to emerge, attempting to bring together the different currents. Mexico began to move toward compromise, while Panama and Colombia, whose policy underwent a substantial change with the election of President Belisario Betancur, moved toward the Mexican–Venezuelan position. An attempt began to be made simultaneously to address the immediate dangers and to find basic principles for peace and co-operation acceptable to all the Central American countries, to address US concerns without directly involving the US or alienating Nicaragua, and to include the Sandinistas in discussions without alienating the US Administration. The first step was the meeting in January 1983 of the Foreign Ministers of Mexico, Venezuela, Colombia and Panama on the Panamanian island of Contadora, from which emerged the Contadora Group. After months of diplomatic efforts, the four Presidents on July 17th presented a first peace plan addressing all issues in general terms, accompanied by an open appeal to Reagan and Castro to help to defuse the situation.

Policy is defined, but undermined

The emergence of the Contadora initiative came at a time when the Administration was under increasing pressure from all sides to clarify its objectives in Nicaragua. In 1982, concern had grown in the House Intelligence Committee as to the real objective of the rebel funding. Chairman Edward Boland attached to the Intelligence Authorization Bill for fiscal year 1983 a classified condition, which at the end of 1982 became a public amendment to a defence bill, prohibiting the provision of 'military equipment, military training or advice, or other support for military activities, for the purpose of overthrowing the government of Nicaragua or provoking a military exchange between Nicaragua and Honduras.' At the beginning of 1983, new moves began to cut off covert funding, centring on a proposal by Boland and Representative Clement Zablocki to prohibit direct or indirect financing by the CIA or any other agency 'involved in intelligence activities' of military or paramilitary operations in Nicaragua. Most Democrats did not dispute that there was some level of Sandinista support for the Salvadorean rebels, and certainly felt some signal should be sent both to the Administration and to the Sandinistas that they were prepared to address legitimate security issues. Nor were they unconcerned at the Cuban and Soviet Bloc military and security presence in Nicaragua, or the level of Nicaraguan military strength. The Boland–Zablocki Amendment certainly hoped that there would be an end to all flows of supplies out of Nicaragua. It proposed open assistance totalling $80 million over fiscal years 1983 and 1984 to 'any friendly country in Central America,' in order, but only in order, and 'to the extent permitted by international law, . . . to interdict the supply of military equipment from Nicaragua and Cuba to individuals, groups, organizations or movements seeking to overthrow governments of countries in Central America'.[47] It was felt that illegal support for groups prominently containing supporters of the deposed dictator Somoza would simply discredit the US, probably only rally more people to the Sandinistas' side, and very probably encourage the regime to dig itself in.

There were certainly some in Congress, and still many in the US public, who remained tolerant and even sympathetic towards the Nicaraguan internal regime but the Congressional moderates' opposition to covert action did not generally reflect any such feelings, and the level of support for the Sandinistas within the US as a whole was not improved by the reception given to the Pope in Nicaragua during his March 1983 visit to Central America. The *New York Times* argued that 'What makes this bad war worse is that it spares Nicaragua from the condemnation it deserves, and not just for its provocative ties with Cuba and the Soviet Union. Its rulers have dishonored their own promises of elections and have driven democratic opponents into exile.'[48] A report in May 1983 by the Democratic majority of the House Permanent Select Committee on Intelligence, while agreeing that the Sandinistas had been supporting the Salvadorean rebels, argued that Administration policy had 'allowed the spotlight of international opprobrium to shift from Sandinista attempts to subvert a neighboring government to a U.S. attempt to subvert that of Nicaragua.' A dissent report from the Republican minority, however, not only disagreed that the covert operation had not been successful in deterring arms shipments, but seemed to indicate the hope that it might do much more: 'The Sandinista Nicaraguan government marks the first foothold of Marxism on the mainland in our Western hemisphere. With only a modicum of help from the United States democracy can flourish in Central America.'[49] It was not clear whether the Administration thought that the rebels could eventually bring about the downfall of the regime, regardless of whether that was its own intention. In late May 1983, the press reported that Enders of the State Department and Casey of the CIA had suggested in secret testimony that the rebels could pick up sufficient popular support to overthrow the Sandinistas by the end of the year. Casey immediately denied this publicly. Indeed, the most alarming aspect of the whole debate was the impression that the Administration did not really know, or would not say, exactly what the objective was with regard to Nicaragua. Republican Barry Goldwater, Chairman of the Senate Intelligence Committee, complained in May that they wanted the President 'to tell us in plain language just what it is he wants to do relative to Nicaragua and the other countries'.[50] The Committee voted for continued funding, but with the condition that he gave by 1 October a new presidential finding defining his objectives in Nicaragua more clearly. The July reports of increased military pressure came at a time of new peace proposals – from the Contadora Group, the Sandinistas themselves and even Fidel Castro, who offered to withdraw all Cuban advisers as part of a multilateral agreement. The reports intensified concern that the Administration was neglecting diplomatic settlement of differences with Nicaragua in favour of confrontation and military escalation with unpredictable consequences. The Speaker of the House, Tip O'Neill, argued that rebel funding would send the wrong message to the President and 'give him an opportunity to flex his muscles' in the region.[51] On 29 July, the House voted, although with no practical effect, to ban rebel funding after 1 October.

The challenge for the Administration was now to present a clearer and generally acceptable definition of its objectives, and to convince Congress and the public that the policy of military pressures and covert action was likely to help achieve them. The Administration's first reaction was simply to stress its interest in finding diplomatic solutions and to state that the Sandinistas, like Castro, would only negotiate if faced with the kind of 'objective conditions' they understood. The President argued that US military exercises 'and the whole appearance that we are not going to back away from what we think must be done down there' were partly responsible for the Nicaraguan and Cuban gestures.[52] Such statements, however, did not clarify precisely what outcome in Nicaragua the pressures were intended to achieve, and within what diplomatic framework it might come about. The Administration was soon afforded some means to respond when, in September 1983, the nine Foreign Ministers of the Contadora Group and Central America met in Panama to consider a 21-point Document of Objectives, covering in general terms the issues of concern to all parties. The document was signed by all Central American Governments, including the increasingly alarmed Sandinistas, despite the inclusion in it of reference to internal politics. Precisely because of its inclusion of pluralist institutions and national reconciliation as integral elements of a comprehensive settlement, the US Administration stated its clear approval. It could henceforth assert that its objectives were entirely compatible with those of the Contadora Group, and claim regional backing for opposing any solutions not including internal political change.

On 20 October 1983, the Sandinistas made another peace proposal in the form of non-aggression pacts between Nicaragua and the US and Nicaragua and Honduras, a regional non-aggression pact and a draft agreement to ease the solution of the Salvadorean conflict, including a verifiable end to all flows of supplies from, and command and control facilities in, Nicaragua. They were rejected as both deficient and inappropriate given the existence of the Contadora forum and the much broader Document of Objectives. In November and December, a series of external and internal gestures were made by the Sandinistas, partly in response to the urgings of the Contadora countries and European Social Democrats, and partly as a direct effort to undermine the US case for continued pressures. They let it be known that the number of Cuban advisers and the level of support for the Salvadorean rebels were to be reduced. According to supposedly captured rebel documents, the November 1983 decision to remove from Managua all but a few Salvadorean rebel representatives and curtail logistic support caused considerable strains between the FMLN and the Sandinistas.[53] A senior FMLN defector stated in 1985 that although a 'secondary directorate' remained, the FMLN General Command had been moved to El Salvador and that, although some supplies continued to flow, the level did drop.[54] For a certain time, there may even have been a total cut. Moreover, the gestures also concerned internal politics. An amnesty was offered to rebel Indians and all those fighting against the Nicaraguan Government except the leaders. A guarantee was offered to private landowners against indiscriminate expropriation. Censorship was lessened on the opposition newspaper *La Prensa*. A dialogue was started with the Church hierarchy. Talks were sought with the internal political opposition. Elections would go ahead in 1985. The Administration at first gave the moves a cautious welcome, but again made clear that its welcome was conditional upon the moves' being the first step toward full and simultaneous implementation of all 21 Contadora objectives. The September Document also permitted the Administration to argue that, just as the Sandinistas had made political commitments to the OAS in 1979, they had again promised the regional powers to establish a fully democratic regime. It could also argue that the Sandinistas had failed to live up to the 1979 commitments, thus proving that pressures were necessary in order to ensure that they fulfilled their promises and that, since the regional powers had failed to ensure fulfilment of the 1979 commitments, there would have to be some element of direct US pressure.

Given the failure of the 1979 'settlement,' any new regional agreement would have to include some international supervision of elections. Since the Sandinistas' failure to live up to its democratic promises had alienated important sections of the population, now represented by the armed opposition, national reconciliation, as included in the Contadora objectives, had to mean negotiation with the rebels. In this respect, the Administration would also be able to point to the demands made in December 1983 – in response to the Sandinista gestures – by the conservative opposition grouping, the Nicaraguan Democratic Co-ordinating Council (CDN), as conditions for participation in elections. These demands included not only an end to the State of Emergency and censorship, and a dissociation of the Sandinista Front from the Army and organs of State, but also that there should be a dialogue leading to general amnesty and the right of the armed opposition to participation in the elections. The Administration would argue that unless an open system was thereby established, Sandinista commitments to end their subversion could not be guaranteed. It thus asserted that rebel pressures on the Sandinistas were necessary precisely to achieve a genuine diplomatic settlement. George Schultz, now Secretary of State, argued that a cutoff of funds 'would virtually destroy the prospect that Nicaragua may agree to reciprocal and verifiable agreements to end assistance to all guerrilla forces operating in the region.'[55]

In the meantime, moreover, the rebel 'Contra' pressures and the demands of the war would keep the Sandinistas occupied in Nicaragua and reduce their capacity to continue providing assistance to the Salvadorean rebels. In the Autumn of 1983, with the Salvadorean rebels posing a strong threat to the US-backed Government in El Salvador, the question of guerrilla assistance was very sensitive. In the wake of the successful US–Caribbean action in Grenada, moreover, there was some increase in political pressure not to be seen to be tying the President's hands as he tried to deal with Communism. In

74

mid-November 1983, Congress approved a compromise measure on funding for the 'Contra' rebels. $24 million was authorised in a military appropriations bill. Access to a reserve contingency fund was specifically prohibited, and the CIA would have to return to Congress in June 1984 for any further funding.

The new definition of objectives, and the tenuous nature of the support for rebel funding, was reflected in the Kissinger Commission's Report. It saw the ideal solution as a comprehensive regional settlement, 'which would not imply the liquidation of the Sandinista Government or the formal abandonment of its revolutionary ideals, but only that it submit itself to the legitimating test of free elections'. This would be agreed between the Central American countries, and include: verifiable commitments on non-aggression; on non-support for insurgents or subversion; on force levels; on the prohibition of all foreign forces, bases and advisers; and a commitment to political pluralism and free elections – all to be effectively and permanently verified. These principles were seen as fully consistent with the emerging Contadora programme. That process should be encouraged, but 'the United States cannot use the Contadora process as a substitute for its own policies', and a 'more specific settlement' than the 21-point programme should be urged. When it came to ensuring Sandinista compliance with this type of settlement, however, the Commission could do little more than reflect the different opinions and possibilities. Financial and commercial incentives were proposed in the form of various US development programmes, Nicaraguan access to aid being 'conditioned on continued progress toward defined political, social, and economic goals,' while 'as part of the backdrop to diplomacy, Nicaragua must be aware that force remains an ultimate recourse'. Beyond urging exploration of political alternatives to continued confrontation and the testing of Nicaragua's stated willingness to negotiate, the Commission could say little more. On the controversial issue of covert support for the Nicaraguan 'Contra' rebels, the Commission simply agreed to differ. The majority believed that rebel efforts 'represent one of the incentives working in favor of a negotiated settlement'. In the appended notes by individual Commissioners, however, Mayor Henry Cisneros suggested testing the Sandinistas' good faith in making the gestures at the end of 1983, and urged suspension of covert aid in order to give them a chance to demonstrate their capacity and willingness to move towards pluralism. Professor Carlos Diaz-Alejandro from Yale University put forward almost the full case for opposing it altogether:

The type of covert support given by the United States government to Nicaraguan insurgents on balance hurts the chances of reaching the goal of a truly democratic Nicaragua. The net effect of such support is more likely to strengthen the most extremist sectors of the Sandinista leadership, and to allow them to claim patriotic motivation for bringing Nicaragua into closer military alliance with Cuba and the USSR. U.S. support to some insurgents is used by Managua to brand all dissidents as pawns of a foreign power, eroding the legitimacy of dissidence within Nicaragua, especially among the nationalistic youth, while giving Managua a handy excuse for economic failures and further political repression. The possibility of accidental war along the Nicaraguan northern border is also increased by these covert operations. Thus, rather than creating pressures for negotiations, U.S. support to Nicaraguan insurgents has made successful negotiations less likely.

By late 1983 there was general agreement in Congress and the US that change in the internal system of Nicaragua was desirable, and would improve the prospects for regional stability and security. However, there was no consensus regarding the policy of rebel support. There was also strong feeling, especially given the suspicion that many rebels were of dubious democratic commitment, that the US should not commit itself to them so long as there was a prospect of a successful Contadora settlement, or indeed that the Sandinistas might actually move toward an open political system through the promised elections. Well before these two possibilities were seen to be explored, however, other developments led to a suspension of rebel funding almost as soon as the Administration had secured its renewal.

Despite continued growth in numbers, the Nicaraguan rebels were failing to make substantial headway in Nicaragua either politically or militarily. They remained disunited. They could not capture and hold a single town, far less establish the promised 'liberated zones' in which to declare a provisional government. There were persistent reports of rebel atrocities and kidnapping of recruits. They were having an effect, but by means which did not increase either their internal or international legitimacy, and which threatened to bring serious discredit to the US. Matters came to a head in the wake of the mining of Nicaraguan harbours, which provoked a wave of protest even from close US allies. The US was taken to the International Court of Justice, and received a preliminary ruling that the US should refrain from aggression against Nicaragua and respect its political independence. Anger in the US concentrated also on the fact that the operations were subsequently revealed to have been directed by the CIA, whose operatives indeed appeared to have got carried away in their dedication, while the Congressional Intelligence Committees had not been kept informed of these actions. The House quickly moved to suspend all further aid to the Nicaraguan rebels. The Senate followed in June.

Doubts and dilemmas of local allies

The US Administration was already having some difficulties over its regional policies even with local friends. The Guatemalan regime resented the continued failure of the Administration to secure military aid, despite its gestures in support of US regional policy and then its formal moves toward democratisation, principally the July 1984 elections to a Constituent Assembly. There had also been an improvement in relations with Mexico, reflected in the latter's agreement to Guatemala's demands to move refugee camps, alleged to be sources of guerrilla support, further from the Mexican–Guatemalan border. Both factors contributed to a retreat from Guatemala's active anti-Sandinista position, and to an apparently greater interest in the rapid success of a Contadora settlement than that of the US Administration. The Costa Rican Government and society remained divided and hesitant about the country's role in the regional crisis. An official policy of neutrality had been declared. There had been reluctance to accept increased military co-operation with the US and there was clear discomfort in many sectors about the presence in Costa Rica of anti-Sandinista groups. The Congressional ban on funding for the Nicaraguan rebels brought new problems, in particular with its key ally, Honduras.

There, at the end of March 1984, officers had ousted the Armed Forces Commander, General Gustavo Alvarez Martínez, because of his political meddling, ambition and extremism, his abuse of the military structure and his role in the handling of relations with the US and El Salvador. Increasingly public statements began to be made of dissatisfaction with relations with the US. Most of the Honduran Government and military, before and after the removal of Alvarez Martínez, believed that the Sandinista regime itself represented a threat to Honduras, and wanted the Reagan Administration's policy to succeed but many had begun to feel uneasy about Honduras' role in that policy. It was embarrassing, and hurtful to nationalist feeling, to be cast internationally as a mere political pawn and military base of the US, and Hondurans were sensitive to their loss of third-world friendships to Nicaragua's benefit. Many were already becoming uncomfortable with the spread of military facilities and the succession of military manoeuvres with US troops, which was becoming a domestic political issue (although popular opposition to the American military presence was limited, and partly countered by the positive impact on the population of the medical action programmes). Many felt that Honduras was receiving far too little from the US in return for its co-operation, especially compared to the amounts being given to El Salvador, which continued to be seen as a long-term security threat and which the US was making very much stronger militarily than Honduras. Whereas Honduran weakness in ground forces was to some extent compensated for by their air superiority over Nicaragua, the same did not apply to El Salvador. Moves began to end the training of Salvadorean soldiers in the Regional Training Centre in Honduras, which was almost universally considered to be unacceptable in view of the unresolved territorial dispute between the two countries, and Honduran fears of a repetition of the conditions leading to the 1969 war. As the economic crisis continued, it was increasingly recognised that the fundamental defence against internal or external revolutionaries had to be the construction of a solid democracy and a more viable and equitable economy – rather than further militarisation. The Congressional ban on funding the Nicaraguan rebels, most of whom were based in Honduras and had received substantial support from the Honduran Government and Armed Forces, raised concern about them to a new level. Serious doubts arose about the credibility of US security commitments in the case of a conflict with Nicaragua sparked off by rebel activities. Some Hondurans feared that the US might reach some bilateral understanding with Nicaragua, or simply fail to go ahead with the prevention of Sandinista consolidation. That might leave in Nicaragua a regime which was not only ideologically hostile but highly armed and resentful of Honduras' past actions, and in Honduras an army of unwanted Nicaraguan guerrillas who did not number much less than the total Armed Forces, and who might pose serious social, political and security problems. If Reagan was unwilling or unable to make his policy work, Honduras did not want to be left to face the consequences alone.

One result was the demand for a new bilateral treaty guaranteeing US defence of Honduras against any aggressor, most immediately seen as being Nicaragua but also perhaps El Salvador, and for an increase in both military and economic aid. Part of the aim of Honduran public statements of discontent with the US, of intent to remove the rebels, and of threats to end Salvadorean training, was to put pressure on the US Administration to provide the treaty and the aid. It also reflected, however, the real dilemmas faced by Honduras. Fears that Reagan might be forced to walk away from Nicaragua brought new tensions into Honduras' attitude toward a Contadora-type settlement. On the one hand, they increased the Honduran Government's interest in achieving some diplomatic agreement. A reduction of regional tensions was vital if Honduras was to recover economically. If the US was not going to get rid of the Sandinistas, and if it could not be counted on to give full support in the case of conflict, then it might be better to find some means of living with the Nicaraguan Government rather than continue to incur the costs and risks of co-operation in a US policy of half-hearted confrontation. On the other hand, if the US could not be relied on, it was all the more important to ensure that any regional settlement was balanced, effective and verifiable.

Dilemmas with regard to the Nicaraguan rebels tended to keep Honduras, however uncomfortably, on the side of the Administration. There were risks of conflict with the Sandinistas if Honduras simply pushed them all into Nicaragua. If all logistic support to the 'Contras' was cut so as to reduce the immediate risks of confrontation, the rebels' prospects would be diminished, and many might try to cross back, thus presenting the Honduran military with the unpleasant choice of armed co-operation with or conflict with the Nicaraguan forces. If logistic support was increased to improve rebel prospects, Nicaraguan forces might attempt direct interdiction, with high risks of conflict. If the Hondurans tried to keep the rebels in Honduras, they might well have to do so by force. If they failed to prevent incursions into Nicaragua, border incidents with Nicaraguan forces would probably continue as well. During the twelve months in which the rebels were deprived of official US funding, the Honduran position remained one of considerable unease, but there was little they could realistically do in the circumstances. The rebels were forced to maintain a lower profile. In May 1985, as the rebels appeared to be flagging, Congress again denied them support. Incidents with Nicaragua reached a new and alarming level, and the Hondurans did take some measures to move the rebel bases further from the border. Otherwise, their tolerance, and practical support, continued more or less unchanged.

The situation not only illustrated the difficulties of stopping the dynamic set up by the rebel forces. It also made a US commitment to the rebels both more likely and even more important for the Administration. US support for the 'Contras' had to some extent become a test of the credibility of US assurances and political commitment to Honduras itself. Concern that Honduran fears might increase its interest in partial settlement strengthened the need to discourage such a settlement, and to avoid any appearance of an understanding with Nicaragua. There was also an additional impetus for the credibility of the Administration's resolve in Central America, and the course of US policy, to be identified not only with opposition to the Sandinista regime in general but with positive support for the rebels in particular.

By mid-1984, the attitudes of the Sandinistas and the US Administration towards the Contadora process were clear, and fundamentally conflicting. The US Administration saw it as one means to bring about internal change in Nicaragua, while the Sandinistas saw it as one means to negotiate an end to the aspects of the crisis which threatened the survival of their Revolution. The former would go along with it so long as it brought sufficient internal change in Nicaragua, did not endanger the Administration's position in the other countries, and did not imply anything more than the withdrawal of Cuba and the Soviet Union. The Sandinistas would go along so long as it prevented external interference in internal affairs and continuation of the US' threatening military presence and political hegemony in Central America, but internal politics were not negotiable. The result was diplomatic manoeuvring around the Contadora process, as both pursued alternative approaches to securing their fundamental objectives. The US would continue unilateral pressures to force change in Nicaragua. The Sandinistas would continue to seek bilateral agreements on external issues, in parallel, and even in contradiction, to their stated position regarding Contadora. Thus, in 1983, the US had shown no intention of substituting multilateral negotiations for military pressures and rebel funding. The Sandinistas, within days of the Contadora Group's July plan, and within weeks of the September Document of Objectives, had presented alternative peace proposals, making significant offers on external issues – but on a primarily bilateral basis, and excluding internal politics.

As Congress banned further official 'Contra' funding, the Contadora Group urged the Administration to hold bilateral talks with the Sandinistas in order to give assurances that the US would respect any diplomatic agreement reached between the Central American countries. In the wake of the scandal over the mining of ports, with US elections due in November 1984, and with a wave of international support for the Contadora process, there was a strong political incentive for the US to manifest diplomatic willingness, and a temporary retreat of the hardest line within the Administration. The Administration agreed, and talks began to be held in Manzanillo, Mexico. The fundamental objective of the Administration remained substantial political change in Nicaragua, inevitably involving some form of negotiation with the rebel forces. If that could be achieved within the framework of a multilateral agreement which acceptably addressed all other issues, most of the Administration was then willing to go along. It did not believe, however, that the Sandinistas were seriously interested in the kind of agreement acceptable to their neighbours, as was currently being negotiated. If nothing else, there might be some diplomatic gain if Nicaragua could be made to appear the obstacle to the peace process.

During the first fruitless rounds of the Manzanillo talks, the Contadora Group was working to incorporate the requested observations of the Central American countries concerning the draft Act on Peace and Cooperation presented in June. On 7 September 1984, it presented a revised Act which it felt had succeeded in reconciling the differences. The Nicaraguan Government at that point still seemed the most reluctant to sign, disliking the Act's proposal for international monitoring of internal political processes and openly unhappy at the prospect of establishing regionally-defined force limits while direct US military pressures and the war with the 'Contra' rebels continued. Of the others, only El Salvador openly expressed any desire for further changes. Within a week the Guatemalan and Costa Rican Foreign Ministers had publicly stated that they would accept the new Act, the latter stressing that it satisfied all Costa Rican concerns through 'obligatory and verifiable' agreements.[56] On 21 September, with apparent Cuban encouragement, the Nicaraguan Government made an entirely unexpected announcement that it would sign the revised Act. It had, in the diplomatic manoeuvring surrounding the process, turned the tables on the US, and was now calling its bluff.

El Salvador, Costa Rica and Honduras now made clear their reservations about the September draft (as did the US Administration) and on 20 October 1984 these three countries presented a modified version at the end of a meeting in Tegucigalpa of their Foreign Ministers. Guatemala attended but did not associate itself with the counter-draft. There seems little doubt that the US Administration did not want the September draft to be signed. US consultations certainly ensured that a decision would be taken to push for a modified Act, and may have been especially significant in the case of Costa Rica. However, it does not appear that the counter-draft was simply dictated by the US, or forced on its local allies. There were obvious reasons for Salvadorean misgivings about the establishment of limits on its force levels and military aid, and the removal of US military advisers. At the same time, the framework for reducing Sandinista forces and removing Cuban and Soviet Bloc advisers from Nicaragua seemed too loose. Honduran opposition to the proposed prohibition of joint manoeuvres, and insistence on better defined limits on force levels, also reflected the perceived need for a more solid regional agreement on security issues, made all the greater because of doubts about the reliability of US security guarantees, as well as a recognition of military dependence upon the US, in view of Honduras' great military inferiority with respect to Nicaragua. An entirely new provision – for the removal from Central America of surrendering irregular forces operating from a State to which they did not belong – largely reflected Honduran concern as the fate of the Nicaraguan 'Contra' rebels if effective agreement on security issues was reached. Nor was there any change, as would have been considered ideal by the US Administration, in the definition of political commitments.

There was legitimate reason to seek improvements in the security and verification provisions of the September draft, and the process did not simply reflect conflict between the US and Nicaragua. Nicaragua's political structure and the size of the military forces protecting it were a real source of concern to both the US and Nicaragua's neighbours. There may also have been differences between them as to a minimally acceptable outcome. That, however, did not change the fact that the US was pursuing its own goals. Contadora was explicitly not a substitute for US national policy. For the Administration, internal political change in Nicaragua was fundamental, and effective external verification implicitly secondary to the establishment of a 'self-guaranteeing' system. With that aim, it was exerting pressures independently of the Contadora process, which was only one framework within which it might take place. The Sandinista argument was thus not unreasonable – in its own terms – that Nicaragua could not accept purely regionally-defined force limits when it faced direct US military pressures; far less could Nicaragua accept a strictly one-to-one basis for the calculation when it also faced the possibility of collective hostility. It would only do so if given a credible guarantee that the US would cease its hostility and not intervene in Nicaraguan affairs. In the end, the issue – whether considered on a bilateral or multilateral basis – was the internal system in Nicaragua. Both the Sandinistas and the US Administration were manoeuvring at all levels to secure conflicting outcomes in that respect.

After Nicaragua's acceptance of the September Act, the Manzanillo talks had a more substantial basis. The Administration made an effort to improve understanding with Nicaragua over the security issues involved in the Tegucigalpa draft. It offered to discuss the level and frequency of international manoeuvres in Honduras and offered flexibility with regard to the downward adjustment to agreed force limits, recognising that immediate reduction for both Nicaragua and El Salvador would be impossible in view of the continuing internal conflicts. However, these issues were not treated in isolation from the question of political developments in Nicaragua.

The Administration continued to stress that establishment of a genuinely democratic system in Nicaragua, through elections verifiably satisfying the standards established in the Contadora Acts, was an essential element of any settlement. Moreover, it directly tied political change to security issues, inasmuch as resolution of the internal conflict was a prerequisite for implementation of security commitments. Especially since the US was not officially supporting the 'Contra' rebels, it could argue that responsibility for resolving the conflict did not lie with Washington, and point to the commitment to national reconciliation included in the Act. There was therefore no alternative to negotiations with *all* rebels to establish the conditions for democratic elections participated in by all national groups, as envisaged by the talks which President Duarte had pointedly held with the Salvadorean rebel groups on 15 October 1984, the deadline for the September Act. This aspect was indeed the key to the US Administration's diplomatic response to Nicaragua's acceptance of the September draft, President Reagan asserting that 'If only the comandantes in Nicaragua would make the same offer to resistance forces there, we would all be much closer to true peace in Central America.'[57] The Sandinistas, however, although moving to accept discussion of all issues concerning security commitments and verification (and even giving signs that they were prepared to back down over their insistence on total US military withdrawal from Central America) were firm that internal affairs should *not* be subject to international agreement. Any national reconciliation plan would be purely Nicaraguan, and there would never be negotiation with CIA-sponsored counter-revolutionaries. They claimed to have no problems in satisfying Contadora political principles, since those were entirely consonant with the stated principles of the Revolution, and elections were in any case due to be held.

The Nicaraguan elections of 4 November 1984, however, were only to make any settlement less likely. They made the US Administration all the more determined to increase pressures and hopeful that it might receive sufficient domestic support to do so. On the other hand, they made the Sandinistas more hopeful of international support for forms of settlement which did not include internal politics. In the final Manzanillo meetings the Sandinistas moved toward discussion of most of the security and verification issues raised by the Tegucigalpa draft of the Contadora Act. However, Nicaragua still saw bilateral understandings with the US and with its neighbours, including international supervision and demilitarisation of the borders, as sufficient for security, and their elections and amnesty offers as politically sufficient and meriting support. They also believed that the Salvadorean, Honduran and Costa Rican Governments were simply being manipulated by the US Administration and that normalisation of relations with the US was what really mattered. Nicaragua therefore offered to come to terms with the US on such issues as foreign military bases and advisers, joint manoeuvres, verified cessation of support for irregular forces, and international border supervision, in return for a normalisation of bilateral relations, involving US action to help to disarm and disband the 'Contras.'

At the same time, however, the Sandinistas insisted that they would only sign the Contadora Act in its September version. This position was unacceptable to the US Administration, since it would have implied acceptance not only of the unsatisfactory September provisions concerning limits on military forces, but also of the internal regime, which the Sandinistas would argue satisfied the Contadora principles regarding elections and was therefore not an obstacle to a peace treaty.

There was indeed one clear FSLN inconsistency: it could not both reach an understanding with the US which permitted international manoeuvres in Honduras, *and* sign a multilateral agreement which specifically prohibited them. It also appeared that the Sandinistas were continuing to seek partial security agreements with Honduras and Costa Rica, and some understanding with El Salvador, which would weaken pressures both for a strong multilateral agreement and for Sandinista negotiation with the Nicaraguan rebels. The Administration believed that Nicaragua was attempting to give the impression to those countries that a bilateral understanding with the US was imminent, which would leave them and the rebels in the lurch. Thus, it would be in their interests to reach immediate agreements, bilateral or multilateral, to remove the source of a mutually disastrous conflict which the Sandinistas emphasised would otherwise be almost inevitable. Given the neutralist pressures within Costa Rica and Honduran doubts as to the Administration's ability to carry out its commitments, it seemed all the more important to counter any precipitate movements toward settlement. In January 1985, as National Security Adviser Robert McFarlane visited the other Central American countries to give them reassurances about the US commitment, the Administration suspended the talks on the grounds of Nicaraguan inflexibility and interest in substituting bilateral for multilateral agreements in order to avoid commitments to arms limits and democracy.

The pattern of developments surrounding the Contadora process over the next six months remained consonant with the conflicting approach of the Administration and the Sandinistas. Some progress was made in negotiating more effective verification mechanisms, and there was some movement towards agreement on most of the security issues. There were other obstacles to agreement of a framework for settlement, such as the US' rejection of the desire of some Contadora and Central American countries for signature of supportive protocols by outside powers, possibly including Cuba and the Soviet Union.

However, the US Administration and the Sandinistas continued to act in fundamentally conflicting manners toward the Contadora process. The Administration continued to urge the drafting of a completely satisfactory document, while waiting to secure renewed funding for the rebels in order to bring about the internal negotiation that it saw as the minimum condition for effective settlement. The Sandinistas, as they tried quickly to break the 'Contras' militarily – in order to avert renewed funding – would play on Honduran fears about the credibility of Administration commitments and the consequences of having the rebels on its territory, and on general concern about border conflicts, in order to push for agreements which ended the rebels' use of neighbouring countries' territory. The Sandinistas therefore in 1985 launched a military campaign aimed at destroying the rebel forces. Should that not prove possible, it was at least hoped that attacks on bases across the frontiers might put pressure on Honduras to control the rebels, and serve as an incentive for quick international action to reduce tensions. Contacts were made with the Honduran Government and further attempts were made to establish a demilitarised zone on the border with Costa Rica. However, there was a real danger that pressure (especially cross-border operations) would increase hostility to the Sandinistas. A serious incident near the Costa Rican border with Nicaragua in mid-1985 had precisely the effect of whipping up Costa Rican alarm and antipathy and strengthening support for anti-Sandinista measures. By late 1985, the positions of Nicaragua and the US with regard to the Contadora process were so clearly conflicting that the prospects for its success seemed minute. For the Sandinistas, the precondition was a US guarantee of non-intervention and an end to support for rebel funding. For the US, it was direct negotiation with the rebels.

The achievement of current policy

The second half of 1984 had essentially been a hiatus in US policy. Throughout the diplomatic developments, the Administration had remained privately committed to the 'Contra' cause, and in its view, the two dimensions – negotiation of a comprehensive regional settlement and pressure for Sandinista negotiation with the 'Contras' – could not be separated. In October 1984, as the Administration manifested an interest in political solutions through support for a modified Contadora Act and for Duarte's exemplary peace talks with the Salvadorean rebels, Congress had approved another $14 million in

'Contra' funding, but had tied its release to a further vote after February 1985. The purely diplomatic options had to be convincingly exhausted first.

However, the 'Contras' had grown substantially in numbers since the cutoff of official funding, and had been receiving sufficient backing from private sources in the US and elsewhere, and from a number of sympathetic governments, to increase their activities and their impact by the end of 1984. They had also become slightly more united, the political faction of the southern-based forces led by Alfonso Robelo having broken with Eden Pastora, who continued to refuse to join with the FDN because of its Somocista elements. Continued 'Contra' activity, quite apart from the Administration's military pressure and diplomatic insistence on their behalf, only helped ensure that neither the international options nor Nicaragua's internal process would develop sufficiently to provide the basis for a durable reduction of tensions between the US and Nicaragua. It was not simply that the Administration did not want alternatives to succeed, but also that the dynamic of the situation made it very hard for them to do so. The first objective for the Administration was thus to ensure that Congress and the US public were convinced of the undemocratic and threatening nature of the Sandinistas and of the impossibility of simple negotiation with them. Crucial in this were the Nicaraguan elections.

International observers agreed that the election on the day was held fairly and without fraud, and indicated continuing popular support for the FSLN: they received 67 per cent of the vote cast, which indicated the support of around half of the registered voters. From the beginning, however, the electoral process had been marked by opposition complaints that the conditions did not exist for fair and free elections. In response to the demands of the conservative opposition grouping (CDN), the FSLN did soften the State of Emergency, but bluntly rejected demands to talk to the rebels. The CDN announced at the end of July that it would boycott the elections. Despite attempts at compromise, the decision was not reversed, while frictions also led the Independent Liberals to attempt to withdraw. The FSLN made another attempt to incorporate the conservative opposition into the process through a short-lived national dialogue in November and December. In early January 1985, the Sandinistas made further moves to increase the prospects for political stability and agreement, and their own international legitimacy, by extending unconditional amnesty to rebel leaders, promising to respect political pluralism and private property and reopening talks with the Church hierarchy. However, although many in Latin America and Western Europe did not share the US view that the elections had been merely a 'Soviet-style' farce, they had not brought the FSLN the international legitimacy they had sought. There had certainly been some abuses, harassment and other unfair practices, while the CDN was weak and politically ineffective. However, the frictions and shortcomings within the process were less important than the fundamental political conflict. Not all *Comandantes* saw the elections as only a tactic on the path to a Marxist–Leninist society, as stated to their embarrassment by Comandante Bayardo Arce. Nevertheless, the FSLN still did not seem to envisage moving immediately to a political system in which it was fully separated from the State and in which opposition parties would have an opportunity to take power. The FSLN could argue that continued restrictions corresponded to the extraordinary circumstances created by the war. The more moderate internal opposition hoped, and would continue to hope, that talks between the Sandinistas and the legal opposition still might eventually bring a more open system. However, many conservatives already believed that the FSLN would only accept such change under strong pressure, if at all and, simply did not want to participate in an electoral process which they saw not only as rigged against them, but designed to institutionalise and legitimise Sandinista rule. In this, they were actively supported, and directly encouraged, by the US Administration.

Had the US suspended all direct pressures, and been willing and able to call off the rebels during 1984, in order to give the Sandinistas a clear chance to show their political intentions without external pressure, it is not certain that the result would have been radically different. But even if most of the Sandinista leadership would not have wanted to make much greater concessions and changes, the continued actions of the armed anti-Sandinista groups only helped to ensure that they would not do so. As it was, the Administration could claim that the Sandinistas had had their chance, especially given the lack of official rebel funding, and had only demonstrated their undemocratic bent. With Sandinista dominance of the National Assembly and internal control not significantly diminished, with two of the three Junta members converted into President and Vice-President, the FSLN directorate still the locus of decision-making, and the police and army still Sandinista in name and nature, little indeed seemed to have changed.

It still remained, however, for the Administration to convince Congress that the Sandinistas were sufficiently threatening, and the Nicaraguan rebels sufficiently credible and attractive, to warrant a new US commitment to the armed opposition. Its handling of the furore raised, a few days after the Nicaraguan elections, by the alleged arrival of MiG fighters clearly revealed an interest in drawing attention away from the Nicaraguan election results, away from the domestic concern about the rebels' unattractive behaviour raised during the scandal over the CIA manual issued to them, and towards the security threat claimed to be posed by a Sandinista regime. With the Nicaraguan elections and Sandinista political concessions seemingly revealed as hollow and the Manzanillo process as futile, but with Congress still appearing certain to reject any further requests for covert aid to the rebels, the Administration moved to a new level of rhetorical attack on the Sandinistas and praised the Nicaraguan 'freedom fighters.' It argued that the rebels were becoming an increasingly strong and legitimate political, as well as armed, force. At the beginning of 1985, Arturo Cruz had first moved to open support for the rebels, and then agreed to become part of their political leadership. By the middle of the year, the United Nicaraguan Opposition (UNO) had been formed, led by Robelo, Cruz and Adolfo Calero, longstanding political leader of the FDN. The rebels' calls for negotiations were also receiving more, and more open, support from internal forces. The Nicaraguan Church hierarchy had called for dialogue between all national groups in a pastoral letter of April 1984 which had, since December 1983, been one of the demands of the conservative opposition in Nicaragua. In February 1985 they issued a statement calling for church-mediated dialogue between the Government and the rebels.

In February, the Nicaraguan Government made new efforts to show that it did not present a security threat, and was genuinely interested in reaching a settlement of security issues. It announced a unilateral moratorium on the acquisition of new arms, including MiG intercep- tors, and the unilateral withdrawal of 100 Cuban advisers. The Administration denounced the moves as a propaganda gesture, believing that the Sandinistas were partly making a virtue out of necessity, since the USSR had probably told them it could not have the MiGs. It also argued that the gestures showed that the Sandinistas were moving to negotiate under pressure, but that these gestures were still insufficient. Continued, and increased, pressures were required.

Many House Democrats, however, remained opposed to any form of rebel aid as ineffective and discrediting. As a joint exercise involving several thousand US troops and, for the first time, tanks, continued in Honduras, Reagan came openly to acknowledge that his objective was the removal of the Nicaraguan regime in its 'present structure'. Many also feared that a continuation of military pressures and covert counter-revolution would inexorably, and unnecessarily, draw the US into direct confrontation with the Sandinistas. They argued that Nicaragua was not the 'totalitarian dungeon' becoming locked behind the Iron Curtain by a brutal dictatorship, as asserted by the Administration, and that the regime did not in itself, if the security issues were addressed by a diplomatic settlement, pose such a threat as to warrant such a dangerous, and illegal, course. Most of all, there were other means to bring about a political opening in Nicaragua. Many Democrats openly objected to the Administration's Manichaean presentation of the situation as unfairly making opposition to covert aid publicly appear synonymous with support for Communism. There was broad opposition to covert aid to rebel forces including many of questionable democratic commitment and atrocious behaviour, at the cost of widespread international condemnation of the US and at the expense of the diplomatic efforts of the Contadora Group. On the other hand, there were those who continued to press for a policy of open aid to the Nicaraguan rebels. The Administration did consider a variety of possible alternatives to covert funding, but rejected almost all as either excessive or impracticable.

The President's first attempt to secure funding was therefore an attempt at compromise with Congress. On 1 March 1985, the Nicaraguan rebels had issued a statement picking up the call of the internal conservative opposition for a church-mediated dialogue, nominating Calero, Cruz and Robelo as representatives, and proposing a ceasefire and acceptance of Daniel Ortega as Head of State pending internationally supervised elections. On 22 March, the Secretary of the Episcopal Conference issued a communique offering co-operation in conciliation. On 4 April, despite reluctance within the Administration to accept Cruz after his previous positions, and despite the fact that many felt that the rebel offer was too generous in accepting Ortega as temporary President, Reagan made a request to Congress based on the new initiative. He asked the rebels to extend the ceasefire offer until 1 June. The $14 million would not be used for arms or munitions during the ceasefire period, but if there was not agreement after 60 days of negotiations, that restriction would be lifted. He reminded Congress that, with bipartisan support, the policy of support for democracy had had considerable success in El Salvador, and had not drawn the US into direct involvement as feared by his critics. He also emphasised that his goals in Nicaragua were consistent with the 21 Contadora goals.

The proposal was immediately rejected by the Nicaraguan Government. It was also narrowly rejected by the House of Representatives on 25 April. Within days, however, the balance of forces in Congress regarding Nicaragua was changed by President Ortega's visit to Moscow in the course of a European trip, in a search for urgently needed economic assistance, and for Soviet oil after Mexico's decision to suspend oil shipments to Nicaragua. The visit was taken as a 'slap in the face' by many on Capitol Hill who had voted against rebel aid days before. To some it may have been confirmation that the depth of the Sandinistas' Soviet ties did indeed make it advisable to ensure change in the internal regime by indirect military pressures if necessary. More important, it helped to create a political climate in which a vote against all measures could present the electoral risk of seeming 'soft on communism.' And for some Democrats unhappy with their situation, it simply provided an excuse to modify it. Reagan quickly responded to the House vote by ordering economic sanctions against Nicaragua, both to maintain the pressure and as a signal to all sides, including the House, that he was firm in his commitment. After several weeks of discussion, a compromise package was reached, and initially approved by the House on 13 June. $27 million would be provided to the rebels, but of purely 'humanitarian' aid, and with the CIA and the Defense Department specifically prohibited from involvement in its distribution.

The Administration seemed finally to have begun to achieve what it wanted from Congress. Support for Administration policy remained tenuous, however, and the Administration was to face strong opposition before securing even preliminary approval for what was the logical next step in its policy, and was to be increasingly obviously necessary if the Nicaraguan rebels were to survive as a credible force, which was US military aid to the 'Contras'.

Notes and References

[1] State Department Special Report on Communist Interference in El Salvador, 23 February 1981.
[2] Alexander Haig *Guardian* 23 February 1981.
[3] White House Counsellor Edwin Meese *Guardian* 23 February 1981.
[4] Abraham Lowenthal 'Let the Latins Have Their Turmoil in Peace' *Washington Post* 28 March 1982.
[5] President Reagan, Address to a joint session of Congress, 27 April 1983.
[6] *Guardian* 23 February 1981.
[7] Ambassador Deane Hinton. Quoted in Raymond Bonner op. cit. p. 238.
[8] *Washington Post* 14 March 1982.
[9] *Washington Post* 24 April 1982 My italics.
[10] ibid.
[11] *International Herald Tribune* 1 November 1982.
[12] Latin America Regional Reports Mexico and Central America, 28 October 1983, p. 6.
[13] 'A New Turn for the Worse.' *Newsweek* 12 December 1983, p. 39.
[14] Cleto Di Giovanni, Jr. and Alexander Kruger 'Central America' *The Washington Quarterly* Summer 1980, p. 176.

15 *Miami Herald* 9 November 1980.
16 Edward L. King *Analysis of Military Situation in Nicaragua* Unitarian Universalist Service Committee, Boston, April 1985, pp. 5-6.
17 *The Military Balance 1981-1982* IISS, London, 1981.
18 The FPL, previously closest to the Cubans and the Sandinistas' 'Prolonged Popular War' tendency, had doubts that conditions existed for insurrection.
19 *Revolution Beyond Our Borders. Sandinista Intervention in Central America* United States Department of State, September 1985, p. 22.
20 ibid.
21 Quoted in Roy Gutman and Susan Page 'A Fumbled Chance for Accord' *Newsday* 1 August 1983, p. 4.
22 Roy Gutman 'America's Diplomatic Charade' *Foreign Policy* Fall 1984, pp. 7-8.
23 Quoted in Roy Gutman and Susan Page, op. cit. p. 23.
24 Michael Getler and Don Oberdorfer 'Pressure to "Do Something" Grows' *Washington Post* 22 November 1981.
25 ibid.
26 ibid.
27 *Washington Post* 17 March 1982.
28 Don Oberdorfer and Patrick E. Tyler 'U.S.-Backed Nicaraguan Rebel Army Swells to 7,000 Men.' *Washington Post* 8 May 1983.
29 Stansfield Turner 'From an Ex-CIA Chief: Stop the Covert Operation in Nicaragua.' *Washington Post* 24 April 1983.
30 Quoted in Lou Cannon and Patrick E. Tyler 'President Admits Aiding Guerrillas Against Nicaragua.' *Washington Post* 15 April 1983.
31 *International Herald Tribune* 10 December 1982.
32 *The Military Balance 1982-1983* IISS, London, 1982.
33 Edward L. King, op. cit. p. 8.
34 *U.S. Military Activities in Honduras*, (Mimeo) American Embassy, Tegucigalpa, 27 March 1985.
35 *The Military Balance 1983-1984* IISS, London, 1983.
36 Philip Taubman 'Reagan Approves Preparation For Large Caribbean Force.' *International Herald Tribune* 25 July 1983.
37 *The Military Balance 1984-1985* IISS, London, 1984.
38 Heinrich-W. Krumwiede 'Sandinist Democracy: Problems of Institutionalization' in Wolf Grabendorff, Heinrich-W. Krumwiede, and Jorg Todt, *Political Change in Central America. Internal and External Dimensions* Westview Press, Boulder and London, 1984, p. 77.
39 *Washington Post* 10 March 1982.

40 *El Nuevo Diario* (Managua) 12 March 1982.
41 Thomas Enders, August 1982. Quoted in Roy Gutman, op. cit. p. 13.
42 *International Herald Tribune* 20 April 1983.
43 Undersecretary of Defense Fred Ikle, 22 May 1985. Quoted in Joel Brinkley and Bill Keller 'Increasingly U.S. Officials Discuss Sending Troops to Nicaragua.' *International Herald Tribune* 6 June 1985.
44 Prepared Statement of Assistant Secretary of State Langhorne Motley, 17 April 1985.
45 President's report to Congress, 10 April 1985.
46 *El Diario de Hoy* (San Salvador) 20 January 1982.
47 Text of H.R. 2760 to amend the Intelligence Authorization Act for fiscal year 1983.
48 *New York Times* Editorial 'A Bad War in Nicaragua' in *International Herald Tribune* 31 March 1983.
49 *International Herald Tribune* 18 May 1983.
50 *International Herald Tribune* 22 September 1983.
51 *Guardian* 29 July 1983.
52 *Guardian* 1 August 1983.
53 *Miami Herald* 22 May 1985.
54 *Revolution Beyond Our Borders* op. cit., p. 12.
55 *Guardian* 21 October 1983.
56 *Uno Mas Uno* (Mexico) 15 September 1984.
57 *International Herald Tribune* 11 October 1984.

3   Current Perspectives for US Policy

Given the depth of the US Administration's commitment in El Salvador and Nicaragua, the size of the problems faced by US policy in those countries, and the powerful dynamics and escalatory interaction of the various dimensions of the crisis, the most likely prospect for US policy in Central America is simply for it to continue within much the same parameters, perhaps throughout the remainder of the Reagan Administration.

The situation in Guatemala is unpredictable and politically volatile, and will certainly present the US with both new and more familiar types of challenge. In El Salvador, the Administration will certainly not give up, but nor will the revolutionary opposition, and there are a multitude of serious problems and dangers yet to be faced. Compared to the period before mid-1984, certainly, the prospects for short-term success seem much improved. However, neither the rate of military improvement and political progress, nor the rate of insurgent weakening, has been as great or as irreversible as the Administration would like to claim, and the situation could still turn against the Government and the US. Most likely in the near future is that the conflict will be continuing, with many of the short-term problems still unresolved, but with the overall trend having gone further against the guerrillas. The crucial question will be whether or not the trend will have gone in favour of internal forces interested in creating new bases for the democratic peace required to achieve longer-term stability. The continuing war will not only maintain El Salvador itself in a state of violence and instability, but also serve to sustain Sandinista tensions with the US and the rest of Central America, and consequently to encourage continued support for the Nicaraguan insurgents.

In Nicaragua, the US Administration has found a new, more specific and globally significant commitment to the rebel cause, which makes it even less likely that the US will change its current policy. It is, of course, possible that the current course could be quickly undermined, and there will be continuing pressures on the Administration to alter it, but it seems at present unlikely. If anything, that policy is likely to become even tougher, and the Congressional votes of June and August 1986 in favour of military aid to the 'Contras' indicated that the Administration will probably be able to secure Congressional support for its policy for some time to come. The indirect costs for the US of that policy, and the possible negative consequences for the rest of Central America, will be perceived by this Administration as unlikely to be sufficient in themselves, or to generate sufficient pressure on it, to bring any early abandonment. There are risks that the situation could get dangerously out of control, but there are also many factors urging restraint on almost all sides. The Sandinista regime is certainly vulnerable, but it is most unlikely to give in to US and 'Contra' pressure unless faced with a threat to its survival. The course of events is unpredictable, but such a threat seems improbable during the remainder of the Reagan Administration's term. In view of the new ideological commitment and definition of much of the Administration regarding the anti-Sandinista campaign, however, the lack of clear prospects for rebel success is all the less likely to discourage its pursuit. So long as the Nicaraguan rebels are in the field and exerting pressure on the Sandinista regime, the Administration will feel able to claim some minimum success for its policy.

In the meantime, it is unlikely that the deadlock over a Contadora peace agreement will be substantially broken. The Sandinistas' reaction to the renewal of 'Contra' funding was to drop their declared moratorium on the acquisition of new weapons systems, to demand that the Contadora forum turn its attention to 'Contra' support and border incidents, and to condition any regional settlement on an end to all US hostilities. A Support Group was formed by Argentina, Brazil, Peru and Uruguay in July 1985, and a new Contadora draft was presented in September. Despite considerable rewording, it contained much the same provisions which had prompted the previous deadlock. Although the negotiations were formally suspended for five months in December, a new initiative was nevertheless made in January 1986, containing a number of elements for reducing tensions which may still be pursued. However, as indicated by the failure to reach any agreement in June 1986, the most immediate obstacles to a settlement, centring on the issues of Nicaraguan politics and the 'Contras', will be unlikely to be overcome until the fate of those forces is determined.

Guatemala

By early 1986, the Administration could point to a number of apparently positive movements in Guatemala in the direction desired by its policy. Although human rights abuse and political violence have continued, and there has continued to be grave international concern at treatment of the Indian population, the situation is certainly better than in the most horrific days. The guerrilla threat appears to have been militarily contained for the present. The military has handed over power to a civilian regime through the elections which took place at the end of 1985. The convincingly elected new President, Christian Democrat Vinicio Cerezo, is of the most moderate centre, thus seeming to support the US Administration's assertion that in 1984, 'Shattering the stereotype of hopeless polarization, the Guatemalan electorate turned out in record numbers . . . to support the political center.'[1] The revolutionary Left has indeed been weakened by the electoral process itself, particularly with the participation in elections of the Democratic Socialist Party (PSD), which had been more or less clandestine since the assassination of its leaders in 1978 but has recently been permitted to campaign openly. So long as that process is not disrupted, the revolutionary forces will probably be weakened by the success of the moderate Cerezo, himself the target of assassination attempts in the past. The process has also weakened the immediate position of the most extreme Right.

However, despite Cerezo's achievements, there is still only limited room for optimism – and none for US complacency. The guerrillas are still there, if territorially restricted. Numbers may have fallen to only some 2000 from around 6000 in 1981–82, but there were 'only' 2000 Salvadorean guerrillas in 1980, and there have been guerrillas in Guatemala in rising and falling numbers for more than 20 years. The elections will bring, at best, the beginning of democratisation in a country which has almost no real civilian institutions. The military have handed over formal power, having had many strong incentives to do so. They could then appear to retire voluntarily and before economic crisis brought total discredit, while failure to retire would have prevented any restoration of full US military aid, the desired increase in US non-military aid and granting of European aid. The military saw the restoration of formal civilian rule in Honduras and El Salvador bringing greater external assistance, and they have not been entirely insensitive to the international pariah status of Guatemala. Many officers also seem to have felt that the demands of administering the country have impeded their conduct of the war, and that political and economic power, including individual enrichment, have threatened the Army's institutional harmony and integrity. However, such incentives cannot necessarily be counted upon indefinitely to keep the military even formally out of power. Were economic chaos to develop and threaten to bring unmanageable social disorder, were the new President to attempt to implement measures which seemed unacceptably to challenge established interests, or were he to challenge the military directly, then another coup is not unlikely. The clear expectation of a total cut-off of US aid in such a situation will be important in dissuading this, but cannot be considered certain to stop such groups in some circumstances.

In early 1986, Cerezo acted quickly, and apparently with Army agreement, against the notorious secret police unit, the Department of Technical Investigations, in immediate response to four death squad killings which greeted his inauguration. Some of its agents may even be investigated and prosecuted for past abuses. However, despite continuing debate as to the legality of the general amnesty decreed by the outgoing military government, Cerezo has implied that he will not risk attempting to bring to justice those in the military most responsible for the massive and criminal abuses of recent years. He will have to be very cautious with regard to such fundamental structural problems and highly sensitive political issues, as land and tax reform. And he will have to be extremely cautious over any possible talks with the revolutionary Left.

Formal removal of the military is only a prerequisite, and only one condition, for stable political progress. The familiar problem remains that the success of the policy depends upon the military's simultaneously withdrawing from politics and 'guaranteeing the political process'. Moreover, the obstacles to establishing full civilian rule, and those to overcoming political polarisation by fostering peaceful reform and development, are not identical. The new Government will have to take into account not only the military's institutional and individual power and interests, but also the powerful business sector and civilian far Right.

Like all other Central American states, it will face these challenges amid dire economic crisis. Debt service claimed 37 per cent of export earnings in 1985, predicted to rise to 50 per cent for 1986, while traditional export prices have been low and markets, particularly in Central America, restricted. National financial reserves are negative, and although taxation is very low (under half the Central American average and mainly on exports), the business sector has fiercely opposed any shift to higher income and corporation taxes. Inflation was around 60 per cent in late 1985, with industry running at only 60 per cent capacity, and unemployment (and underemployment) at over 40 per cent. Public spending has already been cut to 3.8 per cent of GDP, mainly at the expense of health and education,[2] and the

September 1985 rioting against increases in bus fares and bread and milk prices indicated the predictable strength of public reaction to much stronger austerity measures. Even economic stabilisation, quite apart from any possible new social investment or redistributive measures, will put the Government between conflicting pressures of labour and capital. Although organised labour is now relatively weak, still subdued by fear and with limited links to the revolutionary Left, the business sector is powerful, organised and largely tied to the Guatemalan far Right. Social and economic deterioration could well bring greatly increased urban unrest, which could easily take on ideological terms, undermine the current political process, and directly feed the armed conflict.

The new Government's regional policy will also be significant in both relations with the US and domestic politics. Of greatest national sensitivity will be the question of Belize, Guatemala's claim to which has been the source of a long-standing territorial dispute with the United Kingdom. This question remains an important political issue in Guatemala, particularly for the nationalist Right. Belize was not recognised by Guatemala in 1981 when it became independent from the United Kingdom, which has consequently agreed to retain a military presence in Belize in order to guarantee the country against possible Guatemalan attack. The issue of Belize has further complicated US–Guatemalan relations, and brought another dimension to the vexed question of US military ties with Guatemala. In 1983 and 1984, the British Government voiced some concern even over the resumption by the US of arms sales and a limited military training programme. Both the UK and the US, as well as the Government of Belize, are anxious for some agreement to be reached, but progress has been slow.

The Guatemalan position has partly reflected tradition and nationalism, but there is also a central demand for Guatemala to have unimpeded access to the Caribbean. Its small northern coastline opens on to the Gulf of Honduras but is overhung by territory belonging to Belize. After the March 1982 coup, the new military government dropped Guatemala's claims to the entire country, but still demanded the whole southern district of Toledo in exchange for recognition of Belize. Talks between Guatemala and Belize, with the United Kingdom present as an observer, were held in January 1983, and again in May and July 1984. Some further drop in Guatemalan demands appeared to be made, including the possibility of transferring only two small islands or simply changing the maritime boundaries. In the last talks held in February 1985, however, pressures on the Guatemalan Government from hardline military and political sectors brought a return to much the same position as before. By mid-1985, the atmosphere for talks appeared to have improved, but no further movement took place as the Guatemalan Presidential Elections neared. Once elected, however, Cerezo openly stated an interest in reaching what he described as an 'honourable agreement' with Belize, apparently being prepared to drop Guatemala's territorial claims in exchange for 'guarantees for our right to an outlet to the sea'. New talks now seem probable. An agreement ending the territorial dispute could ease a number of international tensions for the Cerezo Government, including some with the US. However, talks leading to an agreement could well provoke hostility to Cerezo from the nationalist Right and part of the Guatemalan military. Moreover, any allegations that Cerezo was bowing to US pressure would complicate, and possibly undermine, other crucial aspects of US policy.

Problems of a different sort may arise from Cerezo's attitude toward Nicaragua. Cerezo will probably try to continue the policy of official 'neutrality', which had already drawn fire on the previous Foreign Minister from the Guatemalan Right for its supposed softness on Communism. He has also begun his term with a burst of diplomatic activity designed to help to reduce political tensions in Central America. This may only increase his many other predictable frictions with the Guatemalan Right and business sector. With regard to Nicaragua, moreover, it also goes against the current thrust of US policy. Any US attempts to bring the new Government into line with its policy in this respect may create further difficulties for Cerezo and exacerbate internal tensions.

The question of US military aid to Guatemala has not created great controversy recently, because it has been clearly rejected or strictly limited by Congress when requested. Only sales of spare parts, and an International Military Training and Education (IMET) programme had been authorised by the end of 1985. Cerezo's inauguration, if there is no dramatic worsening of the human rights situation, will almost certainly permit a limited resumption of most forms of military aid. If requested and given, however, this would draw the US more directly into the Guatemalan crisis, and provoke greater concerns and debates.

There is a military need, or justification, for aid, even though its lack does not immediately threaten the Army's survival. Self-help and alternative sources have sufficed thus far, but supplies are limited, and the Army has significant problems in logistics and mobility. The debate will continue more to concern the behaviour of the Armed Forces and the political implications of aid. Many stress the fact that the withholding of aid has been one factor encouraging a return to civilian rule. Others argue rather that it diminished US political influence and understanding, nearly losing direct contact with an entire generation of Guatemalan officers, while nationalist resentment was one of the factors encouraging Guatemala to be less than fully co-operative in US regional policy. Most Republicans now argue that aid should be fully restored to give the military encouragement and confidence in continuing the political process. It also seems desirable to help deal with the guerrillas as soon as possible and remove at least that threat to the process. Many Democrats, on the other hand, argue that aid, if at all, should be absolutely conditional, and given more in recognition than encouragement of political and human rights improvements. While ensuring military containment of the guerrillas, aid must not strengthen military power and presence, including militarised centres of rural control, and undermine the demilitarisation not only of the Presidency but of the country as a whole.

The key determinant of how US aid of all types is given must be the new Government's own requests, and its views of what will best assist consolidation of its own authority, and of the process of democratisation. Given the power of the military and the business sector, and the pressing economic and social demands of the country, Cerezo is in an extremely difficult and vulnerable position. He has indicated that precipitate receipt of security assistance may not ease the transition process. Whatever happens, the US will face a formidable challenge. US material aid and political commitment will be of central importance in protecting the process but US aid and political pressure are sensitive issues for all parties in Guatemala. Too little or too much could weaken Cerezo's position.

The Administration is aware, and will be constantly reminded, that collapse of the current process and US failure this time round to ensure genuine progress toward democratic institutionalisation and socio-economic reform in Guatemala, would threaten almost uncontrollable conflict and make it very hard to secure aid even in the case of a new revolutionary threat to the regime's survival. There may be fears, or for the Administration perhaps hopes, of embarking on 'another El Salvador', but comparisons with El Salvador are dubious. The Administration can argue that aid to Guatemala will begin after, not before, the peak of guerrilla strength, and when the military is preparing in voluntary and relatively orderly fashion to hand over power. However, the fundamental problems in Guatemala are not identical and are in some respects even greater.

Much will depend on whether – and what – the Administration has learnt from the Salvadorean experience; on whether, among other things, it can prevent ideological sympathy for its local allies in the fight against Communism and the defence of free enterprise and the anti-Communist rhetoric of its regional policy from exacerbating internal conflicts, and – from the beginning – can make an unequivocal, credible and effective commitment to political and social change. The capacity of the US quickly to exert such influence should not be overestimated, especially in view of Guatemalans' strong nationalism, and there are many reasons for it to adopt a relatively cautious and gradual approach.

The situation in Guatemala is so volatile that predictions for the near future are practically impossible. The worst that can be feared is a total collapse of the current political process and resurgence of the past extremes of violence, with very serious consequences for the whole region, and for US policy. The best that can be hoped for is probably that Cerezo will remain in office, the economy will begin to stabilise, the violence and abuses will be reduced, and that the process of civilian institutionalisation will continue, however slowly. If the regional crisis could be settled, and the most favourable external political and economic influences established, the path to democracy and development in Guatemala might possibly still be found.

El Salvador

By mid-1985, the Administration could claim with satisfaction that 'There has been no second Vietnam in El Salvador. And El Salvador will not become a second Cuba.'[3] The prospect that the US might have to face the choice of direct US intervention or revolutionary triumph indeed seemed remote. The Administration could claim progress in the military dimension of its policy and in the political process, movement in the vital area of human rights, continuation of the 1980 reforms and efforts at peace talks.

The Armed Forces have significantly improved in equipment, command and co-ordination, tactical performance, intelligence, training, leadership and morale, if not in logistic planning. The number of effective junior officers and NCOs has begun to catch up with the rapid troop expansion of the last three years, and the Army has become closer to an institution capable of sustained combat in which promotion and prestige depend on military capacity rather than length of service or personal and class loyalties. The greatly expanded helicopter inventory has permitted much more rapid troop movement and reinforcement. The provision of five C-47 airborne fire support platforms (two AFSP aircraft operational and three on strength by the end of 1985), and of helicopter gunships with miniguns and rocket pods, has brought a massive increase in aerial firepower. This improvement in aerial capacity has not discouraged effective action on the ground to the extent feared, and may help end reliance on less selective and increasingly inappropriate aerial and artillery bombardment. Confidence in the rapid arrival of reinforcements and air cover has reduced the tendency of troops to break and run; and rapid evacuation of casualties has raised morale.

The guerrilla forces, on the other hand, have been reduced in numbers, perhaps to between 5000 and 8000 combatants. They are experiencing greater supply problems, internally and externally, and some shortages of food, clothing and medicines. Their areas of effective control are smaller and they have lost, physically as much as politically, much of their once relatively stable and organised popular base in such areas. They have been forced to move much more and to break up into smaller units, concentrating on economic sabotage and disruption, and taking the war more into urban areas. Some aspects of these changed tactics, particularly the increasing number of political kidnappings and assassinations and blunt military response of some groups to the changing political situation, have revealed strains between the guerrilla forces of the FMLN and, more openly, between the FMLN and the FDR, the political wing of the revolutionary alliance.

However, the revolutionaries are by no means defeated, and the war continues. In the second half of 1985, both sides were adapting their tactics and preparing to increase the pressure. Having given the Armed Forces some basic mobility and firepower, US military assistance was now to focus on night operations, in which they have remained deficient, and on 'pink teams' (a reconnaissance helicopter to locate guerrilla units, and then a gunship to hold them down while ground forces are brought in), as well as civic action, Civil Defence, psychological operations and greater co-ordination with the police and para-military security forces. This last element will be strengthened by the funds released at the end of 1985 for the Administration's Regional Counter-Terrorist Programme. However, the FMLN continues its strategy of long-term attrition. While tending deliberately to avoid contact with large Government units sent to dislodge them, the guerrillas still seem able to hold certain 'controlled' areas which they are determined to keep. They are still capable of mounting larger-scale attacks, as most clearly illustrated by the October 1985 attack on an army training centre in the east of the country, with army losses of 42 dead and 70 wounded. They have spread the war more broadly, increasing small-scale activity in urban areas and western regions, and stepping up the campaign of economic sabotage and disruption. And they continue to inflict substantial casualties, even if a large proportion of these, at times as high as 70 per cent, is the result of mines. However, the Armed Forces' casualty rate may have fallen. Official figures for the twelve months from 1 July 1983 to 30 June 1984 were of 1055 dead and 1783 wounded. For the same period in 1984–85 they were of 807 dead and 1885 wounded.

As noted earlier, there can be no quick victory. Given the strength of the US commitment to the government forces, and the current problems with supply and recruitment apparently being experienced by the guerrillas, it may be that attrition in the military dimension will work against the latter in the long run. However, almost all parties recognise that there is no military solution to the conflict in sight, and that the crucial front, both internally and internationally, is political.

By mid-1985, the Administration could point to political progress. The legislative and municipal elections of March 1985 were striking in their results, given President Duarte's difficulties and the appearance of continued polarisation. The centrist PDC won an unexpected, and unassisted, outright victory. Although the Right-wing coalition's failure did not reflect a decline in the base support of the far Right, it seemed to indicate the falling appeal of the extremism typified by D'Aubuisson. The aftermath was to seem even more potentially significant. Whereas the Army had in previous elections been accused of illegally supporting the Right, it was now accused by the far Right of assisting in fraud on behalf of the PDC. The entire High Command went on television to denounce the Right for its 'insulting' and undemocratic political games. The impression was that the Army had broken its traditional alliance with the far Right and the 'oligarchy'. It had certainly not formed an alliance with the PDC instead. It now claimed to identify its interests with the political process itself, the Defence Minister stressing that the Army 'has come to realize that the survival of the institution depends on our not going against the sovereign will of the people'.[4]

In the same period, there had been positive movement in human rights. More credible and unequivocal US pressures seemed to have brought greater acceptance in the Salvadorean High Command that success in the war depends upon the containment of the death squads and a reduction of abuses, which Army representatives asserted were recognised as past 'errors' which only played into the guerrillas' hands. The war in the countryside still brought deaths and abuses of civilians, on the ground and from the air, with resettlement and civic action programmes often having more destructive than constructive impact. However, massacres no longer seem to take place, there was more emphasis from above on winning public support, and the 'reincorporation' of guerrillas. Prisoners were taken, and although the amnesty provision formally lapsed, it continued to some extent informally. The number of overt death squad murders remained relatively very low, and police procedures were changed, with due notification and publicisation of official arrests seeming generally to be made. Moreover, in 1985 and 1986 there has been an increase in guerrilla actions considered by independent human rights groups to be violations, although the number of such violations is still fewer than those attributed to the military, security forces and death squads, while the increasing guerilla use of mines appears to have caused numerous civilian casualties.

However, the improvement has not been as great as the Administration claims and there seemed to have been some deterioration by early 1986. Prisoners are frequently abused and killings and 'disappearances' do continue. These are still well below the worst levels of the past, but sufficient to raise serious questions about Duarte's ability to end human rights abuses and exert full control over the military and security forces.

Progress in the administration of justice has been small. The US is well aware of the crucial importance of establishing a credible and equitable judicial system, and of remedying the tremendous defects in the Salvadorean system's technical base, professional capacity and standing. US programmes in this respect will remain vital to any success of its policy. Justice will have to be seen to be done not only effectively but even-handedly, and with no-one appearing to be above the law. The 1984 trial and imprisonment, at US insistence, of the National Guardsmen who carried out the 1980 murder of four American churchwomen did have a positive public effect. In most such cases, however, justice continues visibly not to have been done, and probably no officer will ever be judicially punished. The High Command may have been willing to bring about changes in many respects but it does not want to go over the past. This is partly out of loyalty to its own, partly to avoid confronting figures and groups out of or still in the Army and Security Forces whose acceptance of the new line is tenuous and who might respond with renewed acts against the current process, and partly because unrestricted investigation and action might be uncomfortable for some of the High Command itself. There may have been an understanding that in exchange for present and future improvements, the past will be forgotten. With the possible exception of the 1981 murder of the Salvadorean land reform official and two US advisers, the US seems willing to go along with that. Since the number of officers who have been removed or transferred by the military itself has been small, this appearance of the military's being above the law will remain a political problem. With all the other problems, and clearly mounting tensions with Duarte, the burden of proof that it has really changed will remain very much with the military.

The 1980 reforms are still in place, and the land reform has had some success. The decree giving 'land to the tiller' ended in 1984, having had limited positive effects and various negative consequences. The Basic Law's first phase, however, has had considerable impact, both in its practical benefits and in weakening revolutionary claims, but it is beset by problems such as the agrarian debt, shortages and shortcomings in credit provision, lack of managerial skills and a large backlog in titling. No implementary legislation for the second phase, affecting medium-size holdings, had been passed by the Constitutional deadline at the end of 1985, and it is doubtful whether it can take effect in the near future, if ever. The Government seems divided as to whether to push ahead with this phase. It will probably, as generally supported by the US Agency for International Development (AID), tend to consolidate and make viable the existing transfers, rather than move to new distribution. The success and effective expansion of the programmes of Phase One will be crucial for the Government's political position in the countryside. However, although demographic pressures may make the generation of industrial employment at least as important as further land distribution, much more will eventually have to be done to respond to rural problems, including the massive challenge posed by the half-million displaced persons.

Finally, the US Administration can point to President Duarte's moves in late 1984 and 1986 toward dialogue with the rebels as evidence of its own interest in a peaceful, political solution.

All these developments have led to a reduction of Congressional opposition to US aid, even if this increased support often is more for Duarte's than for Reagan's policy and Democrats are determined to ensure that their concerns continue to figure in legislation. They have also brought an increase in the international legitimacy of the Salvadorean Government. Both domestic US and international support, however, are still qualified, and easily reversible.

Vulnerabilities of the Duarte Government

Indeed, all these apparent successes, even so far as they have gone, are still tenuous and very fragile. Much of that fragility arises from the disastrous state of the Salvadorean economy. There has been some $1.2 billion (US) in direct destruction since 1979. Despite such signs of confidence in holders of capital as an increase in residential construction, there is still almost no new productive investment as a result of high uncertainty because of the war and because of disagreements and mistrust between government and private sector. Foreign investment has been practically impossible to attract. 'Reform sector' production faces problems of almost every sort. Low prices on coffee, cotton and sugar have only increased the drop in production and export revenue. Service of an external debt of some $1.9 billion accounts for around 30 per cent of falling export revenues. Defence accounts for some 50 per cent of a chaotic budget, while there has been no coherent government economic policy at all. The economy is still nationally inadequate: GDP grew by 1.5 per cent in 1984, and perhaps by 2 per cent in 1985, but population growth is 3 per cent. The economy is also dependent to the point of artificiality: external aid accounts for around one-quarter of GDP. And the social consequences of economic muddle are severe. Inflation is over 50 per cent, and unemployment may be as high as 55 per cent. Living standards remain at half their pre-war level, with acute shortages in housing and other basic needs.

Even without the war, Duarte would face tremendous challenges, being caught between the demands of organised labour, the more radical Christian Democrats, private sector interests, financial constraints and pressures from the US, and powerful conservative opposition. As it is, he must try to bring about economic recovery, social improvement and political stabilisation, while devoting half the budget to the military and facing a determined revolutionary opposition whose open objective is to prevent consolidation of the Government (which many on the far Left recognised as providing a serious *political* challenge) and to put sufficient military, political and diplomatic pressure on both it and the US to force a negotiated solution to the conflict which satisfies their minimum positive demands.

The political battle against the rebels depends on showing continuing progress toward democracy and the satisfaction of legitimate popular demands. The 1984 peace talks seem very distant in late 1986, and certainly can no longer distract attention from pressing problems, while the unsuccesful attempt to hold a third round of talks in September 1986 seems unlikely to ease Duarte's situation much in this respect. So far, the principal instrument in showing democratic progress has been the electoral process itself. After March 1985, there are no more elections scheduled for some years. Moreover, the fact that since the last elections Duarte has had power at all formal levels may not necessarily help him. He now has no formal excuse not to fulfil many of his social promises, while his gaining of total political power only increased the concerns of the private sector and the opposition, concerns which the PDC quickly seemed to confirm with the dubiously legal removal of the Rightist Attorney-General. Duarte must somehow make both social and economic improvements without either further alienating the private sector or seeming to ally himself with business interests. At the same time, the political initiative gained by opening up spaces for greater political and union activities must not be lost by a harsh response to the demands predictably arising, yet Duarte cannot be seen by the private sector, or by the military, to be giving in to radical forces. Both problems were illustrated by the wave of strikes and labour demands in 1985. The disastrous economic situation has not to date led to political turmoil to the extent which could be feared but even PDC union groupings have already been making clear their disillusion, and joining the more radically-led unions in demands for peace talks with the rebels. The austerity measures announced by Duarte in early 1986, including a devaluation, rises in petrol prices of 50 per cent and in bus fares of 20 per cent, were not compensated by the 15 per cent rise in the minimum wage, increase in public employees' salaries and the freezing of prices on some basic foodstuffs. These moves will certainly increase his problems with labour.

There is a possibility that this situation could assist the rebels in their attempts to strengthen their urban base, which would be a significant change in the balance of the war. Whether or not this occurs depends only partially upon more efficient police and security systems. On the one hand, it will be affected by popular reaction to the other aspect of the rebels' urban activities, which is destabilisation through an increase in urban violence. These attacks may have negative political consequences, especially internationally, which counteract the other potential advances. They may increase popular pressure to end the war somehow, but may not endear the revolutionaries to many in a scared and war-weary populace. Nor do they seem to contribute to the process of negotiation. On the other hand, much will depend on the response of the Government to both the strike movements and these urban guerrilla actions. It is possible that too flexible handling of the situation could weaken Duarte's position with regard to the Right and the military. His willingness to exchange his kidnapped daughter for more than twenty captured guerrillas, including senior commanders, prompted clear discontent in the military in late 1985 and fears that the tougher officers could move against the President. By early 1986 there was a broad and clear feeling within the military that Duarte was losing on the political and economic fronts the war which they believed they were winning on the battlefield. Right-wing pressures on Duarte have also increased, although the High Command seems at present to be holding to its new line of support for the Constitutional, and US-backed, President.

However, if the situation brings too harsh an official response or contributes to a resurgence of Right-wing violence, a renewed polarisation is possible which would weaken both internal support for the Government and domestic and international support for US policy. Either or both may be being sought by the rebels.

There are other factors weakening the Government, including the already scandalous corruption of some of its members. Moreover, Duarte himself is a point of fragility. Although PDC support does not depend on him alone, there is almost no other PDC leader with both his national and international standing and relatively honest image. His own history and personality, notably the mutual antipathy between him and the economic elite, make him in some respects an imperfect national reconciler, but there are few other figures who could have done even what he has done.

The prospects for El Salvador

Any hopes that Duarte could reach an understanding with the revolutionary opposition seem to have been dashed, however. The two rounds of talks held in La Palma and Ayagualo in October and November 1984 only emphasised the gulf between the demands of the FDR-FMLN, including some form of provisional power-sharing and immediate military restructuring, and the basic position of the Salvadorean Government and Armed Forces. The failure even to reach agreement over the conditions for a third round of talks, which had tentatively been scheduled to take place in Sesori on 19 September 1986, has made the prospects for productive dialogue seem bleaker than ever. Duarte himself may want a quick and peaceful end to the conflict, realising that effective recovery and development will be impossible while the war continues. However, there is a limit to what he is willing to offer, and he will not talk on the basis of the illegitimacy of his government or his presidency. There are even greater limits to what is acceptable to those upon whom he now depends: the military, the private sector and the US Administration. There is still strong internal and international pressure for talks with the rebels. In the US Congress, the unclear rebel commitment to elections as the primary determinant of power has weakened support for negotiation all the more since the Government has been elected, although pressure for talks with the guerrillas in search of common ground is likely to continue. However, the commitment to prolonged war, and lack of any common ground with Duarte, of most of the FMLN makes it seem unlikely that they will move toward a position which is a generally acceptable basis for peace.

The US Administration accepts that there can be no quick solution. It would resist any arrangement, which is in any case unlikely, appearing to question the legitimacy and viability of a regime which is its Central American 'success story' and in which it has invested so much money and credibility. It will certainly not be willing to legitimise an armed revolutionary movement which it has sworn to oppose and whose success it would perceive as an expansion of hostile forces linked to Nicaragua. Moreover, the Administration believes that any broad coalition government which included the Marxist revolutionary groups would lead to the eventual exclusion of all the others. Its objective is therefore to consolidate the current process and to isolate the rebels politically; to inflict debilitating blows to their military capability and contain the remaining guerrillas geographically; and eventually to offer sufficiently credible and attractive guarantees of personal security and legal political participation to bring in to the system as many revolutionaries as possible. Even if a number of guerrillas remained in certain areas, that outcome is the most that the Administration can, and does, hope for.

At best, it will be a prolonged and nasty winding-down of the war. It is possible that the rebels will be acceptably contained in the near future, but there can be no certainty about that. It may not happen in the next ten years. The extent of the continuing problems poses the risk that the war will be prolonged and nasty without winding down, threatening to reverse even those political and human rights improvements achieved thus far, and bring the country even closer to total ruin.

Even if the war does wind down, the question will remain of whether US policy will have helped to establish the conditions for longer-term stability in El Salvador. Even if the guerrillas disappeared entirely, the problems would not. The direct leverage given by the need for US military aid, however, would be diminished. If the institutional basis for democracy and social development is not thoroughly consolidated first, quite apart from the massive economic problems and the challenge of half a million displaced persons, success would have been illusory. Military and security forces will number well over 50000, while civic action and Civil Defence will have established a thoroughly militarised network throughout the country. Those of the far Right, the economic elite, and those in the military who have in the past fought against change will not have disappeared, and some might well see in a removal of the guerrilla threat only an opportunity to reassert themselves. There will have been no progress without, at least, a credible and effective independent judicial system, an irreversible general acceptance of democratic procedures and new social priorities, and a full and sincere professionalisation, and subsequent reduction, of the Armed Forces. For that to happen, the US will have, at the very least, to provide what the State Department has recognised as the requirement for 'both the reliability of a long-term U.S. commitment and the confidence that this commitment will continue to be tied to equity, reform, and freedom'.[5]

Nicaragua

In Nicaragua, the stated parameters of US policy remain: 'the two extremes the American people want to avoid: a second Cuba, this time on the Central American mainland; and a second Vietnam, with American troops mired in combat'.[6] The Reagan Administration therefore claims to have 'ruled out courses of action that would amount to acceptance of Sandinista goals and abandonment of our own objectives, and direct application of U.S. military force'.[7] Support for the rebels is presented as the only immediate alternative to those two extremes, a 'second Cuba' being seen as the inevitable consequence of US failure to act at all, while direct force 'must realistically be recognized as an eventual option, given our stakes in the region, if other policy alternatives fail'.[8] They are also presented as the best means to work toward the objective of a reliable regime in Nicaragua which would remove all such threats in the long term. The same broad parameters thus define both US policy instruments and US primary, and primarily negative, policy goals. The possible implication that as long as the instruments remain in place, the goals will by definition be minimally achieved, is strengthened by a new global and ideological commitment to the Nicaraguan rebels by much of the Administration.

The original drive to restore US confidence, security and credibility in and through Central America still gives 'geopsychological' importance to the anti-Sandinista campaign but there is now also a greater emphasis by some Administration officials on the global significance of support for the 'Contra' rebels, as well as of general opposition to the Sandinistas. This partly reflected the rhetorical needs of the aid debates, with Reagan asking Congress to 'be consistent and support those who are fighting communism in Nicaragua, just as we support the democratic resistance in Afghanistan and Cambodia'.[9] Such statements helped to parry questions as to the character and prospects of the Nicaraguan rebels, and encouraged wavering Congressmen not to appear 'soft on communism'. But they also both reflected and helped to strengthen a modified ideological approach by many in the Administration: 'If these people can stand up and throw off Communism, it goes beyond Managua. It goes to the gut of our national interest. The way to go after the Soviet Union is through the colonies. We have to find ways to help democratic resistance movements without sending troops'.[10] By mid-1985, the Administration clearly felt that national strength, confidence, and even consensus, had gone a long way toward being restored. With the impact of the Grenadan action, the apparent success in El Salvador, and a number of anti-Communist guerrilla movements throughout the world, the Administration no longer felt so much on the defensive in Central

America, nor saw the global tide running so much against the US. Having been told in the latter 1970s that the US had to adapt itself to the forces of history, which seemed to mean the Left, many now leap at the notion of an era of anti-Communist revolution. 'After years of guerrilla insurgencies led by Communists against pro-Western governments, we now see dramatic and heartening examples of popular insurgencies against Communist regimes. If we turned our backs . . . we would be conceding the Soviet notion that Communist revolutions are irreversible while everything else is up for grabs'.[11] In this respect, Nicaragua in Reagan's second Administration appears to some extent the reverse of El Salvador at the beginning of the first. Helping to 'draw the line' somewhere against the expansion of International Communism then seemed especially important and relatively easy in El Salvador. Helping to push that line back somewhere now seems to be especially desirable, and perhaps possible, in Nicaragua.

It seems to present the eventual possibility of satisfyingly doing right what was done wrong before, or is harder to do elsewhere. On the one hand, it is not only to avoid another Cuba, but to do successfully to the Sandinistas what was *not* done to Castro before he established total internal control and received Soviet commitments and guarantees. On the other it is to help an anti-Communist insurgency to succeed in Nicaragua – which may be easier than in Afghanistan, Kampuchea or Angola against direct Soviet, Vietnamese or Cuban involvement – and even to achieve what might be claimed as the unprecedented reversal of a regime said to be Communist, and even 'behind the Iron Curtain'.[12] It seems possible because of the economic crisis and broad discontent within Nicaragua, and the numbers of the rebel forces. But it may also seem possible, less explicitly, because of Nicaragua's geographic location and international situation.

With Castro's Cuba and the Soviet naval presence, the US position in the Caribbean is no longer unquestioned, but most would assert that US power remains predominant in the region. Part of the Carter Administration had believed that this dominance permitted a relative flexibility in response to internal changes and local challenges to US influence. The increase in Cuban military strength and Soviet naval activities has been one factor encouraging the Reagan Administration to take a firmer position in defence of US strategic interests. However, that continued predominance has also seemed to encourage and permit relative patience and tactical flexibility on the US part in pursuing indirect courses to force internal changes and restore a situation of unquestioned US influence and security at least in Central America.

Part of the genuine concern about Nicaraguan forces levels in regional terms is that it might make it impossible for other Central

American countries alone credibly to deter or respond to 'unconventional attack' through support for revolution and subversion. There is an apparent element in the Administration's case that immediate measures to prevent Sandinista consolidation are all the more necessary in order to ensure that the regime does not reach a situation of such strength that it would become a serious problem for the US itself to deal with. However, it is questionable whether Nicaragua could ever become an unmanageable problem for the US. It is surrounded by US allies, it is a very long way from Moscow and, as the Administration emphasises, as close to Texas and Florida as Washington. Even in the hypothetical case of a military conflict between Nicaragua and US allies in Central America in which the US did not directly intervene, any US ally would have an overwhelming logistic advantage, one reason for the stockpiling of arms in Nicaragua. US officials believe that it would take 'a quantum leap' before the Nicaraguans themselves became a military problem that the US could not 'readily' deal with – and that in any case the Sandinistas would reach their own threshold in terms of economic costs long before they could possibly reach any threshold of concern to the US. No Soviet Bloc combat presence exists or is likely to be inserted. The US is naturally concerned that any action or invasion might provoke involvement by other powers, but it is not generally thought likely that the USSR or Cuba would make any serious commitment to the defence of the Nicaraguan Government. Nor is it certain that the Soviet Union is willing to provide the same kind of open-ended economic commitment to Nicaragua as it gives to Cuba.

There are many reasons for US concern about the Sandinistas' present state, including their ties to the Soviet Bloc and the extent of their resemblance to Cuba in their internal and external behaviour. But, given the differences in the international situation of Nicaragua and Cuba, many critics of the US Administration suggest that it may be inappropriate and unnecessarily restrictive, however appealing, to define policy toward Nicaragua in the terms of the Cuban experience. There is even more tension in the Administration's new global and ideological dimension. It is not only easier to roll back the Iron Curtain where it is not hanging than where it is, but impossible that it can be hanging in Nicaragua, since an Iron Curtain regime is one which the US knows that the Soviet Union will militarily prevent from being reversed. Nicaragua cannot realistically be placed in the same class as Eastern Europe; it will not really even be in the same situation as Angola or Kampuchea, far less Afghanistan, provided that there is no Cuban or Soviet Bloc combat support for the Sandinistas. The Administration can argue that it wants to prevent a Communist regime, but it cannot also claim to want to reverse a Communist regime, far less to show in Nicaragua that 'the democracies simply cannot put up with a Brezhnev Doctrine'.[13]

This new type of commitment will continue to tie the Administration all the more closely to the Nicaraguan rebels, to permit an additional rationalisation of their unclear prospects and of its own inability to offer a precise statement of how it sees their prospects, and to allow it to claim some success so long as they have any prospects at all. While the rebels do continue to operate, direct US military action will be all the less likely, but the Administration's constant assertion of its increased probability in the case of their failure, as an alternative to an Iron Curtain 'second Cuba', will have made it all the harder for the US to explore other options if they do eventually fail. Nevertheless, although the Sandinistas would be as wrong to believe privately that US military action against them is impossible as they have been shown wrong in their repeated public assertions of its imminence, there will remain formidable obstacles to direct US military action in most circumstances.

The Improbability of Intentional Military Action

A decision in Washington to opt for unilateral, armed removal of the Sandinistas is extremely unlikely in current circumstances. This is not to say that it could not be done; rather that it most probably will not. The US would almost certainly feel that regional support was essential, and the chances of any multilateral decision to provide that support are not great. Few OAS countries would lend themselves to such an action. Within *Condeca*, only the Hondurans have forces available. The Guatemalan military are both uninterested and busy with their own revolutionaries, while the Salvadorean forces are tied down with the FMLN. Costa Rica has no army and would find it politically almost impossible to give public support to any such action. Even the US' closest allies hesitate at the thought of invasion, and few of those in Honduras and Costa Rica who do express a desire for the US to remove the Sandinistas want to have to help. Moreover, there has not yet been anything approaching an internationally convincing *casus belli*. A clear US decision with credible multilateral backing to overthrow the Sandinistas by direct military force is likely only in the highly improbable case of Nicaragua's unmistakeably implementing a decision of its own to overthrow a neighbouring government by direct military force.

The US has clearly increased its own military preparedness to deal with all contingencies in the area, including invasion of Nicaragua. Specific plans for invasion may have been drawn up, or revised, although the case is made that in view of US forces' state of readiness and the relative simplicity of the invasion phase, highly detailed plans are not needed. The nature of some joint exercises with Honduran forces has improved their capacity to carry out actions which would be appropriate in any action against Nicaragua: bombing runs and amphibious landings (*Big Pine II*, August 1983 – February 1984); airborne assault and holding of airfields (*Kilo Punch*, March 1984 and *Lightning II*, April 1984). Much of the military infrastructure created in the process, such as the airfields (particularly the improvement of the Palmerola air base to be able to handle anything in the US inventory) and medical facilities, could also be significant in any US action against Nicaragua.

However, the Administration clearly does not want military intervention, less still a unilateral invasion, even if it would probably not lead to troops being indefinitely mired in combat. Durable military control over most of the country could probably be established within a few months, especially since Nicaragua, rather than having any potential equivalent of the Ho Chi Minh trail, is bounded by sea on two sides and US allies to its north and south. However, in view of the predictable strength of national resistance and the difficult terrain within Nicaragua, such a mission would be very costly, far from easy, and probably involve continued commitment of US forces well after the neutralisation of such conventional Sandinista capabilities as exist. Official estimates of the costs of invasion are said not to have been made. An invasion scenario prepared by the Center for Defense Information (CDI) estimates up to 4000 US dead and 20000 wounded over four years, and a total of some $10 billion ($4 billion to pay for the men, munitions and supplies used and to replace lost equipment, and $6 billion for economic reconstruction). Another hypothetical scenario has put the costs of invasion and occupation at 2000 to 5000 US dead and 9000 to 19000 wounded, and at a total cost of $16 billion.[14] General Wallace Nutting, retired Commander of US Readiness Command, from which most of the combat units would have to be drawn, emphasised in late June 1985 that it would be a 'major operation' requiring 'multiple divisions and air support and sea support . . . There would be a big fight to dislodge them', which would drain US forces and distract attention from other parts of the world.[15] Statements reported by the press in June 1985 that, in view of Nicaragua's external geographic characteristics and perceived popular hostility to the Sandinistas, invasion was considered to be 'like falling off a log' are not representative of the assessments of responsible military personnel. Indeed, General Nutting's statements were said to be a response to talk about a possible invasion, which he deplored, 'by civilian members of the Reagan Administration' and to reflect 'a view widely held among senior military officers and echo[. . .] recommendations made by the Joint Chiefs of Staff to the President and the Secretary of Defense'.[16] There are elements in the Administration who are more inclined toward possible military action than the US Armed Services find comfortable. However, this spate of speculation about direct invasion did not necessarily signify any substantial shift within the Administration regarding military action. There was also a strong political interest both in concentrating Congressional minds on the desirability of supporting indirect measures through the forthcoming second vote on rebel aid, and in conveying to the Sandinistas that the Congressional defeat of the first request did not mean that the Administration was any less serious toward them.

The probable direct costs of invasion have increased since 1981, as has the perceived Sandinista military threat which has been part of the cause, and part of the result, of such an eventuality's not being consistently or convincingly ruled out. However, they have not been the principal determinant in consideration of military options. One potential deterrent is the possible increase in regional violence and conflict. If any invasion were carried out in co-operation with Honduran or other forces it would by definition be a regional war. The Sandinistas have claimed that any intervention could not be limited to Nicaragua because of the willingness of revolutionary forces in neighbouring countries to rise in their support or, in the case of the rebels in El Salvador, to take action against Honduran and Honduran-based US forces. There is a high probability that existing Left-wing guerrilla groups in Honduras and the far Left in Costa Rica, elements from which have already been fighting with the Sandinista forces, would take armed action, and that fighting would directly spill over from Nicaragua. The result would be a serious short-term destabilisation of both Honduras and Costa Rica. It is also possible that US forces might be drawn into direct conflict with the rebels in El Salvador. The consequences for Guatemala are unpredictable, but almost certainly negative. Given the small size of the Honduran and Costa Rican guerrilla groups, the Administration tends to see Sandinista promises of regional revolution as exaggerated. Nevertheless, it has no doubt that there would be a surge of 'terrorist' actions against the US throughout the hemisphere, and is aware that, even if the short-term guerrilla response was limited, invasion would in the medium term greatly increase the prospects of guerrilla movements throughout Central America and even beyond.

However, it is principally the political consequences which, if the Administration needs one, are the deterrent. President Reagan has openly recognised that the US' 'own friends and allies south of the border, friendly nations and the Organization of American States would not tolerate our going in with armed force in Latin America'.[17] Those countries could not stop it happening if the US were determined to go ahead, but it is generally agreed that it would 'jeopardize working relationships within the hemisphere'.[18] It would restore the traditional interventionist image of the US, undermine continental co-operation on many important issues, and weaken the 'Inter-American system' more than would the consolidation of the Sandinista regime. Many Latin American Governments would decide, or feel politically obliged, to take an anti-American stand over international issues, and tensions could easily spill over into management of the debt crisis. Invasion would have a serious destabilising effect in countries throughout the hemisphere, and particularly in the case of Mexico, much more so than any designs of international Communism. Even if it did not spark off revolution throughout Central America, it would certainly undo most of what political progress the US has made in the other countries.

Within the United States, there is little support for any use of US forces, except to counter a direct Soviet strategic threat or Nicaraguan direct aggression against America's allies, and practically none for an invasion to overthrow the Sandinistas. Such a course would have serious domestic consequences. It would cause significant divisions, weaken the national consensus behind US foreign policy which the Administration has wanted to restore, and certainly destroy the increased support for its Central American policies. Beyond the Western Hemisphere, it would strain relations with Western Europe, provoke a wave of anti-Americanism, and complicate the management of certain Alliance issues, although it is doubtful whether the future of NATO would be threatened. For the Soviet Union, it would constitute a tremendous propaganda bonus, which might seriously affect many Western interests in the Third World. It would distract global concern and US military resources and attention from other areas. And it would succeed in getting the US to do precisely what it has been trying to avoid: to become 'bogged down' in its own backyard. This, together with the consequences for domestic consensus, inter-American and transatlantic relations, might well outweigh in Soviet eyes any political and potential strategic benefits to be gained from the survival of a Sandinista regime, on which it has been careful not to stake its own credibility.

The Administration is aware of all these factors. Most in it also recognise that, even if a number of Nicaraguans – which appears in reality to be very small – may claim to want a US intervention, such a course would not only fail to solve the political problems, but be politically counter-productive. It would make martyrs of the Sandinistas and reduce the legitimacy of those forces congenial to the US, especially of those willing to participate in a successor government. Above all, it would be ideologically counter-productive for the Administration. It would more dramatically than anything else illustrate the failure of the insurgency to demonstrate the reversibility of 'communist regimes' from within.

It is not likely, as suggested in some quarters, that the Administration would seek some pretext for invasion in order that the President could leave office having honoured his commitment to deal with the Sandinistas. The Administration's ideological commitment and definition will probably continue to allow it to claim some success in Nicaragua almost whatever happens to destabilise the Sandinistas, so long as it is still happening. In El Salvador, the Administration believes that it has 'drawn the line' to the minimum extent necessary to constitute a success. That has not meant a quick and crushing defeat over the revolutionary forces, and a clear and consolidated 'victory for the forces of democracy'. The priority there, and the minimum definition of success has implicitly been only that the other side should not win, and thus seem to push the red line further. Likewise now it is that the Sandinistas should not win, and firmly establish the red line in Nicaragua. In this perspective – and quite apart from any underlying strategic rationale against Sandinista consolidation – to prevent the establishment of that red line, even without securing a more favourable regime, can be presented as sufficient to constitute a minimum success for US policy. Elliot Abrams, now Assistant Secretary of State for Inter-American Affairs, thus argued that despite the rebels' failure by October 1985 to make major military gains, 'they are holding their own and that's important. It means it's impossible for a Communist regime to be consolidated. That is a central achievement'.[19] So long as that can still be said, ideological honour will probably be satisfied.

While the insurgency continues, direct US military action against the regime is highly unlikely. If there were a satisfactory settlement, there would no longer be cause to consider military action. If the insurgency were irreversibly contained, there is a possibility of eventual direct action, depending on other circumstances, but pressures against it would still be strong. US military involvement is more likely in the less likely case of the rebels' approaching success. If this took the form of a collapse of the State and degeneration of the country into chaos affecting neighbouring countries, some form of collective intervention is possible. If the Nicaraguan rebels could establish a credible provisional government recognised by the US, 'military assistance' might well be provided, possibly involving combat troops to the extent necessary to ensure consolidation of the new regime.

116

Risks of Limited Action, Escalation and Unplanned Intervention

Limited US action

There are circumstances in which intentional direct action with limited objectives is possible. The principal of these were made explicit in June 1985 in a modified House amendment to the 1986 Defense Authorization Bill. The President would be free to use US land, sea or air power to 'meet a clear and present danger of hostile attack' against the US or its allies; to 'respond to hijacking, kidnapping, or other acts of terrorism' involving citizens of the US or an ally, and US installations and missions; or to respond to the introduction of MiG fighters or nuclear weapons. The introduction into Nicaragua of Soviet nuclear weapons is almost inconceivable. There is little advantage, even in theory, in having land-based missiles in Central America as opposed to submarine-launched missiles off the US seaboard, and certainly not enough to outweigh their vulnerability and the immense political and strategic risks of such a move. The two most likely causes of US actions with limited objectives and specific targets are therefore the introduction of Soviet fighters, and a terrorist attack on US personnel or installations in Central America.

In the first case, it is probable that the President would order surgical air strikes, even the use of special forces if necessary, to destroy any MiG fighters that had been introduced and assembled. The Sandinistas still hope to acquire jet interceptors from somewhere. It is highly improbable that any Western supplier would agree to sell such equipment. They would almost certainly have to come from the Soviet Bloc. The USSR might agree to supply MiG-21s if, for example, Honduran acquisition of advanced jet fighters were to make Nicaragua's acquisition of interceptors seem justified and their possible destruction by the US an unjustifiable act of aggression, and if the consequences for Soviet relations with the US were seen as acceptable. However, it remains likely that the Soviets will continue to resist Nicaraguan requests for delivery and assembly of the aircraft not least at a time when the Soviet Union seems concerned to mend fences with the US.

The second possibility – of a limited counter-terrorist strike – was aired publicly in the wake of the killing by guerrillas of four US Marines and two US civilians in San Salvador in June 1985. There was some consideration within the Administration of a surgical strike on an alleged base in Nicaragua at which some of those responsible were believed to have trained. Instead, the Nicaraguan Government was warned of 'serious consequences' if there was a further such incident to which the Nicaraguan Government was believed to be linked. If there were an attack on US citizens or installations in Central America which could conclusively and convincingly be shown to have been instigated or assisted by the Sandinistas, and if those responsible could convincingly be tied to some identifiable base in Nicaragua, some counter-measure would be likely. Depending on the nature and scale of the attack, and on the political climate in the US, it is not inconceivable that an attack on US personnel claimed by Left-wing guerrillas in El Salvador might bring some measure against any identifiable element of their organisation in Nicaragua, simply on the grounds that their headquarters were there. However, there is no unanimity within the Administration as to the desirability or prudence of such actions, and considerable difficulty (even for those who believe in them) to establish the necessary conditions in any particular case. The dangers and political counter-productivity, especially with regard to those targeted, of a counter-strike with indiscriminate effects would certainly be emphasised by many in (and outside) the Administration in any further incident.

Surgical strikes are possible in both the MiG and the counter-terrorist case but, especially if anything more than aerial attack were involved, there would be a possibility of accident or unforeseen circumstance leading to direct confrontation and escalation. Even without this possibility the problem would arise of how the Nicaraguans would respond. It would be politically very difficult for them to do nothing. Nicaragua might well break diplomatic relations and expel all US Embassy personnel, which would have the negative consequence of breaking all direct lines of communication. Internment of Embassy personnel, appearing as a seizure of US hostages, would greatly undermine that popular support for the Sandinistas and opposition to Administration policy in the US on which they partly rely, and would obviously risk war with the US. Unless they were killed or seriously mistreated, however, even that would only lead to further escalation if the US Administration wanted it to. There would be pressure from some elements in the Administration to take further action, and even to use the issue as a means to get rid of the Sandinista regime. However, there would be great pressure from those involved in Central American policy and opposed to any direct action, and at that point also from those in the Cabinet not previously involved in Central American policy but believing that the hostage situation did not warrant war. Escalation would be possible, but so would a diplomatic stand-off, during which third parties might secure the safe passage out of Nicaragua of the US personnel. Some entirely unpredictable Sandinista response cannot be ruled out but, while the possibility certainly exists in these cases of a chain of events leading to war, it is by no means a certainty.

There are other imaginable scenarios prompting US action, with greater probabilities of escalation and possibilities of broader conflict. The most obvious is the introduction of Cuban combat units into Nicaragua. Such an action cannot be ruled out but such a step would constitute such a clear escalation of the dangers that it is unlikely that either Nicaragua or the Cubans would contemplate it, or the Soviets condone it, even in the case of a Nicaraguan regime facing a military threat to its survival.

Border conflict

The other main area of concern about escalation is border conflict. It seems almost inconceivable that the Sandinistas would attempt to invade Honduras or Costa Rica but border incidents will continue while Nicaraguan rebels continue to use those countries' territory. There have been a great many incidents on the southern border. There have even been minor direct confrontations between Sandinista and Honduran forces on the northern border, the most dramatic coming in September 1985 when the Hondurans felt obliged to respond to Nicaraguan 'hot pursuit' operations and shellings by sending over *Super Mystère* fighters to attack Nicaraguan artillery positions. Even that incident, however, was controlled, neither side wanting to move to a larger conflict. Despite any Nicaraguan desire to keep their neighbours sensitive to the consequences of rebel use of their territory, they have been relatively cautious and controlled, concerned about the risks of precipitating US action against them. There are some within the Administration and US agencies who might see the possibility, even the provocation, of a border incident as providing a reason to act against the Sandinistas. However, even in the case of a relatively large Nicaraguan Army incursion in hot pursuit of rebel units, which is the most probable escalation of border tensions on the part of the Sandinistas, it remains unlikely that such voices would prevail in the US unless other circumstances were to have significantly changed also. In the case of some much more serious incident leading to a call for external help from a neighbour of Nicaragua, the US would probably restrict itself in the first instance to providing enough assistance for the country in question to feel that it was secure and that the US had responded adequately. It is also likely, particularly in the case of unarmed Costa Rica, that other countries would offer support and reassurance. There have already been talks with Panama and Venezuela regarding the possibility of their assisting Costa Rica in such a situation, perhaps with US logistic support.

To some extent, most parties are using the border issue as an element in diplomatic manoeuvrings, none wanting it to lead to a regional war which would almost certainly entail direct US involvement. The Sandinistas are in part playing up the dangers of border conflict and US intervention in order to achieve agreements about border control and security and to put international pressure on the US. While attempting to counter such efforts, the US Administration often emphasises the dangers and supposed Nicaraguan aggression in order to rally support for its policy. Fears of US invasion are not unwelcome if they might scare the Sandinistas into 'crying uncle', and inspire diplomatic activity with a sense of urgency which might bring increased international pressure on the Sandinistas to reach accommodation with their opponents in order to avert catastrophe.

There are, of course, always risks that the situation could get out of control. Nicaragua could, through miscalculation or desperation, simply go too far. Army actions on the northern border may intensify if there is a sharp increase in logistic support for the Nicaraguan rebels from Honduran territory. Even if they stay at the same level, however, the Hondurans may continue to feel the need to respond strongly. Indeed, it is likely that the larger actions will come from the Hondurans as they feel obliged to show themselves willing and able to defend national sovereignty, against supposedly unprovoked aggression. They did not consult the US before sending over their aircraft in September 1985, in what could possibly have led to further escalation. Although the US stated its approval of the action after the event, there seems to have been some concern about its prudence, particularly as it involved a use of Honduran aircraft which could strengthen Nicaragua's case for the acquisition of interceptors.

The prospects of uncontrollable escalation would seem to be limited, especially given the number of external actors who would move rapidly to prevent it. In the case of the borders – as in the case of limited US actions – it is always possible that events could precipitate a broader military conflict, but there are sufficient restraints in place on all sides for it to seem likely that the US policy will not thus be pushed beyond its current parameters.

US Policy and the Contadora Process

The Contadora peace process continues to be one factor encouraging restraint against escalation of the conflict, but is unlikely to be able quickly to end or even to stabilise the Central American crisis. The US continues to assert that the objectives of its policy are compatible with those of a comprehensive regional settlement and to claim that a satisfactory settlement could serve as the means to end the conflicts

120

with and within Nicaragua. However, the US Administration clearly remains prepared to assist in a regional settlement only if it were to include minimal satisfaction of the central goal of current US policy, which is change of the political system in Nicaragua through Sandinista negotiation with the unarmed and armed opposition. Even while that positive goal is not achieved, the Administration would prefer continued destabilisation of the Nicaraguan Government by the Nicaraguan 'Contra' rebels rather than acceptance of any settlement seen as flawed and insufficient. So long as support for the 'Contras' seems a viable option, the Administration seems unlikely to abandon this or other military elements of its own policy even though the Contadora countries have openly urged it to do so as one element in the broader preparatory process of discussion and reciprocal concession which they have proposed as essential for any eventual peaceful settlement.

The Caraballeda initiative

This view was expressed in the new initiative proposed by the Contadora and Support Groups after a meeting in Caraballeda, Venezuela in January 1986. The decision to hold the new meeting partly reflected immediate concern that the suspension of negotiations announced in December had been a mistake which could only encourage escalation of the confrontation, and the immediate boost to the process provided by the proposals of President Cerezo in Guatemala. However, the initiative also reflected awareness of the need for a new and broader approach.

A comprehensive regional settlement would continue to have the clear potential advantage of simultaneously addressing all the separate issues and levels of issue which have brought that escalatory interaction of tensions which has made the crisis so intractable. However, in large part precisely because of that interaction, treaty negotiations alone had been shown unable to break the deadlock or to create the circumstances in which a settlement will be a feasible means to end the crisis. The new initiative implied that a diplomatic agreement could only formalise and deepen the bases for a durable reduction of tensions, rather than bring them about in itself.

The initiative therefore sought prior movement in four areas, aiming to disentangle and ease the various levels of tension. It urged an end to those particular elements which prolonged the conflict and served to link the different issues and levels of tension. It proposed reciprocal concessions in the opposing material sources of suspicion. It stressed the need for moves to increase confidence and perceptions of common interest, including measures to reduce political suspicions and the perceived political distance between Nicaragua and its neighbours. And it encouraged national moves to end internal political conflict and the local sources of instability.

The Caraballeda declaration defined ten 'permanent bases for peace in Central America':

1 a 'Latin American solution' separating the area from the East–West conflict;
2 self-determination;
3 non-intervention in internal affairs;
4 territorial integrity;
5 pluralist democracy;
6 no armaments or military bases threatening regional peace and security;
7 no military actions by countries of the region, or countries with interests in it, implying aggression or a threat to peace;
8 no foreign troops or advisers;
9 no type of support for groups seeking to subvert or destabilise the constitutional order of Latin American states;
10 unrestricted respect for human rights and all civil, political and religious liberties.

The declaration then defined nine actions required to create the necessary climate of confidence and to guarantee the realisation of the permanent bases for peace, most of which would effectively be unilateral but simultaneous acts partly achieving those bases:

1 the renewal of negotiations for a treaty;
2 an end to external support for irregular forces;
3 an end to support for insurgencies;
4 the freezing and programmed reduction of arms acquisitions;
5 the suspension of international military manoeuvres;
6 the progressive reduction and eventual elimination of all foreign military advisers and installations;
7 unilateral declarations of non-aggression by the five countries;
8 effective steps to achieve national reconciliation and full respect for human rights and individual liberties;
9 promotion of regional and international co-operation to ease the region's economic and social problems.

The Contadora Group and Support Group offered their good offices to promote new steps toward national reconciliation within the legal framework existing in each country, stressing that regional stability depends upon internal peace; to encourage the new Guatemalan president's proposal to hold talks between the legislatives of the region with the aim of establishing a regional parliament; and to bring about renewed talks between Nicaragua and the US.

The Caraballeda initiative was obviously not directed only at the Reagan Administration, nor did it urge concessions only from the US and Nicaragua's neighbours. It obviously sought an end to the Cuban and Soviet Bloc military presence in Nicaragua. If it urged an end to support for the 'Contras', it clearly required the Sandinistas, for their part, to cut all ties with revolutionaries from El Salvador and anywhere else, in Central America and beyond. Its reference to national reconciliation within existing legal frameworks could well seem to be contrary to US demands for Sandinista negotiations with the armed opposition over Nicaragua's political system, assuming the illegitimacy of the current structure and Government. However, it could equally imply that a peaceful solution to the conflict in El Salvador would have to take place within the established constitutional framework and to recognise the legitimacy of the Constitutional President in that country. Moreover, the new Constitution of Nicaragua was still in preparation, such that the 'legal framework' had not yet been fully defined, while Nicaragua was being governed under a state of emergency. Consequently, the proposal for national reconciliation, together with the stress on pluralist democracy and respect for all civil and political liberties, in effect did urge democratisation and political negotiation as necessary for internal stability and regional *détente*. That negotiation, however, need not necessarily take place with any other than the legal Nicaraguan opposition.

Contadora and Nicaraguan politics

There was some continued reluctance within the Contadora Governments to include internal politics, reflecting their own desire to avoid charges of interference in internal affairs and any appearance of applying political pressure on behalf of the US. It can indeed appear that there has been a tension within the Contadora proposals, between emphasis on the right of countries to determine their social and political structures without external interference, and the relatively detailed description given of the type of open and competitive electoral democracy to which all countries are to commit themselves. However, for most of those interested in the success of the Contadora process, there is no necessary contradiction at all between non-intervention and a political structure with the minimum attributes of such a system, these being rather the two dimensions of political

123

self-determination. As phrased in the Caraballeda Declaration, it is 'the independence of each of the Latin American countries to choose its own forms of social and political organization, establishing the regime of government which its population freely decides upon'. Moreover, it is obviously true that there is some international concern about Sandinista actions and intentions quite apart from, and often quite opposed to, current US policy. This concern exists despite all applause for their positive achievements and objectives, recognition that their record by many human rights indicators has been incomparably better than that of El Salvador or Guatemala, acceptance that the 1984 elections were more than a 'Soviet-style farce', and understanding of Nicaragua's circumstances.

The political problem could also be presented in terms of the consolidation of a social revolution, the central question being whether Revolutionary political control should be permanent and exclusive, or temporary and relatively short-lived. After 1979, the Sandinistas did not rush to establish state ownership of the economy or to eliminate the political opposition. However, they did quickly establish a considerable political hegemony and identification with the State which could only provoke concerns that they were aiming at permanent and exclusive power. As discussed above, external factors and considerations were important in shaping Sandinista behaviour. However, quite apart from coming to confront important national sectors with which there was some degree of inevitable tension, it may also be that to some extent 'they unnecessarily alienated the support of many potential allies, out of a misplaced belief that they could thus keep the revolution "pure", and also to consolidate an effective monopoly of power. The question . . . is not whether such a strong and pure revolutionary regime might by some criteria be *desirable*, but whether this schema was ever realistic'.[20] Moreover, it may be that there was some fundamental conflict between the ideological approach of much of the Sandinista leadership and the reality of Nicaraguan society with, among other things, its particularly strong small-scale and peasant sectors. Although retaining considerable popular support, the Sandinistas now face substantial, purely internal, pressures and constraints, as well as the discontent arising from economic crisis. The Sandinistas have not been inflexible in the face of social and economic problems, as has been evident in the changes in economic policies and in the changing pattern of land reform, which has, among other things, recently been modified to respond more to peasant demand for small private holdings. It can also appear that the possibility of greater political opening may not have been definitively removed.

To some extent, the concessions offered by the Sandinistas since 1981 do seem to have been a response to mounting external pressures and US demands. One problem was that however insufficient or insincere those gestures may be considered to have been by some parties, they did not seem to be met with a positive US response or cessation of hostilities.

There was in any case an element of pride and defiance involved, and an understandable sensitivity about US demands. In their – and other – eyes, they seemed to reflect considerable hypocrisy on the part of the US, which never seemed to care much about Nicaraguan elections and human rights while Somoza was there. Nicaragua was felt to have freed itself from the US tutelage which gave it Somoza, while the suggestion of a political agreement, especially with the US, seemed outrageous interventionism. Internal political concessions in a context of war and confrontation with the US could already in 1983 and 1984 seem difficult for the Sandinistas. They could also seem potentially dangerous if they were to be taken as signs of weakness or admissions of illegitimacy, and to lessen the Sandinistas' control while they faced internal and external enemies suspected to be implacable opponents of the Revolution. The Sandinistas will not 'give in' to the US.

By the end of 1985, the prospects of the Sandinistas' ever perceiving and accepting the political issue in terms which are not related to international confrontation, and of their being willing and able to make definitive moves towards a more open political system, could appear only to be reduced by a continuation of US pressures and the 'Contra' war.

Such a dilemma is felt by some in the legal opposition, who have tended to argue that the opening which still exists is partly due to such pressures, but also that US pressures and armed conflict make any peaceful political solution between Nicaraguans all the less likely. It permits the association of internal political differences and demands with international conflict, a perceived 'hegemonic' intransigence by the US, and armed attacks on Sandinista authority. Many in opposition have therefore suggested that stronger political pressure from the regional powers and Western Europe would be preferable and more effective on both national and political grounds. However, the association of political change with US hostility also makes it more difficult for the Contadora countries themselves to exert political pressure. Indeed, the tendency of many Sandinistas to see the pluralism issue as reflecting US interests and the Contadora initiative as reflecting Latin American nationalism in the face of the US, has often seemed to mean that they see the Contadora Groups' inclusion of political issues at all as mainly the result of US pressures or an attempt to keep the Americans happy while getting them off Nicaragua's back.

The objective of US support for the 'Contra' rebels is supposedly to provide the necessary pressure to force acceptance of demands which the unarmed opposition shares, but is unable to achieve by peaceful means because of Sandinista intransigence. The implication of Contadora proposals to disentangle the various dimensions of the conflict is that the result in practice is likely to be the reverse. The Sandinistas will be all the less likely to make concessions which are also demanded by US-backed anti-Communist insurgents, even if many are in fact simply coincident positions, some of which are expressed even by the Nicaraguan Socialists. They will also be all the more likely to continue their censorship and restriction of mobilisation in support of such demands.

Proposals made by the legal opposition indeed had many features in common with the rebels' March 1985 plan, the crucial difference being that the Sandinistas would not have to make concessions directly to the rebel leadership. The legitimacy of President Ortega would be recognised. In exchange, all citizens' rights and guarantees would be restored, and there would be new elections, with no exceptions and a restructuring of the Supreme Electoral Council, to a Constituent Assembly in which all parties would have real political influence. Other steps would then be the 'nationalisation' of the Sandinista Army and the Sandinista Police and the transformation of the local Sandinista Defense Committees from a party organisation into a means of community development, as was indeed contemplated by the FSLN leadership. Given the depth of the economic crisis and the level of popular discontent, some opposition leaders have expressed a 'moderate optimism' that some internal agreement might eventually be achieved. However, any possibility there may have been in the Spring of 1985 of new elections to the Constituent Assembly seems to have been ended with the US embargo and renewal of rebel funding.[21] It is highly unlikely that the Sandinistas will now agree to new elections. Moreover, the tightening of the State of Emergency in October 1985 prompted both the Independent Liberals and the Socialists to walk out of the discussions of the terms of the new Constitution.

Nevertheless, even if all the opposition were to walk out of the Constitutional discussions, it is still possible that the Sandinistas might make much the same concessions. There would be room for future openings, provided that the Constitution did not institutionalise those aspects of a Sandinista State which are common complaints of the unarmed opposition and the legitimate political figures in the armed opposition, and of varying levels of concern to most regional and European governments. So long as there was at least the prospect for the legitimate opposition of gaining genuine political influence and a fully equal opportunity in future elections, the opening would not seem to have been definitively closed even if emergency measures continued in the meantime.

It may be that finalisation of the new Constitution will be postponed until there is some end to the war and relaxation of external tensions. Both the opposition and some Sandinista leaders have claimed that they do not want the legal framework of the country's future to be dictated by a State of Emergency. It seems highly improbable that there could be any rapid political opening before an end to the war and to US hostility is at least in sight. The Sandinista leadership may well be concerned that this might be seen not as generosity or flexibility but as weakness and an implicit recognition of failure or illegitimacy. While the war continues, any such interpretation would risk strengthening the position of those fighting for their full political downfall, however relaxation of control in itself will predictably be feared to bring increased internal destabilisation. The Sandinistas may also believe that the economic crisis and the external influences on the current political situation would militate unfairly against them in the event of any precipitate political opening. They generally believe not only that the 'Contras' are primarily creatures or agents of US interests, but also that the depth of the economic crisis, which has given rise to such growing discontent in 1985 and 1986, is primarily the result of US destabilisation and 'economic aggression', and the demands of the war. They also increasingly see certain opposition sectors as both sympathetic to the rebels and tied to the US. These would be among the most active, articulate and well-financed in politically exploiting that discontent and other problems in an open political campaign. Indeed, between December 1984 and March 1985, the National Endowment for Democracy, a federally financed foundation established by the Reagan Administration, had approved a total of $300000 in grants to the CDN, the independent Permanent Human Rights Commission, and *La Prensa*.

The Sandinistas might eventually, as still hoped by part of the internal opposition, give more of a free and fair chance to other parties. However, just as the Sandinistas explicitly reject the notion of a reduction of armed forces until US hostilities end, one implicit argument will be that they will open up the system only when hostilities end, when the US withdraws its support for both armed and unarmed groups, and when they have a free and fair chance to satisfy popular demands and thereby strengthen, or win back, their popular support.

Just as US military pressures and support for the 'Contra' war seemed to make it impossible for the Sandinistas to reduce their own military forces and ties to Cuba and the Soviet Bloc, US pressures and insistence on negotiation with US-backed insurgents seemed to be making any other forms of negotiation and understanding all the less likely.

A similar difference was reflected in the Contadora initiative's aim to counter the escalatory interaction between internal and sub-regional political tensions. In this respect, it could be accepted that Nicaragua's existing internal situation was a source of suspicion and fear, but it could equally be suggested that the perpetuation of Nicaragua's isolation might only help maintain Nicaragua in that situation because of fears on the Sandinistas' own part.

The US Administration and many sectors in Nicaragua's neighbouring regimes argued against increasing Sandinista confidence, on the grounds that the Sandinistas would only negotiate seriously under pressure, and indeed out of fear. There was also the implication that there could be no lasting confidence or common interest with Nicaragua while it was under a Marxist–Leninist government. The implication of the Caraballeda initiative, on the other hand, was that the prospects both for a more democratic Nicaragua and for sub-regional concord could be improved only by an increase in political discussions, co-operation over matters of common social and economic concern, and confidence over the possibility of effective agreement over security issues. Indeed, it could be argued that there was little constructive alternative if the Sandinistas were not going to negotiate with the 'Contra' rebels and the 'Contras' could not overthrow the Sandinistas.

US policy was not seen as the only obstacle to the peace process. Responsibility could also be attributed to a measure of extremism, inflexibility and provocation on the part of the Sandinistas. There were also doubts within the Contadora Governments as to how far the Sandinista leadership really was prepared to go towards pluralist democracy and away from the Soviet Bloc. Nevertheless, it seemed possible that much greater openings and understandings might still be achieved. It seemed certain that this possibility could not be fully explored so long as the US continued its current policy.

The 'Latin American solution'

Moreover, US policy could not only be seen as responsible for some of the difficulties encountered in bringing a peaceful national solution to the internal conflict. It could also be seen as one element impeding the efforts of the regional powers to achieve regional peace and co-operation, and to establish a new regional framework for regional security. With regard to this dimension, and the notion of a 'Latin

American solution' to the crisis, the Contadora attitude had yet more problematic implications with regard to US policy towards Central America.

The implication at the internal level was that the US should cease its own direct pressures and involvement, and allow internal and regional forces to bring about a more stable and generally acceptable solution. A successful solution of this nature would permit regional stability and be at least minimally compatible with US political interests. Indeed even its pursuit was more likely than was current US policy to improve the prospects of the eventual outcome's not appearing a political defeat for the US. There would, however, have to be one fundamental concession by the US, namely the renunciation of any 'traditionally' or globally perceived right on its part to influence the course of internal affairs. If the Sandinistas were to accept the virtues of a competitive electoral system of political self-determination and to abandon their internal hegemony, it would be both necessary and right that the US should abandon all 'hegemonic' political interventionism and accept that it could not be a direct guarantor of an internal political structure.

At the regional level, the implication was likewise that the US, as well as the Soviet Union, should reduce its direct presence and pressures as a global power, in order to permit movement toward a regional solution which would prevent Central America from being a source of global concern and confrontation. Most immediately, this reflected the widespread feeling that an excessively anti-Soviet focus in US policy has exacerbated the internal and regional problems; the desire to counter the increased polarisation caused by association with the international ideological conflict; and the belief that it will simply be extremely difficult to reduce either Nicaraguan force levels or Soviet Bloc military assistance to the Sandinistas unless there is some reciprocal reduction in US military pressures against Nicaragua. Additionally, the current US attachment to the 'Contra' rebel cause as an anti-Communist insurgency of world-wide significance does not seem to help regional efforts to disentangle the Central American crisis any more than have assertions by the Sandinistas or their foreign friends of the Nicaraguan Revolution as a milestone in a global anti-imperialist struggle.

The ideal alternative proposed at Caraballeda was for both the US and the Soviet Bloc to cease all support for destabilising and irregular forces, and gradually, simultaneously and reciprocally to withdraw their own military presence from Central America. At the same time, the US would reach a preliminary understanding with Nicaragua over issues affecting US security interests as a global power. This would take place in the context of a comprehensive process of concession and negotiation mediated by the regional powers. So long as both the US and the USSR were prepared to refrain from unilateral involvement of a global strategic nature, the regional powers, with impartial international support, would themselves guarantee local compliance with the subsequent diplomatic settlement between the Central American countries.

Such a 'Latin American' solution could establish regional security and stability, and be compatible with the fundamental strategic interests of the US. Regional 'non-alignment' and separation from the 'East–West' conflict could never imply equivalence in regional relations with the US and USSR, and most countries would neither expect nor want such equivalence. In terms of historically-perceived US strategic interests, no challenge would be intended to the twin premises that the Caribbean region should be secure for US passage, and that there should be no presence of its global adversaries such as to threaten either the US itself or its capacity to project its power. There is no less of a regional desire for the removal of the Soviet Bloc military presence in Nicaragua or the prevention of any Soviet destabilisation. The parallel desire to have no US military presence in Central America either does not necessarily conflict with US interests, another long-standing US strategic concern being precisely not to have to distract military resources and attention to the area.

Those proposing a 'Latin American solution' could also argue that it is by movement in this direction – beginning with an end to support for the 'Contra' rebels – that the prospects are more likely to be improved of avoiding any eventual choice between an outcome which appears a strategic setback for the US and direct US intervention, with all its negative political and strategic consequences.

There would, however, have to be a fundamental concession by the US, and a redefinition of US relations with the region. In immediate terms, this would imply a subordination of direct and unilateral US action to the efforts and responsibility of the regional powers. The US would have to accept the primary role of the regional powers in guaranteeing both the peace process and the eventual settlement, even if the nature of the process was such that the precise outcome could not be guaranteed in advance and involved a gradual reduction of the instruments with which the US would alternatively have sought to guarantee its own interests. In broader terms, the redefinition would entail abandonment of the traditional assumption of the region's political exclusivity and international alignment with the US, in exchange for a regional commitment to prevent threats to the US of a clearly global and strategic nature from arising within the region.

The Caraballeda initiative, and such proposals for a 'Latin American solution' of the crisis, could to some extent be seen as a plea for all parties to help in breaking the escalatory spirals of tension and suspicions which have developed since 1979, and to try to start again. Indeed, many actors themselves have tended to use 1979 as a point of reference, whether in terms of the 'original programme' of the Revolution or of a break in US imperialism, to argue that if only the other side would return to it, there would be no problem.

Back to the future?

In many respects, one can indeed see the situation of late 1979 as revealing a potential for peaceful compromise and understanding which was then frustrated and distorted, largely for reasons which could be considered as being to a greater or lesser extent avoidable. Consequently, it can appear that if there could be more favourable circumstances, and if all sides would be prepared to make the necessary concessions, it would be possible to revive that potential for compromise and understanding.

However, quite apart from the manifest difficulties now involved in bringing about the steps required, there are two fundamental obstacles to even trying thus to start again. First, the present US Administration not only remains unconvinced by the general notion of a 'Latin American solution', but believes that events have proved the Sandinistas to be irredeemable. Second, there were inherent problems which were not likely to be overcome in 1979 even if all else had succeeded.

To some extent, Nicaragua was an exceptional case and the Nicaraguan Revolution simply could not be stopped. Moreover, it was to some extent a forced compromise on the part of the US and the Sandinistas, barely concealing a multitude of differences and suspicions, exaggerated expectations, and in some cases ulterior motives. Nonetheless, compromise it was, and one which momentarily seemed to establish many of the circumstances and broad parameters for peaceful co-operation – and for a process of change at both the internal and regional level – which would imply and ease a process of redefinition of US relations with the region. In essence, the US would accept that process of change and redefinition, which was sought by most of Latin America. The US would be willing to work with the government which emerged from a national and nationalist revolution. That government's commitment to political pluralism, a mixed economy and non-alignment was supported, and might be guaranteed, by the regional powers.

It all went wrong. Leaving aside the simple assumption that the Sandinistas had always been totally lying about their intentions, although not necessarily denying it in individual cases, there are three circumstantial reasons for which it was then almost bound to go wrong.

First, the behaviour of both sides and the credibility of, even the rationality behind, their positions, suffered from the very impact of the revolutionary triumph. In Nicaragua there was a euphoria, exacerbated by inexperience; in the US there was a shocked, emotional reaction, bitterness of debate and recrimination, exacerbated by broader domestic divisions and sensitivities.

Second, changing circumstances made it all the harder to overcome the multiple suspicions, fears and temptations present. With Guatemala also smouldering, a burning situation quickly emerged in El Salvador to tempt, or force, Nicaraguan and other revolutionary hands, and further to colour US responses with fears of the collapse of Central America, its hemispheric alliance and its global credibility. Developments in Afghanistan and Poland inevitably altered the global context in which Central America would be perceived, and increased the temptation to see it as a global test-case and one, moreover, which the US could do something about.

Third, there was a certain amount of globally motivated Soviet activity involved, with some degree of simple opportunism and probably some degree also of subversive support and political solidarity perceived as a response to US actions with regard to Afghanistan.

It is conceivable that circumstances in these three respects could become more favourable, thus easing the process of compromise over some of the central issues involved, and helping to overcome another barrier to any understanding. That was – and still is – the exacerbatory influence of deep suspicions arising from perceived historical experience, and consequent assumptions about the probable course of the other's behaviour. In the US, the assumption was that Left-wing revolutionaries would be dominated or manipulated by Soviet-leaning Marxist–Leninists bent on monopolising power and exporting revolution. For many regional revolutionaries, the assumption was that the US would always be intransigently opposed to radical reform and greater independence in the US' global sphere of influence. Unless a Revolutionary government took appropriate precautions, it risked being destabilised or overthrown. These complementary suspicions were intensified by the fact that Nicaragua then had, to its immediate north, military regimes which were perceived by the US as highly vulnerable, and by the Sandinistas as probably hostile. Such ingrained suspicions, quickly confirmed and strengthened by tensions over other issues, did contribute – with some measure of hypothetical avoidability – to a widening of the political distance to the current point of perceivedly irreversible incompatibility. It might therefore be hoped that, in more favourable circumstances, steps might be taken simultaneously by the Sandinistas and the US to disprove such suspicions, and to ease the separation of their differences from the global confrontation.

The possibility of such steps being successfully taken, however, clearly depends on two things. The first, which constitutes a fundamental dilemma for the Contadora Groups, is that there should exist a framework of guarantees which is sufficiently credible to both sides for each to believe in the safety of taking such preliminary steps without risking everything and to believe that the other would indeed respond. Many on both sides always doubted that the situation promised in 1979 could work, or did not want to accept as permanent the implicit compromise if it did. Thus they did not take all the appropriate steps and perceived risks required to give it a fair chance of doing so. They did not respond to the informal regional framework by refraining, unilaterally but simultaneously, from doing many of those things which the Contadora Groups are now formally urging that they should, unilaterally but simultaneously, stop doing. The regional powers were neither able nor willing to stop it all happening, mostly because of the strength of the dynamics set in motion, and because of differences with the US and between themselves over precisely what should be made to happen or not to happen. The Contadora Groups do not now seem to have sufficient leverage or credibility to bring about such reciprocal confidence-building steps. The Sandinistas assert that they do want to isolate the area from the 'East–West' conflict and would like to be able to co-operate in everything required to bring a 'Latin American solution' to the crisis. However, they explicitly state that they will not take the steps required over security issues until the US itself provides a credible guarantee that it will cease its hostilities. The US Administration, even as it has appeared to be seeking a hegemony restored, has obviously had to take into account the regional powers' initiatives and interests, and would for the most part see new forms of co-operation by and with them as desirable and beneficial. The problem is that they would only seem desirable while they did not appear to threaten US interests as a global power. The US does not believe that either the unarmed Nicaraguan opposition or the regional powers can stop the Sandinistas from themselves creating problems of an 'East–West' nature, including a Marxist–Leninist state in Central America. Rather, it is felt that the Sandinistas have fulfilled, internally and externally, almost all US fears about the consequences of their taking power, and that the regional countries have been unable, and to some extent unwilling, to stop them getting away with it. Any argument that the US should step back in order to allow solutions of a non-'East–West' nature to appear thus tends to seem simply naive.

A second requisite for the success of such confidence-building steps is obviously that there should not in fact be an irreversible incompatibility of interests, and that it should be possible to separate the internal and regional dimensions of the crisis from the global conflict. In most respects, both might be believed still to apply at least in principle. However, even if the issue of Nicaragua's non-military relations with the Soviet Bloc and the consequent increase in the Soviet political presence in the region could be overcome, the question of Cuba would still seem to present a fundamental obstacle, which will continue to plague the efforts of the regional powers. Almost whatever else had happened in 1979, the question of Cuba would have created tensions.

The inevitable problem of Cuba

While US–Cuban relations remain in a state of frozen hostility, and the two countries' interests are perceived as mutually exclusive, then any situation in which Cuba is involved, whether internal conflict or regional agreement, will to that extent appear as a threat to the US, and inevitably one of a global nature in view of Cuba's ties to the Soviet Union. Any definition of non-alignment which seems akin to that of Cuba – or even to include close relations with Cuba – will thus seem highly suspect, and the democratic commitment and strategic reliability of any Government however fairly elected, will tend to be seen in large part as a function of its interest in ties with Cuba. Even if the Sandinistas were to accept and fulfil all the commitments of a Contadora plan, they would certainly, during the time that they were in power, refuse to end friendly relations with Cuba. While Nicaragua's neighbours see any Cuban presence there as inevitably threatening in view of Cuba's commitment to revolution, it will be all the harder to achieve those permanent bases for peace in Central America. The regional powers have in differing ways and from different points of view attempted to address the problems posed by the question of Cuba's role, but there has been little change in the situation. How the Cuban dimension should be dealt with by the US will present a serious challenge in the case of any foreseeable type of settlement reached with a Sandinista government. It is the type of challenge which current US policy is intended precisely to avoid.

Current perspectives for Contadora

Whether the renewed energy of the Contadora Groups in early 1986 continues or whether the Contadora governments come to give a lower priority to the Central American issue, it is unlikely that the process will be formally abandoned. However, it is also unlikely that any substantial progress will be made in the immediate future, either in the preliminary steps proposed at Caraballeda or in the negotiations for a diplomatic settlement.

It may be that there can be no such progress until the armed conflicts in both Nicaragua and El Salvador are more decisively fought out. So long as the war in El Salvador continues, the US Administration and the Salvadorean Government, will not want to remove the military advisers or endanger US military assistance to El Salvador. The Salvadorean conflict will probably continue to be a point of perceived confrontation and serve to maintain tensions and suspicions, until it seems closer to resolution. Until the line against the spread of revolution seems finally to be secured in El Salvador, the US presence in the area and US pressures on Nicaragua are all the less likely to be reduced. Other Central American Governments may likewise see continuing revolution in El Salvador as a function of Sandinista activity and as an indication of the need for radical change in Nicaragua. And unless Congress halts all aid to the Nicaraguan rebels or the rebels are suppressed on the ground, it is unlikely that the present US Administration will abandon its commitment to them in order to explore an alternative course.

It may also be that the ideal peace process and vision of a 'Latin American solution' proposed at Caraballeda can never come about. However, a Contadora settlement, if it can be made to deal effectively with security issues and the question of mechanisms to ensure compliance, is likely to remain an important element in any resolution of the immediate crisis. Moreover, despite a degree of wishful thinking, much in the Contadora Groups' initiative can certainly be considered as an alternative approach which may in some respects be more realistic than current US policy, and may indeed be more likely to improve the US' own longer-term options. While current US policy continues, the most that can probably be expected with regard to the steps called for at Caraballeda is that the remaining openings for a durable reduction of tensions within Nicaragua and between Nicaragua and its neighbours are not further closed. However, the course of the Contadora process in the meantime, particularly as it affects Nicaragua's political appearance, will be important in shaping the development of US policy if the 'Contra' rebels are brought to the point at which they no longer present a viable option for the US even to maintain pressure on the Sandinista regime.

Rebel Prospects

The Sandinistas would be unlikely even seriously to debate the possibility of negotiation with the rebels unless faced with a considerable threat to the survival of their regime. The rebel forces do not currently pose such a threat. The US Administration is manifestly unclear as to just how and when they might, and apparently inconsistent as to how it expects the Nicaraguan Government to respond to increasing pressures. The simple casting of the Sandinistas as Communist, and of the rebel campaign as a test case in the reversal of Communist Revolution, provides one easy rationalisation of the rebels' uncertain prospects and the Administration's own inability to state how it sees the precise course and outcome of the policy. In October 1985, Assistant Secretary of State Elliot Abrams acknowledged that four years of rebel attacks had not achieved significant change in the Nicaraguan regime, but he argued: 'I would reject the view that that means the policy isn't working. I would take the view that we simply have not provided enough pressure . . . It is our view that the Sandinistas are Communist, and that they do not believe in democracy and they do not want it.' Any action, such as allowing the newspaper *La Prensa* to remain open, 'is in the nature of a concession under pressure'. He saw in the US 'complete consensus that the Sandinistas are really reprehensible people, that they are Communist and that something needs to be done to force them to compromise.' Acknowledging that the Administration's view has been that Communist governments by definition do not compromise, he said: 'This would be a first. That is why it takes so much pressure'.[22] A similar suggestion is made by some to explain further why events in Nicaragua are impossible to predict: this is uncharted political territory, a new process of historical learning about how Communist regimes change.

Administration officials do argue, more convincingly, that it is simply impossible to predict what will evolve from the situation. The US does have a definition of what is an acceptable outcome, in the four points of US policy: cessation of Nicaraguan support to insurgent movements in other countries; reduction in Nicaraguan armed forces; withdrawal of foreign advisers from Nicaragua; and establishment of a pluralist democratic structure in Nicaragua. Rebel support, among other strong pressures, has the highest chance of achieving a negotiated solution satisfying those points. There are numerous paths by which such a solution might come about, and the US not only does not know, but does not particularly mind, which it might be. There might be a sudden mass uprising, a gradual transfer of national control, a collapse into chaos leading to a negotiated process of political reconstruction, an outright Sandinista acceptance of the March 1985 proposal, a reconciliation plan within a multilateral diplomatic framework or any number of other imaginable scenarios. So long as there is a negotiated solution which also satisfied the US' fundamental concerns, it would not insist on any particular form of settlement, even if the Nicaraguan opposition and the other Central American countries had settled for a negotiated solution which was not ideal for the US. Furthermore, it is considered mistaken to believe that the US Government should necessarily be able to predict events at all, since it does not totally control the situation: the war in Nicaragua is fundamentally an internal conflict, while the US does not dictate the course of the regional negotiations in which it is not even a direct party. The fact that the course of events cannot be predicted is therefore not seen as reason to doubt either the rightness or the potential success of the policy. Nor is the fact that such success may not take place in the very near future. Officials emphasise that the Administration is not so impatient. It is prepared to wait for as long as it takes. If a positive outcome seems remote in current circumstances, the perceived implication is that the circumstances, not the policy, should be changed. So long as the pressures on the Sandinistas do not decrease, time is not on their side. The longer the pressures continue, the greater their cumulative effect in undermining the regime and establishing the conditions for its eventual transformation by one means or another.

Nevertheless, statements by Administration officials have recognised, explicitly or implicitly, that much will have to change before the Nicaraguan Government will face economic collapse or a serious military challenge, at least one of which would be necessary for their survival to be threatened.

Sandinista economic weaknesses

Nicaragua's economic situation is certainly perilous, with serious social consequences and implications for Sandinista support and control. The prolonged war will continue directly to bleed the economy and the budget, of which an official 40 per cent and an overall proportion of over 50 per cent was devoted to military expenditure in 1985. There is a drastic shortage of foreign exchange. Direct destruction and loss of production, dislocation and diversion of resources, adverse market prices and natural disasters – on top of business sector tensions with the government – all helped to reduce Nicaragua's exports earnings to under $400 million and to create a balance of payments deficit on current account of around $500 million in 1984. The exchange crisis, heavy pressure on the currency, the lack of economic growth in 1984, and high inflation forced a series of drastic measures in February 1985, intended both to boost production and to reduce an unmanageable budget deficit of over 20 per cent of GDP. The currency was massively devalued. Interest rates went up. Public spending was cut in almost all areas except defence. Prices for agricultural produce were raised, and state subsidies cut. Food prices increased, on regulated goods by an average of some 200 per cent and on unregulated goods by as much as 600 per cent, and the price of scarce petrol rose by 150 per cent. The wage structure was adjusted, but the various increases in minimum wage levels were insufficient to compensate for the loss of purchasing power. There was, however, little prospect of an improvement in the foreign exchange situation, crucial for economic stabilisation. The $402 million in foreign aid raised from both halves of Europe in the Spring of 1985 was neither large nor liquid enough to allow Nicaragua to fund the level of imports needed simply to keep the economy turning over. The US economic sanctions have created further problems for Nicaraguan trade, although a wide variety of countries have agreed to take parts of the sales lost to the US market.

New agreements with Comecon made in October 1985 will not much ease Nicaragua's financial situation. Although the Government has been careful to honour all obligations to the IMF, in order to avoid possible suspension, it has no possibility of meeting service payments amounting to $1.4 billion in 1985 alone on a growing foreign debt of nearly $5 billion in 1985, more than Nicaragua's GDP. The freeze on credit from the World Bank and US efforts to block loans from the Inter-American Development Bank have made all the more difficult Nicaragua's efforts to obtain external finance. By August 1985, even the Sandinista Labour Confederation (CST) was arguing that the package of measures had not brought the desired results, with agricultural and industrial production falling, and workers' standard of living plummeting further.[23] The State's economic crisis has led to a further surge in the informal sector, alternative mechanisms of economic activity and exchange, and the black market. Many wage earners have protested at the continued profiteering, and many workers and peasants who do generally support the Sandinistas have expressed resentment at the austerity measures, which are felt to make them bear the brunt of the crisis while senior officials continue to live in apparent style. A new series of economic measures was therefore adopted in early 1986, aiming to stimulate production and partly restore real wage levels, as well as a stronger campaign to curb informal and black market activities.

Nevertheless, the economic situation in Nicaragua has become notably worse, the hardship felt by the people moving to a new level, and hitting such fundamental needs as health care. Many Nicaraguans do not accept the Government's arguments that the crisis is primarily the consequence of the war and US hostility; the Government is blamed for economic mismanagement. The increase in popular discontent and the erosion of active support for the regime during 1985 and 1986 has been unmistakeable.

The regime would certainly feel threatened if a situation seemed imminent of such economic collapse and hardship that order could be maintained, if at all, only by military law or other overtly forceful control of the population, thus putting at risk the determination and loyalty even of members of the Sandinista Front. Such a situation would come closer if, as desired by the US Administration, all Western aid and trade would cease, or be made absolutely conditional on negotiation with the legal and armed opposition. European aid has already fallen substantially, and there has been a generally adverse reaction to the hardening of the state of emergency. However, it seems unlikely that Western European, Canadian and Latin American economic ties would be cut except in the case of some dramatic external change, or of more physically abusive and politically unacceptable measures against the civilian population and legal opposition. While Nicaragua still faces US hostility and US-backed insurgency, and does not go beyond the limits at which political concern and distaste would outweigh the domestic pressures and diplomatic arguments for maintaining ties, economic relations will probably continue. Even if they were to begin to diminish seriously, the expected effect would probably not provoke immediate considera-tion of political negotiation with the rebels while containment of the insurgency seemed possible. Moreover, economic collapse would still only be certain and imminent if all non-Western assistance was also greatly reduced, or cut. Soviet Bloc support will probably remain at little more than the minimum necessary to ensure Nicaragua's immediate economic survival and counter-insurgency capability – such as oil, food, a certain amount of basic goods, and arms. However, that support, being domestically unquestioned and primarily a function of the USSR's international interest in the survival of the Sandinista Revolution, will not be affected on political grounds by anything they might do to maintain internal political control. It can therefore probably be counted on in most circumstances short of US military intervention, at least so long as Nicaragua faces US hostility and an insurgent threat, and unless the Soviet interest in Nicaragua is substantially altered by external considerations.

The Sandinistas are clearly aware of the social and political dangers of their deteriorating economic situation, and know that it cannot quickly improve. In October 1985, the Nicaraguan Government announced the suspension of many civil liberties, and a widening of the state of emergency which had been in force since March 1982, but considerably softened in August 1984. The measures were somewhat reduced two weeks later, in response to almost universal protest in

Nicaragua and the apparently surprising depth and breadth of international concern. A number of judicial freedoms were restored, but rights such as those to strike, outdoor assembly and freedom of expression remained suspended. Censorship was subsequently increased, and a large number of people picked up for interrogation, although most were released unharmed. The President justified the measures publicly with the need to counter efforts to form an 'internal front', arguing that 'agents of imperialism, which act from some political parties, communications media or religious institutions are redoubling their actions to sabotage the effort of military defence of the homeland and to provoke discontent'.[24] This was widely considered a rhetorical justification for an over-reaction to attacks on the draft in a Church newspaper, and to labour protest and agitation for reinstatement of the traditional Christmas bonus payment. However, these measures, like the indefinite closure of *La Prensa* and the expulsion of two church leaders in mid-1986, clearly did reflect Sandinista awareness of a need both to maintain political control in a potentially volatile situation and to discourage the establishment of ties with the armed opposition groups. They also showed the Government's determination not to allow manifestations of discontent to grow into a political groundswell within the country, while it was fighting rebel forces which had not yet been defeated.

It is by no means impossible that the economic crisis will breed such discontent that the regime will eventually crumble. In the short term, however, despite the undermining of active support for the Sandinistas, it is unlikely to lead to such ungovernability or to translate into sufficiently broad active support for the rebels to threaten the regime, unless the rebels increase their own threat to the Government.

The 'Contra' threat

The US Administration accepts that the 'Contra' rebels do not (mid-1986) have the capacity to overthrow the Nicaraguan Government by their own direct military force alone. Although some in the Administration may believe it possible or desirable for them to acquire such a capacity, it has generally been argued both that military overthrow is not the desired objective, and that direct armed force is not expected to be the only instrument in transforming the Sandinistas. The armed opposition is the source of effective pressure on the regime and the core around which the population will rally because of economic discontent, political repression, clashes with the Church, or ethnic problems. With sufficient rebel links to both internal and external democratic forces and enough public pressure in Nicaragua, it is thus argued, the Sandinista regime can be forced to accept national reconciliation and political evolution. However, often even in the same presentation, a contrary expectation and a clear catch in the argument is evident. Presumed to be 'dedicated Marxist–Leninists' and afraid of free elections which they know they would lose, the Sandinistas are not thought willing to accept the course of peaceful political evolution. And it is recognised that the population will only rally around this 'core' provided that they see that the armed opposition has enough strength to win.

In this respect, there may be a circularity to the argument: the rebels can only receive sufficient popular support to present a serious threat to the regime, if they can demonstrate that they do present such a threat. Thus far, the broad discontent in Nicaragua has not translated into anything like equally broad support for the rebels. The Sandinistas still retain the active support of perhaps one third of the population. Through the army, militia, police and mass organisations, they exert a thorough, if relatively restrained, political control. Control over many scarce resources and social opportunities provides further powers of dissuasion. Much of the Nicaraguan population simply does not want to get involved in the conflict, on either side. And relatively few, especially in the cities, will take the risk of going to arms against the Government unless life becomes intolerable and the rebels seem to present both a credible and an attractive alternative.

The rebels are not an insignificant force, having grown to around 17000 by mid-1985, of which perhaps 10000 were active combatants. They cannot any longer be simply considered as Somocistas and mercenaries. The proportion of former National Guardsmen and those directly associated with the Somoza regime in the FDN has fallen with time, and falls further with the level of seniority. Former Guardsmen constitute perhaps 90 per cent of the military general staff and senior leadership, and at least 32 per cent (the figure given by the FDN) of the overall military leadership, but probably less than 10 per cent of the total combatants. Most of its political leadership were not Somoza supporters, while the armed Indian groups on the Atlantic coast, and the groups which have operated in the south of Nicaragua have practically no connection with the Somoza regime. Nor, despite the proven resort to forced recruitment, even of children, can this account for a majority of the rest. Much of the increase in their numbers has been of those coming of their own volition or persuaded of the rightness of the cause. Large sections of the peasant population of the northern mountains in particular have been disillusioned, resentful of government policies, and receptive to arguments that the Sandinistas are atheistic Communists who abuse the Church, will expropriate their land and steal their produce. Many Sandinista officials recognise that by 1984 the FDN had established some 'social base' in certain of these areas, in which they could move and find support with relative ease and confidence. The FDN has received recruits, in lesser numbers, from other social sectors, and some ex-Sandinistas. Significant internal groups, and most importantly the Church hierarchy, continue to call for reconciliation and dialogue with the 'Contras'.

The rebels have inflicted great human and economic losses on the regime, diverted its resources and helped to create conditions in which its popular support has been undermined. The renewal of US funding encouraged the FDN to mount a series of offensives in the late summer and early autumn of 1985, which inflicted substantial losses on government forces and showed that the rebels could operate throughout large areas of the country. Communications and intelligence appeared to have improved and there also began to be some improvement in the rebels' equipment, notably the acquisition and first successful use toward the end of 1985 of surface-to-air missiles (SAM-7s).

However, the Sandinistas' own military capacity has notably improved since 1984, and not only in numbers and heavy equipment. There is more constant patrolling, and by better troops, and strengthened militia presence, within a reorganised defence structure. The fast-moving Irregular Warfare Battalions and new special units have proved effective in response and pursuit on the ground, while there has been a newly effective use of helicopters, both of the Mi-8s for rapid troop movement and of the Mi-24 gunships acquired since November 1984. Fighting was heavy during most of 1985. The two sides' casualty figures for 1985 differ wildly. The FDN claims to have killed 5677 Sandinista troops and wounded 3979, receiving 414 defections, but does not offer figures for its own losses. The Government claims to have killed 4608 rebels and wounded 1101, with some 500 captured and 1,000 surrendering, admitting 1143 losses.

By the end of 1985, the military initiative appeared to lie with the Sandinista forces. The rebels had still been unable to take and hold a single town, and the areas in which in 1983 and 1984 they were able to mount persistent attacks and maintain a relatively constant presence were shifted and diminished during 1985. By the end of 1985 the Sandinistas had established a much stronger presence in the northern mountain areas, in which the rebels had been able to count upon a significant degree of local support and into which infiltration and resupply from Honduras was relatively easy. There was a more constant and effective Sandinista military presence in these areas. Much of the peasant population which had been affording support to the rebels was relocated, and efforts were made to regain local support through greater economic assistance, social programmes and land distribution. On the other hand, rebel actions increased in the central areas during 1985, reflecting a continued capacity to move along the sparsely populated central uplands and attack economically important targets, but also increasing dependence on air drops of supplies from Honduras in order to maintain their activity. Although they seemed to find some local support from the peasant population in these areas, they did not threaten government control of population centres.

Even if the rebels were, as they claim is possible, to double in numbers, and the strength and effectiveness of the Sandinista forces were not to increase further, a number of other things would have to be achieved before they could begin to pose a credible military threat.

First, they would either have to establish effective control over border areas from which gradually to expand, or at least to be able to maintain a strong internal infrastructure, in order not to have to move back across the borders when they run out of supplies or depend on vulnerable air drops.

Second, they would have to have an effective southern front from which to mount co-ordinated offensives. In this respect much depends on the position of Costa Rica, without the increased co-operation of which the establishment of such a front would be very difficult. The failure of the more vigorously anti-Sandinista Social Christian candidate in the February 1986 Costa Rican Presidential Elections seemed to indicate that, despite widespread dislike and mistrust of the Nicaraguan regime, there remained considerable reluctance on the part of Costa Rica to adopt a more active role against it. There will probably remain some degree of tolerance of rebel activities, but it seems unlikely that there will be sufficient connivance, and even support, for the southern front to acquire the military significance of the north, which has been made possible only by Honduran co-operation. Indeed, shortly after the February elections and a slight improvement in relations with Nicaragua, it was announced that Costa Rica and Nicaragua had agreed to the presence of an international monitoring commission along their border.

Third, the 'Contra' rebels would need much better training and a significant upgrading of their military equipment before they could defend any fixed lines and positions, successfully confront the Sandinista forces in any strength, and even begin to challenge them in the crucial Pacific littoral where most of the population is concentrated. For this, they will require substantial military assistance from the US Government.

In the last months of 1985, it was already clear that the Administration was preparing to request military assistance at some point in 1986. It was also clear that Congressional resistance to this remained strong.

Among the factors which would predictably alter the situation would be Nicaraguan acquisition of MiGs, or other 'unacceptable' Soviet Bloc equipment, the presence of Cuban or other foreign combat troops, and some sharp deterioration or brutalisation in Sandinista internal behaviour. The Administration was therefore quick to emphasise all developments which seemed to constitute moves in these directions. The October tightening of the state of emergency prompted broad condemnation of the Sandinistas in the US for revealing 'the totalitarian core of their philosophy', giving Reagan 'an enormously useful ready-made case to take to Congress',[25] and showing their 'True Colors . . . Their avowal of repression is the biggest victory of the "Contras" so far'.[26] In November, Administration officials made public reports of a 'steep increase in the amount of incoming shipments' of Soviet Bloc arms through Cuba, increasing Nicaragua's 'very offensive military capability, designed to intimidate' its neighbours,[27] and making it ever more of a Soviet arsenal. Pentagon assessments were given of the Nicaraguan inventory, estimated to include some 150 tanks and 200 other armoured vehicles, 200 anti-aircraft guns, 300 missile launchers, 100 anti-tank guns, 24 multiple rocket launchers, 145 howitzers, and 32 helicopters, of which 6 were Mi-24 gunships.[28] In December, in the wake of reports that two Cubans were among those killed in the Mi-8 helicopter shot down by the rebels, the Administration, while recognising that Cuban combat troops were not involved, argued that Cuban military advisers were actively engaged in combat operations. Assistant Secretary of State Elliot Abrams openly stating his hope that this development would encourage greater support for the rebels.[29]

Indeed, the House vote in November 1985, authorising the supply of unarmed aircraft, helicopters, vehicles and sophisticated radio equipment, had seemed to indicate some further drop in Congressional opposition to rebel funding. However, when the Administration confirmed in January 1986 that it would be requesting military assistance, the extent of continued resistance became apparent. While questioning the Administration's assertions of the enormity and immediacy of the threat posed by the Sandinistas, opponents did not deny the need to ensure protection of regional and US security interests. Nor did they argue that Nicaragua was not in need of national reconciliation and democratisation. Many in Congress opposed any form of support for the Nicaraguan 'Contras' as dangerous, discrediting and probably ineffective. US military assistance, especially if it were to involve training by US personnel, was widely feared only to escalate the conflict, and to draw the US into direct confrontation with the Sandinistas.

The Administration argued that stronger 'Contra' pressure was

144

needed precisely in order to avoid any eventual direct action by the US and to bring about a serious negotiated settlement which would bring long-term security and stability. Administration critics countered that the Sandinistas refused to negotiate with the 'Contras' and the 'Contras' alone could not defeat the Sandinistas. An open US military commitment to the rebels could therefore lead only to an eventual choice of US defeat or US intervention, or at best to a state of permanent conflict with dangers of escalation which would be even harder to control. The critics argued that such a commitment would preclude other efforts to bring about a generally acceptable negotiated settlement, stressing that the Contadora countries were now openly calling on the US Administration not to press for more aid to the Nicaraguan rebels. Indeed, in February 1986, the eight Governments comprising the Contadora and Support Groups directly appealed to Secretary of State Schultz for the US instead to back their new peace initiative. US opponents of 'Contra' aid further emphasised that support for this course now seemed to be waning even within the other Central American countries. The new civilian President of Guatemala and the President-elect of Costa Rica were publicly unenthusiastic, subsequently reacting against assertions by the US Administration that their countries generally favoured aid to the rebels. Likewise, the new Honduran Foreign Minister was publicly to deny suggestions that his Government had authorised aid to be channelled to insurgents.

The Administration pressed on with its campaign, President Reagan making extraordinary personal efforts to sway Congress and public opinion. The debates of March 1986 provoked even more controversy and bitterness than those of April and May 1985. Administration officials suggested that the Democrats were ignoring regional realities and failing in their own responsibilities to US security and the cause of democracy. Congressional opponents complained that the President was resorting to misrepresentation and abuse in his obsessive campaign to secure assistance to the 'Contras'. Many Democrats were angered, in particular, by the manner in which Administration presentations of the issue tended to identify opponents of military aid as 'soft on' and even co-operative with International Communism.

The President's request, for $30 million in 'humanitarian aid' and $70 million in military assistance, was approved in one House Committee and turned down in three others in early March. The plan was rejected in the House by 222 votes to 210 on 20 March, despite a last-minute offer by the President to delay disbursement of $75 million of the package for 90 days, after which it would be supplied unless there had been a regional peace settlement or a 'serious internal dialogue' in Nicaragua. A new vote in the House only came in late June. While opponents of the proposed aid package added to their arguments demands to investigate the allegations of involvement in drug trafficking and of misuse of US 'humanitarian' aid by 'Contra' leaders, President Reagan again made great personal efforts to win support for the proposal and the Administration again stressed all developments in Nicaragua which might reduce Congressional resistance. It was asserted that political repression and confiscation of properties had intensified, that the Soviet Union had resumed direct arms shipments to the Sandinistas, that a Soviet reconnaissance aircraft had been assisting Nicaraguan counter-insurgency operations, and that foreign military advisers had increasingly been carrying out support roles in Nicaragua.

On 25 June, the House of Representatives approved the aid proposal by 221 votes to 209. A practically identical proposal was approved by the Senate on 13 August by 53 votes to 47, thus requiring only final action by a Conference Committee of the two houses and signature by the President to go into effect. While a further $300 million in economic aid would be given to El Salvador, Honduras, Guatemala and Costa Rica, $30 million in non-military aid and $70 million in military assistance would be given to the Nicaraguan rebels in three phases. Training could be directly provided to the rebel forces by US military personnel, who would be prohibited from going within 20 miles of borders with Nicaragua. However, the CIA seemed likely to be given supervision of the programme, and again to be legally permitted to conduct covert operations against the Nicaraguan Government.

Military assistance is certainly necessary if the Nicaraguan rebels are to increase, or even maintain, their level of military activity. Military assistance itself, however, cannot help overcome all the rebels' weaknesses even in the military dimension. Despite claims to have issued a code of conduct and to have disciplined those responsible for atrocious behaviour, many of the rebel forces have continued to conduct themselves in often undisciplined and brutal ways which neither convince many Americans of their respect for human rights, nor seem likely to increase their broad popular appeal within Nicaragua.

While their military credibility will be a key element in determining their internal support, it is not likely that the rebels will be able to gain significant popular support, nor begin to establish an urban base unless this and other aspects of their political weakness are corrected. They would also have to demonstrate greater political unity among themselves, more convincingly displace the ex-Somocista elements, and give more prominent and effective control to the more legitimate and democratic opposition groups. They would have to present a political programme which is convincing, appealing and clearly not an

146

excuse to return to the old regime. This will have to go beyond assertions of the need for elections and democratic structures and to show what more they would do than have the Sandinistas to satisfy popular needs and demands, and how they would do it. They would also need to make some token but material demonstration of their capacity and willingness to deliver on their promises. They need to have an 'internal front', and to do a great deal more to develop urban cadres and show even some presence in urban areas. In order to present any threat of an uprising such as that which toppled Somoza, they would also have to establish active ties with the internal opposition parties and sectors. To the extent that many of those groups, and of course the Church, are urging dialogue and reconciliation, some such pressure does already exist. However, the Sandinistas have thus far shown themselves willing to stifle it, and made clear that opposition groups even making contact or identifying with the armed groups will be considered and treated as 'Contras'. Finally, the rebels would need to have a much broader and more effective 'international front.'

Some moves have already been made to try to correct these political weaknesses, including an agreement reached between the 'Contra' leadership in Miami in May 1986, which was said to provide for greater civilian control over FDN military operations, and prevented a possible open split of the UNO leadership. Moreover, steps towards overcoming the rebels' clear political as well as military weaknesses are envisaged under the Administration's $100 million aid package.

While largely devoted to providing much-needed equipment, the proposed aid programme was reported to give priority to military training and the establishment of a logistics apparatus with which to ensure constant resupply of forces operating within Nicaragua. However, there would also be instruction in civic action in order to win popular support, aiming at a reduction of civilian casualties and abuse, and including such measures as medical assistance by teams accompanying rebel forces. Another objective would be precisely to help set in motion the crucial interaction between military threat and popular support by convincing the Nicaraguan population that the 'Contras' present both a serious challenge to the Sandinista Government and an attractive political alternative for Nicaragua.[30]

If the new package of US aid is indeed finally approved in Washington, and if there are no serious obstacles to its effective provision on the ground in Central America, it is very likely that there will be an intensification of the fighting in Nicaragua. Better training, more secure supply and the acquisition of many more surface-to-air missiles, in particular, would greatly increase the problems of the Sandinistas forces in combatting the 'Contra' threat, and place stronger pressures on the Nicaraguan regime. Such increased US assistance would certainly ensure that the Nicaraguan rebels would not be contained, if at all, for a considerable period.

Nevertheless, the Nicaraguan rebels face tremendous obstacles and, although President Reagan may have succeeded in securing Congressional support for US military assistance to them, that support remains tenuous. It was given in a significant number of cases more from frustration with the Sandinistas than from faith in the 'Contras' or in the Reagan Administration's policies, and there remain strong constraints and pressures against any significant escalation of direct US involvement in the war against the Sandinistas. Were the 'Contras' to fail to show that they had sufficient political support and virtue to deserve sustained US assistance and sufficient strength to increase pressure on the Sandinista regime with their own forces alone, support for current US policy could well begin to be withdrawn.

A crumbling of the Nicaraguan regime before 1988, through internal collapse rather than military overthrow, is not inconceivable, while the possibility of negotiation cannot be ruled out. The conflict could be continuing in 1988 with at least the same level of intensity, if there had by then been no serious problem with Honduras, a major and sustained increase in assistance to the rebels, and a broadening of their popular base in Nicaragua. If there had also been a significant internal weakening of the Sandinistas and a drop in their external support, and if rebel aid, Sandinista isolation and Nicaraguan economic crisis were to continue into the next Administration, a future crumbling of the regime or turn to negotiation in some form and framework might occur.

There could, on the other hand, be a rapid collapse of the 'Contra' rebels, and of current US policy. It is possible that all aid could again be stopped during the Reagan Administration, especially if the rebels were to commit some unacceptable outrage or the Administration were in some manner to overstep the limits imposed by Congress. It is also possible that developments could bring direct US action against the Sandinistas. However, the most likely course is for the Nicaraguan conflict simply to go on – and for US policy to continue within the same parameters – perhaps throughout the remainder of the Reagan Administration. Many in it frankly state that there may simply be no better alternative than continued pursuit of the goal of a negotiated solution, using the rebels to maintain pressure on the Sandinistas, and accept that the conflict could go on for years without a final outcome.

There will continue to be domestic and international pressures against prolongation and escalation of the 'Contra' war. At present, the US Administration seems willing and able to resist those pressures so long as the Nicaraguan rebels remain a minimally viable force. It also appears to see the current indirect costs of its policy, which are emphasised by some critics, as being acceptable or not really costs at all.

However, unless there is some significant change in the current constraints on the level and nature of direct US support, and even if the 'Contra' rebels are boosted for a while by an increase in US aid, it is unlikely that they will be able to pose a direct threat to the Sandinista Government. The pressures against continued support for the rebels may become irresistible if it becomes undeniably clear that they are approaching irreversible containment.

International Pressures and Costs of Current Policy

Global perceptions

Critics of current US policy stress that there are significant costs for the global image of the US. It has invited comparison between the US position in Central America and that of the USSR in Eastern Europe and Afghanistan, and between US support for anti-Communist insurgents and that support for revolutionaries and terrorists which the Administration condemns in Cuba and the Soviet Union. Despite the case made at the World Court, it has also put the US on the wrong side of international law, and the US continues to draw condemnation in international fora. There is a widespread public perception even in allied and neighbouring countries that the US Administration is manifesting an alarming and often hypocritical obsession in its attitude towards Nicaragua. Its apparently indiscriminate and exaggerated condemnation of Sandinista policies, much of the social dimension of which has drawn considerable sympathy and support in Western Europe and Latin America, has only seemed to confirm Sandinista accusations and broader Latin American suspicions that the US is implacably opposed to radical social reform in Central America in itself. However, there is no indication that the Administration, which does not see itself as in the wrong or as behaving like the USSR, will be substantially swayed by this.

Relations with Western Europe

With regard to official relations with Western Europe, differences have diminished in the case of El Salvador, but there remains substantial divergence with regard to Nicaragua, despite increased disillusion and concern in Europe about the course of Nicaraguan politics. The US embargo against Nicaragua was not joined, nor viewed as a positive or even effective step, by European countries. Indeed, in December 1985, six NATO allies[31] ignored a US appeal and voted in favour of a General Assembly Resolution calling for the lifting of the US economic sanctions on Nicaragua. The European Governments have showed no sign of offering support to the Nicaraguan rebels and they did not receive kindly the US efforts to persuade them to exclude Nicaragua from agreements between the European Community and Central America.

Both the US and Western Europe have been disturbed and disappointed by steps taken by the other, and by the failure to present a common Western position. Many Europeans have resented a perceived US failure to consult them, some seeing the credibility of the Western Alliance as undermined by US unilateralism, and others fearing a distraction of US attention and commitment to Europe. Many in Washington have resented Europeans' failure to support the US in a matter seen as of common concern for Western security and of particular concern to the US, while some US unilateralists have found fresh cause for criticism of European irresponsibility. However, although the Grenadan action had some influence on public opinion concerning the prudence of US leadership, in only two cases has the Central American crisis seemed openly to become an Alliance issue. In early 1981, the issues of El Salvador and the deployment of intermediate missiles seemed to converge for the Left-wing of the ruling Social Democrats in West Germany, and in 1985 and 1986 opposition to US policies in Nicaragua merged with opposition to NATO in the period preceding the Spanish referendum on NATO membership.

Since the clashes of 1981 and 1982, however, both sides have preferred to play down the differences. The US has ceased to seek public commitment by the Europeans and most Europeans have muted their criticisms, tending to avoid direct confrontations and channelling their relatively restrained diplomatic activities into support for the Contadora process. Most European Governments are not prepared to make any open and direct stand against the US, especially on behalf of a regime whose democratic commitment remains to be confirmed. No senior European delegations attended the inauguration of President Ortega. However, it is unlikely that ties with Nicaragua will be cut or that such aid as is still being given will be ended. For the US Administration, this is an irritant, and to some extent an obstacle, which it would ideally like to see changed but it will not make an issue of it. Nor will it abandon its policy because of European attitudes, or because of the need to present a common Western position. The perceived costs of continuing tension in Central America for transatlantic relations will probably seem greater in Europe than in Washington.

Regional implications

With regard to Central America, the Administration does not see its policy as having the negative domestic political consequences for Nicaragua's neighbours suggested by its critics, or accept that the negative consequences for the region should be attributed to US policy rather than to the Sandinistas and their external backers.

In both Honduras and Costa Rica, the role that they play in US policy and the consequences of that role have become an internal issue placing the Governments under pressure and seeming to add strains to political stability. The presence and activities of the Nicaraguan rebels have created multiple domestic problems. Continued tensions with Nicaragua and fears of exported Left-wing subversion will help to sustain the central role of the Armed Forces in Honduran politics and could bring a danger of internal political violence. Resources will continue to be diverted to security needs and away from pressing social and economic needs. In Costa Rica, there had arisen by the end of 1985 a striking new level of political conflict in ideological terms. Extreme Right-wing organisations and private armed groups had emerged. Part of the extreme Left had been talking of possible armed actions within Costa Rica, and there had been calls from some quarters to restore an army. There had been a substantial strengthening of Costa Rican security forces, causing widespread concern about the possible beginning of militarisation of this uniquely non-military society.

The Administration's response is that these immediate political consequences should not be exaggerated in either case. Given the depth of Costa Rica's economic crisis and the political strains arising from the regional conflict, the country's stability and democracy have thus far only proved their resilience. The strengthening of the security forces is an unwelcome development, but the Costa Ricans themselves argue that they must take these steps to adjust to the new reality which they face – of border problems, the threat of terrorist activities and the increase in armed crime. They cannot be considered as 'militarisation', or as assuming an aggressive posture against Nicaragua, or as establishing permanent US military presence and control. The security forces' training and arms have been upgraded, from a previous state of considerable inefficiency and ill-equipment. The Civil Guard's inventory has been substantially expanded, particularly in patrol craft, light planes and helicopters. It has also received some 200 rocket launchers, and a number of mortars and anti-tank weapons. Forty-five Costa Ricans received counter-insurgency training at the regional centre in Honduras prior to its closure. In May 1985, 24 US military advisers for the first time began training Costa Rican personnel at a new centre. Some 750 men are to form new border patrol and counter-insurgency units. However, it is argued that this rate of security improvement will probably not continue. Only some 150 men are scheduled to be trained at the new centre in 1986. It is also emphasised that the US military advisers are not to be permanent, but are only training Costa Ricans to train indigenous units. US military aid, which began with $2 million in 1982, rose to $9 million in 1984 and $11 million in 1985, but it is expected to fall to $2.5 million in 1986. Moreover, training and equipment have been received from a number of countries other than the US, including Israel, Taiwan, Panama, Venezuela and West Germany.

In Honduras too, it is argued that the militarisation and potential destabilisation of the country should not be overstated. Indeed, good relations with the US and security co-operation on equitable and respectful terms are not an issue for most parties and sectors. Unless there is some dramatic change in its level and nature, it is unlikely that the US military presence in itself will be a major source of political destabilisation. The Honduran Armed Forces themselves have not increased in anything like the proportions of those of El Salvador and Nicaragua, and remain relatively small, while there is nothing like the Civil Defence of El Salvador and Guatemala, by which civilians in rural areas are organised by the military into armed patrols. The military retain a central role in politics, but it is likely that they would have done so even without the continuing regional conflict, while to some extent the restoration of civilian government has been a result of the regional crisis. The first years of the new Government were certainly marred by abuses of all sorts, with much of the real power clearly in the hands of the Head of the Armed Forces General Alvarez, but army officers removed him and his most extreme colleagues in 1984. In 1985 the Armed Forces behaved with considerable political restraint and responsibility, indeed more so than some civilians. They showed no interest in taking advantage of the constitutional crisis to restore themselves to power, and were one of the influences encouraging President Suazo to modify his political ambitions and manipulations. Despite the confusions and frictions caused by the subsequent political and electoral compromise, the elections in November 1985 took place with no major fraud and high popular participation. For the first time in Honduran history, one democratically elected government had handed over power peacefully to another.

Yet, even if there may seem to be no immediate cause for alarm, there is a broader argument. So long as the isthmus is torn by ideological confrontation and so long as Nicaragua remains a focus of international tensions and in a state of armed conflict, it will be impossible to restore the regional stability, security and co-operation necessary for economic stabilisation and development. There will be even fewer prospects for real stabilisation and growth of Honduras and Costa Rica in particular, which will thus depend on US aid all the longer. Ideological tensions may endanger the development of stable democracy in all the other countries, and make still harder the difficult beginning of democratisation in Guatemala. The Administration accepts all this, but argues that the solution lies in Nicaragua ceasing to be a focus of international tensions and armed conflict. It should also cease to be the exception to the trend toward democratisation; it should compromise with its opponents. The US is only helping those opponents, and will continue to strengthen the democratic develop-ment of Nicaragua's immediate neighbours as well as their security until the situation changes in Nicaragua. The Administration clearly hopes that the proposed provision of a further $300 million in economic aid to the other Central American countries together with military aid to the 'Contras' will help to satisfy concerns in this respect. With regard to the specific social problems posed by the presence in Honduras of large numbers of Nicaraguan rebels, the Administration's tacit response is that Congress should authorise sufficient assistance for most of them to stay and fight in Nicaragua.

Provided that there is no setback to democracy in Honduras and Costa Rica, the domestic implications of policy toward Nicaragua for the other Central American countries may not be a major factor increasing opposition to it in the US, especially while the Nicaraguan regime appears not to be moving in the direction of greater democracy. Moreover, Sandinista ties to the rebels in El Salvador and tensions on Nicaragua's borders can always be made to support the view that Nicaragua is the most direct source of regional conflict. Nevertheless, it seemed clear by 1986 that the issue of support for the Nicaraguan rebels had become a source of serious discomfort even for Central American allies of the US, and was creating frictions in US relations with them.

The renewal of US funding for the 'Contras' in June 1985 helped to reassure the Hondurans that the US was not backing down on its commitments, and thus to encourage them to continue their tacit co-operation. However, there continued to be concern and discomfort in Honduras about its role, which the Hondurans have wished to remain covert and plausibly deniable, in what had become overt US assistance to the Nicaraguan rebels. In August, the Honduran Foreign

Minister stated that the US Embassy in Tegucigalpa would not be permitted to channel assistance to the rebels, the US responding that it would respect Honduran sovereignty, and that none of the aid money would be distributed to the rebel forces while they were in Honduras.[32] In October 1985, the first 14 tons of new supplies purchased with US 'humanitarian' aid were seized by the Hondurans, the private aircraft carrying the shipment having arrived at the country's main international airport with a film crew on board. The Honduran Government continued to block shipments of supplies, while in November moves were apparently made to close the FDN's main training and supply centre, allegedly housed within Honduran military installations, after detailed reports about it emerged in a Honduran newspaper. Amid a series of visits by high-level US officials and changes in Honduran military positions, which seemed to reflect a strengthening of more conservative sectors, the frictions seemed to be being overcome. At the same time, however, Honduran discomfort seemed to be increased in early 1986 by the fact that the bulk of the 'Contra' forces had again retreated back into Honduras. As the debates about military aid intensified in the US in March 1986, the new Honduran Foreign Minister publicly denied suggestions by the US Administration that his Government had authorised aid to be channelled to the 'Contras'. Following Senate approval of the military aid package in August 1986, he again openly stated that Honduras would not allow military assistance to be provided to the Nicaraguan rebels on Honduran territory. Indeed, the Salvadorean Government quickly followed with an announcement that it would not permit military training to be given to the 'Contra' forces on Salvadorean territory either.

The Costa Rican Government has also expressed continued concern about support for the 'Contras'. 'Contra' efforts to establish an effective southern front will continue and will be encouraged by the US. The Costa Rican agreement in early 1986 to an international monitoring commission on the border with Nicaragua seemed to present a potential obstacle to the development of such a front, and a possible cause of frictions in the event of future incidents involving use of Costa Rican territory by US-backed rebel forces. President Oscar Arias, since his election, has publicly questioned the provision of military assistance to the 'Contra' forces, and implied that they would not be allowed to operate from Costa Rican territory.

The attitude of these countries does not reflect hostility to the US or a desire to weaken their own ties to the US. Both the Costa Rican and the Honduran Governments continue to support most aspects of US policy in Central America, and are themselves anxious to bring about political changes in Nicaragua. Although the extent of their opposition should not therefore be exaggerated, however, their apparent lack of enthusiasm about the 'Contras' cannot be dismissed as public posturing. It is more a reflection of their own dilemmas. Both Governments have come to question whether the Nicaraguan rebels, especially with such tenuous support in Washington, can ever be an effective force. They also have genuine concerns about an escalation of external support to make the rebels more effective, which causes alarm about the implications for their own countries and the possibility of war. Both countries want to ensure that any regional settlement will guarantee their security and stability and bring greater democracy to Nicaragua, and suspect that without strong pressures the Sandinistas might not make sufficient concessions. At the same time, a US military commitment to the Nicaraguan rebels, with a demand for Sandinista negotiations with them as a precondition for any broader agreement, would seem far from certain to bring closer any peaceful settlement at all.

In the case of Honduras in particular, the Administration's argument is true that official expressions of concern about the 'Contras' partly reflect doubts about both the rebels' prospects and the credibility of US commitments. It may therefore be the case that if the rebels were all to move into Nicaragua and to demonstrate serious military capacity and political support, and if there were to be solid backing in the US for the Reagan Administration's policy, the Hondurans would be much less reticent about their own role. Conversely, of course, if Honduran discomfort, doubts and dilemmas were to grow, their reluctance to co-operate in 'Contra' support and their interest in exploring alternative paths might increase.

However, as discussed above, the Hondurans' options are limited while their concerns about Nicaragua and their interest in US aid are considerable. They may complain and present obstacles, but they will probably be neither able nor entirely willing to remove the 'Contras' or stop all flows of aid. Unless there also begins to be a decisive shift in 'Contra' prospects and support in Washington, Honduran discomfort will probably not be an unmanageable problem or cost for the Administration. Likewise, given Costa Rica's own concerns about the Sandinistas and its economic dependence on the US, the Government there will continue to have considerable disincentive to any strong opposition to US policy.

Moreover, although Guatemala is likely to try to continue its 'neutral' stance, El Salvador is likely to continue its support for US policy and the 'Contras'. Honduras and Costa Rica will probably want to maintain their common negotiating position with El Salvador. The issue of Sandinista ties both to Cuba and the Sobiet Bloc and to the rebels in El Salvador will also help maintain their own fears about the implications of a consolidated Sandinista regime, and consequently their acceptance of continued military pressures on Nicaragua.

So long as the US Administration can maintain support in Congress for the Nicaraguan rebels and the rebels are not decisively suppressed by the Sandinistas, there will probably not be sufficient pressures from within the rest of Central America to prompt reconsideration of current US policy. If there were to be greater 'Contra' effectiveness, greater Congressional consensus and a radical hardening of the Sandinista regime, it is possible that the support and enthusiasm of Nicaragua's immediate neighbours for the 'Contra' option might increase. This might in turn help reduce Congressional opposition and thus lead to a progressive strengthening of the necessary bases for a US policy of insurgent support. Perhaps more likely, however, is for a reverse process gradually to take place, by which continuing Central American concern, Congressional disagreement and limitation of 'Contra' aid, questionable 'Contra' progress and waning 'Contra' morale would interact to produce an eventual undermining of that course.

So long as the Contadora process had not been abandoned, this might well translate into preference for the type of approach proposed in the Carabelleda initiative, or even for simple acceptance of a regional settlement not entailing formal provisions for supervised political change in Nicaragua. To what extent, or how quickly, will be largely determined by current perceptions of the political situation in Nicaragua and of the capacity of the Contadora proposals to guarantee Central American security, and by the capacity of the Contadora countries to convince the US to accept their alternative.

In early 1986 the Reagan Administration clearly did not see the possible costs for US relations with the rest of Latin America as sufficient to warrant abandonment of its current policy toward Nicaragua. Certainly, and much more than in the case of Western Europe, it has felt it necessary to try to avoid any appearance of ignoring Latin American opinion, and the Administration has endeavoured to make its policy appear entirely compatible with Latin American interests and initiatives. There has, however, been a significant divergence with many Latin American Governments to add to the other problems endemic in inter-American relations. The Caraballeda Declaration and the open request by the eight governments comprising the Contadora and Support Groups for the US Administration not to press for military aid to the Nicaraguan rebels seemed to indicate that differences were becoming larger and more open. It also seemed that there might be an increase in Latin American efforts to exert diplomatic pressure on the US.

However, despite the resurgence of the Contadora initiative after premature announcements of its death, the earlier signs of disillusion or discouragement among the Contadora Governments themselves were an indication of the limits to their determination. Quite apart from the Contadora Governments' own concern about the Sandinistas and consideration of the internal opposition to their Foreign Ministries' attitude, continued failure, or increased costs on their part, might well prompt them to give a lower priority to Central America. Moreover, given the present economic situation in most Latin American countries, there may be little they could do, even if they seriously wanted, to increase pressure on the US over Central America. While the US must be concerned that direct US intervention might adversely affect management of the debt issue, most Latin Americans have no interest in linking the issue of the current level of US activity to immediate economic issues. To the extent that such linkage may already have occurred, indeed, it seems rather to have been made by the US with the aim of putting pressure on them.

If the point were to come at which the US Administration is brought to abandon the 'Contras' and to explore alternatives offered by the Contadora Groups, it would not simply be because the Latin American countries would have been able to exert greater direct pressure on the US. It would be more the result of an interaction between waning 'Contra' fortunes and morale, international pressures and domestic opposition, eventually leading to an acceptance that there was simply no better alternative. In the meantime, however, it seems likely that US support for the Nicaraguan 'Contras' will continue whatever Latin American critics of this course may say.

Notes and References

1 State Department report on Central America, 12 April 1985.
2 *Financial Times* 13 June 1985.
3 Prepared statement of Langhorne A. Motley, Assistant Secretary of State for Inter-American Affairs, before the Subcommittee on Western Hemisphere Affairs of the House Committee on Foreign Affairs, 17 April 1985.
4 *Sunday Times* 7 April 1985.
5 State Department report on Central America, 12 April 1985.
6 Prepared statement of Langhorne Motley, 17 April 1985.
7 President's report to Congress 'U.S. Support for the Democratic Resistance Movement in Nicaragua.' 10 April 1985.
8 *International Herald Tribune* 18 April 1985.
9 Radio address to the nation, 20 April 1985.
10 Quoted in Shirley Christian 'Reagan Aides See No Possibility Of U.S. Accord With Sandinistas' *New York Times* 18 August 1985.

11 Secretary of State George Schultz. Quoted in Doyle McManus 'U.S. Shaping Assertive Policy for Third World' *Los Angeles Times* 18 August 1985.

12 George Schultz to House Foreign Affairs Committee *International Herald Tribune* 21 February 1985.

13 ibid.

14 Theodore Moran 'The Cost of Alternative Policies Toward El Salvador 1984-1989' in Robert Leiken (ed.) *Central America: Anatomy of Conflict* Pergamon Press, Oxford 1984, p. 156.

15 Quoted in Richard Halloran 'U.S. General Opposes Nicaragua Invasion' *International Herald Tribune* 1 July 1985.

16 Richard Halloran, loc. cit.

17 Quoted in Bernard Gwertzman 'Schultz, Seeing "Tyranny", Asks Aid to Guerrillas in Nicaragua' *International Herald Tribune* 25 February 1985.

18 General Wallace Nutting. Quoted in Richard Halloran, loc. cit.

19 Quoted in Joanne Omang 'Press Sandinistas Harder, A U.S. Official Advises' *International Herald Tribune* 12/13 October 1985.

20 Laurence Whitehead 'The Prospects for a Political Settlement: Most Options Have Been Foreclosed.' Paper prepared for the Conference on the Conflict in Central America sponsored by the Friedrich Naumann Stiftung in co-operation with the Inter-American Institute for Human Rights, San José, Costa Rica, 1-6 December 1984, p. 11.

21 In April 1985, there were reportedly informal contacts between Sandinista and legal opposition leaders, during which the possibility was mentioned of negotiation leading to new elections. This was said to have been dropped in the wake of the US embargo.

22 Quoted in Joanne Omang, loc. cit.

23 *Le Monde* 30 August 1985.

24 *Guardian* 17 October 1985.

25 *Washington Post* Editorial 'Backward in Nicaragua' in *International Herald Tribune* 22 October 1985.

26 *New York Times* Editorial 'True Colors in Managua' in *International Herald Tribune* 19/20 October 1985.

27 Quoted in Shirley Christian 'U.S. Says Moscow Ships More Arms To Nicaraguans.' *New York Times* 5 November 1985.

28 *Washington Post* 6 November 1985.

29 *Financial Times* 7 December 1985.

30 Richard Halloran 'Green Berets will be sent to train "Contras", U.S. says.' *International Herald Tribune* 22 August 1986.

31 France, Spain, Denmark, Greece, Norway, Iceland.

32 Latin America Weekly Report 6 September 1985; *Washington Times* 2 September 1985.

Conclusions

US policy goals are unlikely to change in El Salvador or Guatemala. As long as progress towards achieving those goals continues, the central issue for American policy towards Central America over the next few years will remain that of Nicaragua. The course of the 'Contra' campaign there will determine both US policy options and, consequently, the possible outcomes to the Central American crisis.

While developments in Nicaragua cannot be predicted with any certainty, the Sandinista Government is not likely to face any dire challenge to its survival in the near future. Although the Sandinistas will remain under strong economic and political pressure (from both inside and outside), the Nicaraguan rebels are unlikely to be able to pose a threat direct to the regime.

However, the 'Contras' will not quickly be suppressed, especially while US aid is received, and may be boosted for a time by an increase in US assistance. The Reagan Administration may view the maintenance of this continuing pressure on the Sandinista regime as a minimum success and sufficient justification in itself for continuation of current policy. Domestic and international pressures on the Administration are presently insufficient for it to abandon its strong commitment to the 'Contra' rebels. These pressures will probably not change while the level of direct US involvement does not significantly increase, the 'Contras' remain a minimally viable force, and the Sandinistas fail to do more to convince the US Congress and many Western Governments of their ultimate commitment to non-alignment and open democracy. So long as the US provides support for the 'Contra' rebels, maintains military pressures on the Sandinistas, and insists upon both direct Sandinista negotiation with the 'Contras' and Sandinista negotiation with its neighbours under pressure as conditions for any form of agreement, the deadlock over a peace settlement will probably continue.

Nevertheless, the point may well be reached when the United States will have to adopt a different policy. This could occur if, for example, more decisive containment of the 'Contras' by the Sandinistas were to combine with increased domestic and international pressures to force a withdrawal of US support for the rebels or if there were to be other significant changes in the Central American situation – perhaps in El Salvador or Honduras. The manner in which such a point is reached will obviously influence the US choice of options.

In all events, strong opposition will exist in the US to any policy which might fail to satisfy fundamental US security concerns in Central America, jeopardise the position of the Salvadorean Government, or seem to constitute a humiliating defeat for the US. This will hold for any future Administration, and a Democratic Administration will not be anxious to lay the Party open to charges of definitively 'losing' Nicaragua at the second attempt. Any process of policy change with regard to Nicaragua is not likely to be simple, easy or quick. The possibilities if the 'Contra' option becomes unviable will be limited and none of them will appear free of risks or costs. But these other options need to be analysed as dispassionately as possible, notwithstanding the strong divisions and emotions which have been aroused in the United States over Central America. This chapter will consider alternative assumptions about the nature and flexibility of Sandinista intentions, analyse the policy choices for the United States over the next few years, and conclude with a series of recommendations.

Alternative Assumptions about the Sandinistas

Are the Sandinistas intransigently committed to a hostile Marxist–Leninist regime – as argued by the Reagan Administration – or are there grounds for believing that Sandinista intentions are more flexible and still susceptible to external moderation? Few in the US disagree that there has been strong Leninist influence on Sandinista ideology and behaviour, and strong Sandinista sympathy with Cuba. The debate in the US revolves around assumptions as to the extent of the Sandinistas' ambitions, the importance of the other influences and pressures on them, and the likelihood of their eventual moderation by outside forces.

The Reagan Administration argues that Sandinistas have a unanimous and irreversible commitment to the eventual establishment of a full Marxist–Leninist regime, tied to Cuban and Soviet Bloc interests. They are bent on spreading subversion and exporting revolution to the extent that they are not prevented from doing so. They have the internal capability and necessary Soviet backing to carry out these ambitions whatever the consequences would be for Nicaragua's relations with its neighbours and the West in general. If US pressures are removed they would consolidate such a Communist state, and no longer even pretend to have any interest in democracy and non-alignment. Only under strong pressure from the 'Contra' rebels and the US will the Sandinistas negotiate seriously, if at all, even over security issues.

An alternative view is that a stable Communist state in Nicaragua should not be considered inevitable, whatever desire there might be for such an outcome within the Sandinistas, for at least three reasons – even in the absence of 'Contra' and US pressure.

First, the USSR will not necessarily be willing to back the Sandinistas entirely or indefinitely, although so long as the costs are not high, the chances of Soviet abandonment are low. Second, Nicaragua will remain in dire economic straits, and the regime will be under strong pressure to satisfy popular needs and demands. Unless it wished and were able to opt for total integration into Comecon (which seems unlikely), it would have a strong interest in increased economic ties with Latin America and the developed Western countries, and – eventually – normalisation of relations with the US itself. Third, although the Sandinistas' current hegemony and control permits them to stifle discontent, the permanent imposition of total control and a monolithic polity would not easily be accomplished in any circumstances. Organised labour has not been fully controlled, and the important influence of the small-scale sector in Nicaragua will continue. The influence and activism of the Church would inevitably remain strong. The opposition parties would have sufficient base not to be suppressed entirely or indefinitely. The Government would fear the total flight of private capital and qualified persons, and many in the business sector would retain their determination to stay in Nicaragua, rather than leave and hand over to the state, as in Cuba.

In this alternative view, it is not argued that the Reagan assumptions can be guaranteed to prove wrong in all respects. It is of course conceivable that the Sandinistas might seek to turn away from Latin America and Europe, to eliminate all effective internal opposition and to tie themselves to Comecon. The Soviet Union might indeed be willing to provide full subsidy to Nicaragua. However, the Reagan Administration's stated assumptions about even the Sandinistas' internal course should not be considered inevitable.

A further alternative assumption, indeed, is that although the

Sandinistas refuse to negotiate with US-backed 'Contras' or to accept a regional peace treaty while under direct US pressure, they are under sufficient other forms of pressure to agree to a generally acceptable settlement at least over security issues in the context of a broader process of negotiation involving withdrawal of US support for the 'Contras' and of direct US pressure.

The problem, of course, is that these assumptions can be tested only if the US were willing gradually to abandon both its current instruments of pressure and, as an inevitable corollary, its insistence on directly forced political change in Nicaragua as a pre-condition for a withdrawal of those instruments. Likewise, the problem is that the Sandinistas' intentions, and the unavoidable consequences of their being left in a position to carry them out, can only be tested for certain if the Sandinistas are left in precisely such a position.

US policy options

The range of US policy options is not itself affected by the assumptions that one holds about the Sandinistas. Indeed, they may not be determinant in any eventual US choice among those options. However, assessments of the costs and risks entailed in those options will clearly depend upon the assumptions that one makes about the critical issue of Sandinista intentions. If the current US policy of support for the Nicaraguan 'Contras' is brought to a halt, such that the US is simply forced to adopt an alternative course, what are the realistic US policy options?

Option one: military intervention

The option of military action to remove the Sandinista regime, whether in the form of a US invasion or of a collective security action, merits consideration only if one holds the Reagan assumptions. It would present some risks of broader conflict, and could be guaranteed to have both high political costs for the US – domestically and internationally – and adverse consequences for regional stability. Direct military action would not only exclude any role for the regional powers, but be a massive blow both to their foreign policies and to the prospects of achieving any new framework of regional security which might strengthen US regional interests in the long term. It would also have a negative impact on the Western Alliance, on East–West relations and on America's position in the world.

Such military action might just conceivably produce within a few years a stable, friendly, democratic government in Nicaragua, with similar governments in the rest of Central America, thus achieving the best possible outcome for US interests in the long term, despite seeming the most costly option in the short term. More likely, however, would be an unstable regime in Nicaragua with limited legitimacy and depending on a long-term US military and political commitment for its survival, with the rest of Central America likewise volatile and insecure.

Option two: containment and coercion

The second broad option would be to continue to oppose any outcome that does not entail radical change in Nicaragua's political structure and government either before or as an integral and internationally supervised element in a comprehensive settlement.

The instruments of such a policy might include a massive increase in Honduran military strength, a further strengthening of Costa Rica's security capability and the establishment of a US military presence in Costa Rica, a strengthening of the internal security capabilities of all the other Central American countries, a revival of *Condeca*, increased US military exercises, the provision of firm US security guarantees and a large increase in US military and economic assistance, as well as continued economic coercion and diplomatic isolation of Nicaragua.

Its stated goals would be twofold. On the one hand, it would aim to counter the presumed intention of the Sandinistas to attack or subvert Nicaragua's neighbours once relieved of rebel pressures. On the other hand, it would attempt to maintain strong pressure on the Nicaraguan regime by increasing the other elements of pressure in current US policy. Expanded US military assistance, presence and guarantees would also be necessary to counter the possible growth of interest by Nicaragua's neighbours in settlement with the Sandinistas if the US were seen to abandon the Nicaraguan rebels.

Although one assumption in the Reagan view is that the Soviet Union is willing to prop up the Sandinistas, Soviet failure to do so could not only increase the prospects of Sandinista collapse but also affect global perceptions of the reliability of Soviet commitments. An additional rationale behind this policy option could thus be to outlast the Soviet Union and Cuba.

This option would make sense only on the basis of Reagan assumptions about the Sandinistas, or if the reduction in direct US assistance to El Salvador entailed in a security settlement would threaten the survival of the Salvadorean Government. In this case, containment would be a necessary, but temporary, measure before choosing among the other options.

In this containment option, the possibility of a negotiated settlement would be left open if the Sandinistas would agree to hold internationally supervised elections. Such a step by the Sandinistas, however, would in this context be tantamount to open surrender to the US, and therefore be highly unlikely.

Such a policy would preclude exploration of any remaining openings for future understandings, and only help to fulfil many of the assumptions in the Reagan view. Nicaraguan force levels would certainly not decrease. They could even further increase in response to the strengthening of the forces in the region, especially if there were renewed moves to revive and activate *Condeca*. If the Sandinistas are committed to establishing a Marxist–Leninist regime, a situation of permanent isolation and external hostility would only encourage and assist them in doing so. They might well not take further steps to reduce support and haven for regional revolutionaries but increase such activities in response to such escalated hostility. Also, although the Soviet Union would be unlikely to attempt to establish permanent military bases or introduce advanced offensive weapons (while such moves remained obviously an unacceptable challenge to US security interests), Nicaraguan ties to Cuba and the Soviet Bloc would be guaranteed to continue for as long as the latter was willing to pay.

The Soviet Union's interest in a complete and open-ended economic commitment, and in any defence commitment, must in any case be questionable. It would almost certainly continue to avoid committing its credibility to the survival of the Nicaraguan regime. However, in view of the various political benefits to be gained from such a situation, especially in Central America, as well as the costs for the USSR's global revolutionary image of abandoning a beleaguered regime, it would probably continue to provide minimum military and economic support for as long as Nicaragua remained under US pressure. The economic costs may be unwelcome even at present levels, but provided that there was sufficient geopolitical incentive, they might not seem prohibitive even if most Western ties were cut. Moreover, the Soviet leadership might with some reason believe that it would have less difficulty in financially outlasting the US than the US Administration would have in outlasting Congress.

The possible outcomes of this option would probably be an internal collapse of the Sandinista regime, a precipitation of direct US action or, most likely, a permanent situation of controlled tension and frozen hostility.

Even if the Salvadorean guerrillas had been decisively contained by the point at which it was adopted, the containment option would have adverse consequences for regional stability. Any massive expansion of Honduran forces and militarisation of Costa Rica could well bring all

164

the negative consequences for those countries' stability and democracy feared at present. The demilitarisation of El Salvador and Guatemala, which is so important for the long-term development of democratic civilian institutions there, would probably not take place. The continued state of tensions would tend to discourage new economic initiatives and investment. Mounting economic problems would breed further political and social unrest. Strengthened military and security apparatus, accompanied by a permanent identification of internal instability with external subversion, would threaten increased repression and polarisation even in Costa Rica. Also the increase and spread of the US' military presence and ties to the security forces would threaten to draw the US directly into the internal problems of these countries. The US commitment would be long-term, but might consist primarily of permanent security co-operation and economic support for economically unviable and politically volatile countries. An isolated Nicaragua would be as close to a 'second Cuba' on the mainland as it is likely to be. The US would not only have 'lost' Nicaragua but would risk only 'holding' the other countries at high economic and political cost. There would be permanent risks of conflict. Failure to continue containing would always be feared to bring Sandinista-inspired insurgency. If the consequence of such containment were to have been positive setbacks for development and democratisation in the other countries, the potential for a resurgence of violence and turmoil would indeed be there.

Finally, this option would have some of the same consequences as the intervention option for the regional powers, as well as foregoing the possibility of establishing new patterns of security co-operation in the region. Such a course would solve none of the existing problems, while creating many new ones, and it could probably not be a permanent state of affairs. Indeed, the US Congress might not be prepared to provide the necessary funds for a sustained containment policy.

No US Administration or neighbouring government actually wants an outcome which simply freezes Nicaragua, or Central America as a whole, in its present situation. Moreover, the other Central American Governments will continue to have a strong interest in reducing regional tensions, especially in view of their deep economic problems. The Hondurans in particular would probably have some concern about what is supposed to happen to any remaining 'Contras' under this policy. There are also widespread sensitivities regarding their national roles and images in the case of any such permanent military alliance with the US in another institutionalised arena of East–West confrontation in Latin America. A simple shift from a policy of support for the 'Contra' rebels to one of 'containment' might not be easily accomplished, especially if the dropping of 'Contra' support were to raise serious doubts as to the likely durability of the US commitment to 'containment'.

Option three: settlement

The third broad option is for the US, in conjunction with Nicaragua's neighbours, to abandon its insistence on political change in Nicaragua both as a condition for a reduction of pressures and as a specific, binding and enforceable commitment in any negotiated settlement. The United States would agree gradually to withdraw all instruments of direct pressure (support for insurgents, unilateral military intimidation, economic coercion) and to hold bilateral talks over security issues with the Sandinistas, as part of a process of regional negotiation. While also agreeing to accept the regional powers as guarantors of both the process and the settlement itself, the US would maintain diplomatic support for the other Central American countries in securing a strong multilateral agreement on security commitments and strong mechanisms for verification and enforcement. The US would also make clear to the Sandinistas that any clear breach of the agreements which constituted a direct threat to the US would be met with a US response.

No-one is going to pretend that a regional settlement will be easy to reach or simple to enforce. Any regional settlement would have to include specific, binding and enforceable commitments with regard to the immediate security concerns of all parties together with a mechanism for arbitration of inevitable disputes: non-aggression, border security, prohibition of foreign military bases, prohibition of support of any sort for insurgents, irregular forces, terrorists and all groups seeking to destabilise other countries, withdrawal of foreign military and security advisers, prior negotiation on maximum military force levels and agreed programmes for reduction to those levels would all have to be covered, difficult though this will be, if any settlement is to be acceptable and durable. It would be agreed that El Salvador, Guatemala and Nicaragua would phase the reduction in their force levels taking into account the level of guerrilla conflict in their own countries. International military exercises would not be formally prohibited, but would be limited in some form of confidence building agreement which would be understood to preclude any Cuban or Soviet Bloc military activity in Nicaragua, while clearly aiming at the practical elimination of all such exercises.

The agreement might call for national reconciliation, but only as an agreed objective of amnesty and guarantees of political participation

166

within the respective national legal frameworks. The immediate willingness of rebel groups within each country to lay down their arms and take up such offers would not be made a condition for implementation of the international security commitments. With regard to internal politics, the same broad principles as in the Contadora draft treaties would still be emphasised and included, but definite political change in Nicaragua would not be specifically mandated or internationally supervised. It would take place, if at all, only after an end to hostilities and resolution of the immediate security issues. The US would accept that it would not have an absolute guarantee that such change would in fact occur, and would be constrained from resuming pressures on Nicaragua whatever happened internally.

While difficulties will inevitably arise in reaching such an agreement and in establishing effective regional mechanisms for verification and enforcement, these will be assumed to be overcome in assessing the implications of this option for the US. A regional security settlement will depend upon the Sandinistas' having sufficiently strong interest in achieving an agreement of this nature to be flexible over outstanding differences over security issues, as well as sufficient diplomatic sense not to insist on any regional condemnation of the US or unilateral US declaration.

On the Reagan assumptions, this option will appear as only slightly less of a 'worst case' than simple acceptance of the Sandinista regime in its current state. In the alternative view, this option might still turn out to be a 'worst case', but it is probably the best 'worst case' available to the US. Moreover, the possibility would be left open of settlement not turning out to be so bad.

In either view, this option would entail some degree of immediate political cost for the US. The US would appear to have visibly failed in its principal stated objectives, having accepted the legitimacy of the Sandinista regime and abandoned the Nicaraguan people into 'totalitarian' hands. Having staked its credibility on the prevention of a 'second Cuba', the credibility of US commitments elsewhere in the world might be questioned. Whatever the subsequent political developments within Nicaragua, however, this type of broader political cost will need to be considered against the specific costs entailed in the other options – a direct military intervention or permanent 'containment' of Nicaragua. The latter would not only be expected to 'lose' Nicaragua but also fail to bring any of the compensatory broader political benefits which might be expected to accrue from the US, visibly refraining from political interventionism and co-operating with the regional powers in the peaceful diplomatic pursuit of regional security and stability. Moreover, so long as the

Sandinistas and the Cubans could see the prudence of not attempting to use the settlement process to humiliate the US, the consequences of choosing this option for US credibility and prestige would to some extent be only as great as the US made them appear.

The implications of Sandinista survival for the rest of Central America are at the centre of concerns over the dangers of such an option. However, a security settlement would cover almost all the external consequences which might be feared from a consolidated Sandinista regime, Marxist–Leninist or not. The questions of whether the Sandinistas are committed to a Marxist–Leninist regime and of whether such a regime could be trusted would be put to the test, but in relatively controlled circumstances. If the US and Nicaragua's neighbours were willing to make a genuine effort to live with Nicaragua, international opinion could be expected to be supportive. The credibility of US efforts to live with Nicaragua and to make the settlement work would require clear US acceptance of the fact that further internal conflicts, and any continued fighting in El Salvador or Guatemala, could not necessarily be attributed to secret violation of security commitments by the Sandinistas or anyone else, just as the Sandinistas would have to accept that continued pressures against their regime could not necessarily be attributed to covert action by the US.

Assuming that the Reagan Administration is correct about the Sandinistas' internal political intentions, would the subsequent Marxist–Leninist regime comply with the settlement once it had been implemented?

If the Nicaraguan Government was unmistakeably and without provocation to break its security commitments despite specific pledges to the Central American countries, the regional powers and the international community, steps would have to be taken. If the provisions for enforcement failed, or were not duly applied, and the Nicaraguan violation was sufficiently serious to bring a threat of conflict with its neighbours, the settlement would obviously collapse. The US, together with Nicaragua's neighbours, would probably then have to choose between the other two broad options. However, even such a failure of the settlement option would have its advantages, if it was internationally recognised to be the responsibility of the Sandinistas and not a US manoeuvre to find a pretext to act against the regime because of its internal policies. If the Nicaraguan Government is as irredeemable as many in the US believe, it would finally be showing itself as such to the world by breaching the peace despite being given security guarantees and a genuine chance to make a fresh start in its external behaviour. And by seeming to validate the premise that Sandinista power is incompatible with regional stability, actions against Nicaragua would receive much more of that broad and positive international support, the lack of which is one factor reducing the prospects for the success of current US policy. The problem, of course, will be to provide the kind of unimpeachable evidence of Nicaraguan transgression that would be needed to trigger a regional response. This is likely to be a messy process and not a clear indictment.

If the Nicaraguan regime were to become 'Communist' but was prepared to abide by the security commitments of a settlement, and if it were to prove possible for the US and Nicaragua's immediate neighbours to coexist with it on the basis of such a settlement, then a certain stability could come to develop in the region. A successful settlement could accelerate a reduction of the conflict in El Salvador but, so long as Nicaragua was verifiably not involved in any form of support for the Salvadorean rebels, continued fighting need not cause the settlement to break down. Once the internal conflicts had been controlled, the reduction of regional tensions and force levels would have some positive consequences for regional stability. Demilitarisation and democratisation in El Salvador and Guatemala would be boosted, militarisation of Costa Rica more likely to be avoided, and many of the strains on the Honduran political process eased. If those countries were to become stable and relatively prosperous, as would be more likely than in the case of indefinite crisis or the 'containment' option, the US would also have achieved the political containment of the revolutionary tide and be exerting political pressure on Nicaragua if only by force of example.

On the basis of an effective settlement which eliminated the external justifications claimed for continued Sandinista political hegemony and control, it would also be possible for the US to test, and for other internal and external forces to influence, Sandinista political intentions. If in this context the Sandinistas were nevertheless to impose a totalitarian Marxist–Leninist regime, the Reagan view would sadly have proved correct in that respect, although the external consequences might not be so disastrous as assumed on that view. If, on the other hand, they were not to do so, and the Sandinistas moved towards a political structure which might be less than the liberal democratic ideal but nonetheless a more open structure based on broad national consensus, there would clearly be no reason or justification for US concern.

The argument could still be made that, even after a settlement over immediate security issues, a Marxist–Leninist Nicaraguan Government sympathetic to the Soviet Union could be a potential strategic asset for the Soviet Union. In the case of global crisis or conflict, any agreement might simply be ignored, and there would be possible costs even in peacetime.

Nicaragua could only acquire the means itself to pose any potential conventional threat to Caribbean SLOCs (Sea Lines of Communication) or the Panama Canal by openly breaking the regional settlement. The Nicaraguans would nevertheless retain, or could secretly acquire, the capacity for mining and sabotage. In peacetime, however, even a Marxist–Leninist Nicaragua sympathetic to the USSR would have no incentive to carry out such attacks, quite apart from the fear of a devastating US response. Nicaragua has been one of the nations with the highest proportions of its trade using the Panama Canal, having had as much as 77 per cent passing through it.

The more serious fear would revolve around the opportunities provided to the Soviet Union. Although a settlement would presumably prohibit Soviet military installations, no formal impediment would exist to an increasingly regular utilisation of Nicaragua by the Soviet Union to extend its naval and reconnaissance activity through port calls and aircraft operations. This type of activity would be made more likely if Nicaragua were to be closely tied to Comecon, or fully subsidised by the Soviet Union, thus reducing its interest in the development of positive relations with the US and the West in general. Even if this were generally to seem to be an abuse of the settlement, strong pressures would exist against abandoning the agreement so long as the letter of the agreement had not been broken, and no direct threat to Nicaragua's neighbours or offensive threat to the US were presented.

In view of this possibility, the US might wish to accompany a regional settlement with a global understanding with the USSR over the nature of Soviet activities in Nicaragua, even though one of the fundamental drives behind current US policy is *not* to have another regime in the hemisphere regarding which any strategic understanding with the Soviets seems remotely necessary. However, the US would have another potential course, which would be to increase Nicaragua's own interest in having a positive understanding with the US. Even if Nicaragua were Marxist–Leninist, the immediate extent of Nicaraguan integration into Comecon would probably depend in part upon the attitude adopted by the US itself. All current indications are that both the Sandinistas and the Soviet Union would prefer Nicaragua also to have normal economic relations with the West, including especially the US. If the US were to accompany a regional settlement with a restoration of such relations in order to test Sandinista intentions, then Nicaragua's possible interest or acquiescence in assisting Soviet strategic activities and in breaking any settlement could be influenced not only by threats of reprisal but also by the provision of incentives and a strengthening of Nicaraguan interest in continued stability and normal relations. In both respects, the role of the regional powers and Europe would be extremely important. Were Nicaragua also again to have substantial and valued economic relations with the US and be made aware that such relations were conditional on Nicaragua's not abusing any settlement, then even if the Soviets were prepared to pay for Nicaragua's survival, the Nicaraguans themselves might well be very reluctant to move in that direction.

Absolute confidence in this respect will probably not be attainable. In the settlement, the US would have security guarantees, but might simply have to live with the fact that Nicaragua will never have that unquestionable international reliability of the past. The strategic value of Nicaragua in the event of global crisis or conventional conflict would objectively be limited. Any use of Nicaraguan facilities by the USSR would prompt an immediate US response, and possible action attempted by Nicaragua in war against SLOCs or the Canal would be suicidal. Some hypothetical risk would remain. However, if the regime cannot be removed, it must surely seem preferable to have Nicaragua as it would be after a successful regional settlement, especially if normal relations had been established, than to have Nicaragua in a state of hostility with the US, highly armed and with a Soviet military presence, especially if US resources and forces were committed to its containment.

Perhaps the clearest and most unavoidable challenge for the US in the event of settlement would be that of Cuba, for it could exacerbate tensions between Washington and Havana. On the other hand, there is also the possibility, however remote it may seem at present, that a successful regional settlement could help to reduce tensions with Cuba. Moreover, the US will almost certainly sooner or later have to seek new ways to face the challenge of Cuba's regional role if it is ever to achieve durable bases for regional stability. Whether or not any greater understanding with Cuba can ever be reached depends, of course, also on the Castro regime. The circumstances in which to resolve the Cuban question would probably be more favourable in the case of settlement than in the case of either of the other broad options left open to the US if the 'Contra' option is effectively closed.

Even on the assumption that the result of a move towards this type of settlement would be a 'Communist' Nicaragua, this is arguably the best option for the US, unless the Salvadorean Government would risk collapse if US advisers were withdrawn. This type of settlement would entail some political costs, extremely limited strategic risks, and a lack of absolute certainty and reliability for the US in the area. However, the extent of the costs and risks could in part be controlled and influenced by the US itself. The eventual result could be made a strengthening of regional security with positive long-term benefits for the US in the hemisphere, and some positive global implications for regional management of security issues.

Recommendations

Governments rarely address policy options quite so starkly and tend to pursue existing policies until events force them to change. The Reagan Administration's special commitment to the Nicaraguan 'Contras' makes this especially true in the case of US policy towards Central America. While it is possible that the Sandinista regime may eventually crumble or give in, it is more likely that the US course of support for the 'Contras' will eventually be undermined, thus forcing the US to consider alternative options. At that point, military intervention or containment may be attempted or precipitated. However, unless there is some significant change in the external situation, an effective security settlement with a Sandinista Government is both the best option for the US and indeed the most likely to commend itself, whatever assumptions the Administration may hold as to subsequent political developments within Nicaragua.

The immediate issue then is whether the US should continue its current policy, in the hope that it might yet achieve an outcome which is more attractive than the options remaining in the event that the 'Contras' fail. Or should the US begin to change its policy now, on the assumption that it will probably be forced to do so at some point anyway?

Beyond preventing 'Communist consolidation' for as long as possible, why should the US continue its current policy, even assuming that it probably will not succeed and cannot continue for ever? First, continuation of current policy might gain time for the rebels in El Salvador to be contained before the US was forced to consider reducing its assistance to the Salvadorean Government. However, while US interests would not be served if the result of a security settlement were to be an increased risk of collapse of the Salvadorean Government, the timing of a security settlement should not be tied to the prior containment of the Salvadorean rebels. A settlement which ended all external support to the guerrillas – and would be more effective in cutting off supplies than the 'Contra' war, which the US Administration has partly justified by that argument – could directly contribute to a reduction of the armed conflict. Moreover, the simple containment of the guerrillas is not and should not be the objective of US policy in El Salvador. Greater material and political disentanglement of the Salvadorean conflict from the other elements of the crisis, within the process of regional negotiation, could also broaden the possibilities of national dialogue within El Salvador. Unless there is a sharp reversal of the current trend in the Salvadorean conflict, the benefits for US policy in El Salvador of continued hostilities against the Sandinistas will not be greater or more certain than those of a security settlement, nor be sufficient to outweigh the other arguments for changing policy towards Nicaragua sooner rather than later.

A second argument for continuing current policy is that it might nonetheless increase the Sandinistas' internal weaknesses, such that the pressures for political change would be all the greater by the time that the direct 'Contra' threat disappeared. However, continued US and 'Contra' pressure is likely to encourage the Sandinistas to strengthen their internal control. Moreover, were popular discontent to be increased as a result of these pressures, the Sandinistas might see increased dangers for them in any precipitate opening of the political system. If the opportunities remaining to establish bases for greater understanding between the Sandinistas and the legal political opposition in Nicaragua are not explored, the more likely it will be that Sandinista hegemony might be perpetuated and eventually institutionalised. If strengthened internal control and ties to the Soviet Bloc were to alienate further the Sandinistas from Latin America and Western Europe, the Sandinistas' eventual susceptibility to the influence of those countries might only be reduced. Indeed, the longer the current situation and the diplomatic deadlock continues, the greater the possibility that the present level of regional efforts to address all dimensions of the crisis may not continue. There will probably be no radical or definitive change in the political situation of Nicaragua before a process of settlement is begun, now or later. Whatever the ultimate ambitions of the Sandinistas, the establishment of an open democracy is unlikely in any case because of the war and the confrontation with the US, but the declaration of a one-party state is also unlikely if only because of the Sandinistas' need to maintain a minimum level of support from Latin America and Western Europe. Although far from certain, the prospects for an eventual opening of the Nicaraguan political system would seem on balance to be greater if current US policy changes sooner rather than later.

There is a broader and more positive argument, along similar lines, for changing US policy sooner rather than later. There may still be potential openings to increase confidence and perceptions of common interest between the Central American countries themselves as part of a broad process of concession and compromise. If some progress could be made in this respect, as well as in encouraging some preliminary political movement within Nicaragua, in parallel to negotiations over the security commitments of an eventual settlement, then the prospects could be improved for such a settlement to be viable and to be the basis for future understanding and co-operation. Any such opportunities, both internally and regionally, may be running out.

Continued pursuit of current US policy may only impede anyone's improving the prospects of an eventual settlement with the Sandinistas being less costly and risky in practice.

There is finally the simple, but strong, argument that it is better to end the costs entailed in continuation of current policy as soon as possible. These include the costs in human life and suffering resulting from the war; the instability and lack of development in Central America; the controversy and divisions with the US; the frictions in US relations with Latin America; and the discredit for the US in much of the world caused by support for the 'Contras'.

To argue against military pressures and support for the 'Contras' is not to argue against all forms of pressure on the Sandinista regime. However, the current US course only weakens, and in some respects discourages, other pressures which could be more appropriate and more successful in promoting political understanding within Nicaragua and in helping to secure peace and stability in Central America. A prolonged and increased commitment to the 'Contras' does not seem more likely to further US interests than an increased and immediate willingness to take the chance – which is both risk and opportunity – of conceding greater initiative and responsibility to the Contadora Groups.

Consequently, the US should phase out its support for the 'Contras' and cease its insistence on negotiation between them and the Sandinistas as a precondition for other forms of negotiation. It should begin now to make the necessary moves implied on its part to make the settlement option as safe, painless and potentially productive as possible. It should maintain diplomatic (and, where necessary, military) support for Nicaragua's neighbours while pressing for a strong and workable agreement on security issues. It should also convincingly co-operate with the regional powers in their efforts to disentangle the crisis and to keep open the remaining openings for greater internal and external understandings.

An immediate move by the US in this direction does not and should not imply precipitate acceptance of a diplomatic treaty alone. It would be better in all respects if there were to be more of a broad and gradual process of concession and confidence building, in which appropriate external influence and political pressure could and would be effectively exerted, particularly by the regional powers and Western Europe, and the Sandinistas might make the preparatory moves toward compromise at all levels that are required on their part. It is by beginning now to encourage and participate in such a process that the US may avert the difficult choice of perceived 'worst cases' that is the probable alternative.

There is still a ray of hope that some settlement can be achieved in and over Central America, with the necessary concessions and changes accepted by all sides for eventual peace and co-operation. In 1986, it seems little more than a glimmer on the horizon, but it should not be allowed to die.

Index

Abrams, Elliot   116, 136, 144
accommodation policy   14-17, 20-28
Afghanistan   20, 21, 23, 29, 132
Agency for International Development
   (AID)   104
Alliance for Progress   8-9, 25
Alvarez Martinez, General Gustav
   77, 152
American Institute for Free Labor
   Development (AIFLD)   41-2
amnesty   47, 96
   in Nicaragua   73, 74, 83, 87, 166
Angola   64
Arce, Bayardo   87
Argentina   68
Armed Forces
   certification   28, 39, 42, 48-9
   Honduran   36, 59, 152
   Nicaraguan   59, 144, 145
   Salvadorean   23, 38-9, 41, 43-4, 47,
   100-103, 109
arms   11
   build up (Nicaragua)   3, 54-6, 58-60,
   142, 144, 152
   limitation   18, 84, 88
   traffic   28, 44, 52-5, 57-8, 60-61

Barnes, Michael   35
Bay of Pigs   10
Belize   69, 97, 98
Bermudez, Enrique   57

Betancur, Belisario   70
Big Pine I (Ahuas Tara I)   59
Big Pine II (Ahuas Tara II)   60, 113
Blandon, Adolfo   44
Boland, Edward   70-71
border conflict   76, 119-20, 143, 152
Britain   97
Brezinski, Zbigniew   16
Bush, George   49
business sector
   El Salvador   26, 49, 50, 105-6, 107
   Nicaragua   20, 61-2, 137, 161
Bustillo, Juan   44

Calero, Adolfo   88, 89
Caraballeda initiative   121, 122-3, 124,
   128, 130-31, 135, 156
Caribbean Basin   10-13, 169
   Initiative (CBI)   67, 68, 69
Carter Administration   14
   Central America   15-30
   El Salvador   22-30
   Sandinistas   18-22, 28
Casanova Vides General Carlos
   Eugenio   44
Casey, William   57, 72
Castro, Fidel   11, 12, 18, 52, 72
Central American Defence Council
   (Condeca)   60, 112, 163, 164
Central American Democratic
   Community   69

Cerezo, Vinicio 95-6, 98, 99, 100, 121
Certification process 28, 39, 42, 48-9
Chamorro, Pedro Joaquin 16
CIA 18, 22
  'Contra' support 56-8, 60, 71, 75,
    76, 88, 90
Cienfuegos incident 10, 12
Cisneros, Henry 75
Civil Defence 101, 108
Cold War 6, 8
Colombia 36, 69, 70
Comecon 138, 161, 170
Comintern 23
Communism 7, 116, 136
  anti- 8, 27, 42, 45, 47, 109-10, 126
  El Salvador 9, 23, 25, 27, 33, 38-9,
    42, 45, 47, 172
  Guatemala 8, 98, 99-100
  Nicaragua 18-19, 65, 74, 109-10,
    146, 161, 169, 171
Contadora process 89, 94, 120, 150,
    156-7
  Act 81-5, 86, 94
  compromise 131-4
  'Contra' threat 140-49
  Cuban role 134-5
  current perspective 135-6
  Document of Objectives 73-4, 75,
    80, 89
  emergence 36, 67-70
  Latin American solution 122, 129-
    31
  Manzanillo talks 80-85
  Nicaraguan politics 123-9
  objectives, US policy and 70-77
  Support Group 85, 121, 122
  see also Caraballeda initiative
containment policy 41, 63, 68, 102-3,
    163-6, 167, 169
'Contra' rebels
  containment of 165-6
  funding, see military aid as military
    threat 140-49
  negotiation pressures 82-4, 154-6,
    161-2, 172-3
  Nicaraguan Democratic Force 86,
    88, 141-2
  prospects 136-7
  United Nicaraguan Opposition
    (UNO) 88
  US support 3-4, 121, 123, 125-30,
    135, 159-60, 172-4

Corinto, 64
Costa Rica 51, 77
  border conflict 119, 120, 143, 151
  democracy 2, 36, 37, 65, 69, 154
  invasion of Nicaragua
    (consequences) 112, 114
  militarisation 163, 164-5, 169
  peace talks 81, 83, 84, 85
  US policy (implications) 151-5
covert action 56-8, 71-2, 75-7
Cruz, Arturo 55, 62, 88, 89
Cuba 1, 2, 12-13, 29, 34
  El Salvador and 25, 28, 33
  Nicaragua and 3, 18-22, 51-2, 54,
    56, 59-61, 65, 68-9, 71-2, 110-12,
    123, 144
  Revolution 6, 8, 10-11
  role (regional settlement) 10-11, 18,
    134-5, 167, 171
  Sandinista ties 20-22, 66, 128, 164

D'Aubuisson, Roberto 23, 27, 41-2,
    48, 49, 102
death squads 7, 22, 26, 40, 47-9, 96
  containment 41, 102-3
democracy, pluralist 65, 122, 123,
    128, 137
Democratic Alliance 8
Democratic Forum (1982) 69-70
democratisation 1, 13, 19
  Central America 15, 69
  Costa Rica 2, 36, 37, 65, 69, 153
  El Salvador 9, 25, 27, 40-41, 43,
    45-6, 50, 105, 108, 169
  Guatemala 8, 36, 37, 77, 96, 98-100,
    153, 169
  Honduras 2, 36, 37, 153-4, 169
  Nicaragua 57, 61-5, 71-4, 76, 82-4,
    155
  Sandinista 62, 74, 76-7, 159, 161,
    169, 173
Diaz-Alejandro, Carlos 75
dictatorships 7-8, 14, 17, 19
Dominican Republic 70
Duarte, José Napoleón 9, 26, 47
  presidency 27-8, 41-2, 49-50, 83, 86,
    102, 103
  vulnerabilities 28, 104-7

economic
  coercion 163-5
  crisis 67-70, 127, 137-40

elite 8, 9, 22, 26-7, 41, 43, 107-8
relations (Caribbean) 12-13
situation (El Salvador) 104-5, 106
situation (Guatemala), 96-7, 99-100
see also mixed economy
economic aid 2, 14, 78, 95-6
El Salvador 2, 27, 39, 48, 104-5
Nicaragua 15-16, 20-22, 35, 53-5,
  67, 71-2, 138, 139
El Salvador 7, 8
agrarian reform 26, 41, 104
Arena (Nationalist Republican
  Alliance) 42, 43, 49
arms 52-5, 57-8, 60-61
Carter Administration 15-16, 22-30
Christian Democrats (PDC) 9, 24-
  7, 41-3, 47, 49, 69, 102, 105-7
Democratic Revolutionary Front
  (FDR) 26, 27, 68
democratisation, *see* democratisation
economic aid 2, 27, 39, 48, 104-5
economic situation 104-5, 106
elections, *see* elections
Farabunds Martí National Liberation
  Front (FMLN) 26, 27, 28, 38, 40,
  47
military aid, *see* military aid
National Conciliation Party (PCN)
  43
ORDEN 23
peace talks 69, 81, 84, 85
People's Revolutionary Army
  (ERP) 23, 25
Popular Forces of Liberation (FPL)
  23
Reagan Administration 33-54, 93,
  100-109
Sandinista involvement 71, 73, 74,
  77-8, 123, 154-6
Secret Anticommunist Army
  (ESA) 47
Security Forces 23, 25, 27, 39,
  40-41, 49, 103
Social Democrats 9
elections
El Salvador 9, 15, 39-41, 46, 48-51,
  102, 105, 124
Guatemala 15, 77, 95, 98
Honduras 36, 153
Nicaragua 52, 73-6, 83, 86-9, 126
USA 23, 27, 35
see also democratisation

elite, traditional 8, 9, 22, 26-7, 41, 43,
  107-8
Enders, Thomas 35, 46, 54-5, 63, 72
escalatory spiral 58-63, 65
Europe, Western 3, 13, 115, 125, 139,
  150, 170
European Social Democrats 66, 73

FDR-FMLN 28, 38, 40, 47, 52, 54, 61,
  101
'Finlandization' of Nicaragua 63
Foreign Aid Bills 39, 48
Foreign Assistance Act 20
Foreign Military Sales (FMS) 11
foreign policy, *see* US policy
Franco-Mexican Declaration 40, 68

García, Jose 44
geostrategic shifts 13
Germany, West 40, 43
global powers 150
credibility 2, 5-6, 12-13, 18-19, 132-
  4
Latin American solution 129-31
Goldwater, Barry 72
Gorman, General 50
Grenada 18, 34, 60, 74, 151
Guantánamo 11
Guatemala 7, 52, 60, 70, 81, 155
current perspectives 93, 95-100
demilitarisation 165, 169
Democratic Socialist Party (PSD)
  95
democratisation, *see* democratisation
Department of Technical
  Investigations 96
elections 15, 77, 95, 98
guerillas 2, 36, 95, 99, 114-15
human rights 36, 61, 95, 98, 99
invasion (consequences) 114-15
military aid 15, 36, 77, 95-6, 98-9
guerillas
containment 108, 163, 164-5, 172
El Salvador (FMLN) 7, 22-3, 25-9,
  33-4, 38, 43-5, 53, 60-61, 71, 73-4,
  93, 101-3, 105-8
Guatemala 2, 36, 95, 99, 114-15
Gulf of Fonseca 25, 62

Haig, Alexander 32, 41, 56
Helms, Jesse 35
Hinton, Deane 42, 46

Honduras 7, 15, 142, 163, 164
  anti-Sandinistas 68, 77-9, 142-3
  border conflict 119, 120, 143
  democratisation 2, 36, 37, 154, 169
  elections 36, 153
  Goloson airbase 59
  invasion of Nicaragua
    (consequences) 112, 113, 114
  military aid 28, 59, 78
  Nicaragua and 51, 69, 71, 73, 81-2
  peace talks 81-5 *passim*
  US military activity 51-2, 59-61,
    142-3
  ✓ US policy (implications) 150-5
human rights 28, 127
  Carter policy 14-16, 24, 25
  Contadora process 122-5, 148
  Guatemala 36, 61, 95, 98, 99
  Nicaragua 127, 146
  Reagan policy 38-9, 41-3, 45-8, 50,
    100, 102-3

IMF 138
Immediate Reaction Battalions 44
imperialism 18, 20-22, 51, 54, 129-31
Intelligence Authorization Bill 70-71
Inter-American Development Bank
  138
International Military Education and
  Training programmes 11, 98
invasion scenarios (and costs) 112-17
Iran 18, 23
Israel 43

Jamaica 69
Japan 13
justice systems 26, 45, 48, 61, 103, 108

Kilo Punch 113
Kirkpatrick, Jeane 19, 44-5
Kissinger Commission 37, 48, 50, 65,
  67, 75

La Prensa (newspaper) 55, 73, 127,
  136
land reform 9, 26, 39, 47, 96, 104
  Agency (murders) 27, 42, 103
'Latin American solution' 122, 129-
  31, 133, 135
Lehman, John 56
Lightning II 113

Long, Clarence 35

McFarlane, Robert 84
Magaña, Alvaro 41
Majano, Adolfo 27
Managua 54-5, 62, 65, 69, 73, 76
Manzanillo talks 80-85, 88
Martí, Farabundo 7, 23-4, 26
Martinez, Maximiliano Hernandez 7
Marxism 18-19, 23, 25-6, 29, 33-4, 62
Marxism-Leninism 55, 87, 132
  El Salvador 34, 40, 45, 48
  Nicaragua 63, 65, 66, 128
  Sandinista 18, 29, 34, 54, 62, 141,
    160-61, 164, 168-70
Mather, General 6
Mexico 12, 13, 17-18, 33, 77, 115
  in Contadora 36, 68, 69-70, 89
  Manzanillo talks 80-85, 88
military
  intervention 1, 3-4, 112-21, 162-3
  profile (US) 1-3, 4, 5-10, 11, 14
  regime, Salvadorean 8-9, 22, 24-8,
    41-3, 47-50, 108
military aid 6-7, 11, 14
  'Contra' 74-7, 80, 85-90, 94, 109,
    143-9, 156
  Costa Rica 152-3
  El Salvador 2, 15-16, 26-9, 35, 39,
    41-50, 62-3, 78, 135, 172
  Guatemala 15, 36, 77, 95-6, 98-9
  Honduras 28, 59, 78
  Nicaragua 16, 71-2, 75-7
Military Assistance Programme
  (MAP) 11
Misquito Indians 57
missile crisis 10
mixed economy 18, 19, 61
Monroe Doctrine 5

National Bipartisan Commission 37,
  48, 50, 65, 67, 75
National Endowment for Democracy
  127
National Guard
  El Salvador 27, 49, 50, 103
  Nicaragua 7, 16, 17, 51, 57, 141
National Security Council 27, 56, 62
nationalism 10, 12, 15, 24, 76, 77, 97,
  98, 99, 100, 125
NATO 115, 150
neutrality laws (exiles) 55

180

New Deal   8
Nicaragua   7, 98
   agrarian reform   62
   border conflict   119-20
   Broad Opposition Front (FAO)   16
   Carter Administration   15-19, 29
   Church   55, 73, 87-8, 140, 141, 142,
      147, 161
   Cuban relations, *see* Cuba
   democratisation, *see* democratisation
   economic aid, *see* economic aid
   economic crisis   67-70, 127, 137-40
   El Salvador and   25, 28, 29
   elections, *see* elections
   military aid, *see* military aid
   Permanent Human Rights
      Commission   127
   Soviet relations, *see* Soviet Union
   State of Emergency   62, 74, 86,
      126-7, 139-40
   see also Contadora; Sandinistas
Nicaragua (Reagan Administration)
   covert action   56-8, 71-2, 75-7
   escalation   51-5, 58-63, 65-7
   internal regime (changes)   63-7
   local allies   77-9
   military action (US)   3, 112-19
   policy (costs)   149-57
   policy (current perspectives)   94,
      109-12
   policy (development)   2-4, 33-7, 85-
      90
   policy (objectives)   70-77
   policy (options)   159-60
Nicaraguan Democratic Co-ordinating
      Council (CDN)   74, 86-7, 127
Nicaraguan Democratic Force (FDN)
      57, 86, 88, 141-2
Nixon Administration   11
non-alignment   131, 134
   Sandinistas   18, 19, 21, 159, 161
Nutting, General Wallace   113-14

Ochoa, Sigifredo   44
oil   11-12, 17-18, 33, 89
O'Neill, Tip   72
Organization of American States
      (OAS)   12-13, 16, 19, 56, 68, 74,
      112, 114
Ortega, Daniel   22, 89, 126, 150
Ortega, Humberto   51, 64

Palmerola air base   59, 113
Panama   36, 70, 120
Panama Canal   5, 7, 11-12, 169-70, 171
   Treaty process   17-18
Pastora, Edén   62, 86
peace
   proposals   43, 69-70, 72-3, 80-86,
      100, 105
   see also Contadora process
Pezzullo, Ambassador   54, 56
Pickering, Thomas   48
Poland   56, 132
political systems
   El Salvador   37-41, 43, 45-6, 100,
      102, 105-8
   Guatemala   77, 96, 98-9, 100
   Honduras   36, 151, 152, 153
   Nicaragua   37, 61-5, 67, 80-83, 86,
      115, 116, 121, 123-8, 167-8
   open, *see* democratisation; elections
   pluralist   18-19, 61, 65-6, 73-6, 86,
      124, 125-8, 132
   self-determination   122, 124, 129
Portillo, José López   68-9
private sector, *see* business sector
Puerto Rico   11
Punta Huete airfield   64

Reagan, Ronald   17, 19, 22, 27
Reagan Administration   30
   Central America in   32-7
   Contadora process and   120-49
   El Salvador in   38-51
   international pressures   115, 149-57
   military intervention   162-3
   see also Nicaragua (Reagan
      Administration)
Regional Counter-Terrorist
      Programme   101
regional policy   67-70, 97, 100, 150-7
regional settlement   3, 4, 10-11, 74-5,
      121-3, 128-31, 133-5, 154-6, 166-71
regional stability   4-7, 10-15
   Caraballeda declaration   122-5, 156
   Contadora role, *see* Contadora
      process
   reforms for   1-2, 8-9
Rio Treaty   56
Ríos Montt, Efraín   36
Robelo, Alfonso   20, 51, 62, 86, 89
Romero, Carlo Humberto   22
Roosevelt, Franklin D.   7

SALT II 18
San Salvador demonstration 23
San Vicente 46
Sandinistas (FSLN) 16-18, 21, 34,
  51-3, 62, 68, 84, 86-7, 126
  alternative assumptions 160-71
  anti-(campaign) 54, 56-8, 68
  Carter Administration 18-22, 28
  Contadora role, *see* Contadora
    process
  'Contras' and 3-4, 74-5, 77-9, 85,
    87-8, 109-12, 135-7, 140-43, 155,
    159-62, 172-4
  covert action 36, 54, 56-8, 61-2,
    68-73
  Cuban ties 20-22, 66, 127, 164-5
  democratisation, *see* democratisation
  economic weakness 137-40
  military intervention 112-20
  peace talks 72-3, 80, 82-4, 131-4
  political system 66, 73-6, 87, 124-8
  power 66-8, 89-90, 111
  Reagan Administration 34, 37, 51-
    6, 63, 65, 70
  Salvadorean support, *see* El Salvador
  Soviet ties, *see* Soviet Union
Sandino, Augusto 7
Schultz, George 74, 145
sea lines of communication (SLOCs)
    6-7, 11, 64, 169, 171
self-determination 122, 124, 129
social reforms 8-9, 15, 24-7, 99, 108
  see also land reform
Socialist International 40
Somoza, Anastasio 7, 8, 16-17, 18-19,
    21, 71, 125, 141
Soviet Union 1, 2, 25, 33, 34
  in Afghanistan 20, 21, 23, 29, 132
  Cienfuegos incident 10, 12
  Nicaragua and 3, 51-2, 54, 56, 60,
    63-4, 71, 123, 139-40, 144-6
  Sandinista ties 18-22, 28-9, 66, 89-
    90, 110-12, 117-18, 128-30, 161,
    163-4, 170-71

US action (factors) 115, 117-18
Spanish War (1898) 5
stability, *see* regional stability
Stone, Richard 46, 47
Suazo, President 152

taxation reforms 9, 96
Tegucigalpa 81, 82, 83
terrorist activity 16, 18, 26, 53, 117,
    118, 151
  see also death squads
Toledo 97
totalitarianism 18, 45, 56, 61, 167
Turner, Stansfield 57

United Nations 17, 21, 55
United States
  military activity 1, 3-4, 112-21, 143-
    5, 162-3
  military profile 1-3, 4, 5-11, 14
  traditional influence 1-3, 5-10
United States policy
  Central America (problems) 1-4
  changes 13-15
  Contadora process and 120-49
  costs 149-57
  current (development) 32-90
  current (origins) 5-30
  current perspectives 93-157
  options 159-60, 162-74
  traditional 3, 5-10

Venezuela 13, 36, 68, 69, 70, 119
  Caraballeda initiative 121-3
Vietnam War 11, 14

White, Robert 29
World Bank 138

Zablocki, Clement 71